SLOW TRAVEL

Isle of Man

Local, characterful guides to Britain's special places

Emma Craig

EDITION 1
Bradt Guides Ltd, UK
The Globe Pequot Press Inc, USA

First edition published January 2026
Bradt Travel Guides Ltd
31a High Street, Chesham, Buckinghamshire, HP5 1BW, England
www.bradtguides.com
Print edition published in the USA by The Globe Pequot Press Inc,
PO Box 480, Guilford, Connecticut 06437-0480

Text copyright © Bradt Travel Guides, 2026
Maps copyright © Bradt Travel Guides Ltd, 2026; includes map data © OpenStreetMap contributors
Photographs copyright © Individual photographers, 2026 (see below)
Project Manager: Emma Gibbs
Cover research: Pepi Bluck, Perfect Picture

Thank you for buying an authorised edition of this book published by Bradt Travel Guides. For over 50 years, Bradt Travel Guides has encouraged adventurous, immersive and responsible travel, and this is only possible because of the support of our readers. By purchasing our books, you are enabling us to continue to commission expert authors who genuinely know and love the places they write about, and who write their books after thorough, on-the-ground research.

The author and publisher have made every effort to ensure the accuracy of the information in this book at the time of going to press. However, they cannot accept any responsibility for loss, injury or inconvenience resulting from the use of information contained in this guide. All rights reserved. No part of this book may be reproduced, scanned or distributed by any means without the written permission of Bradt Travel Guides, nor used or reproduced in any way to train artificial intelligence technologies/models. Bradt Travel Guides and the author unequivocally reserve this work from the text and data mining exception, as per Article 4(3) of the Digital Single Market Directive 2019/790.

ISBN: 9781804693148

British Library Cataloguing in Publication Data
A catalogue record for this book is available from the British Library

Importer to the EU: Freytag-Berndt u. Artaria KG, Ölzeltgasse 3/10, 1030 Wien, Österreich

Photographs © individual photographers credited beside images & also those from picture libraries credited as follows: Alamy.com (A); Dreamstime.com (DT); Shutterstock.com (S); Superstock.com (SS); Wikimedia Commons (WC)

Front cover The castle and harbour at Peel (David Chapman/A)
Back cover Maughold Head (Creative Imagineers Ltd/S)
Title page Castletown (David Chapman/A)

Maps David McCutcheon FBCart.S. FRGS

Typeset by Ian Spick, Bradt Guides
Production managed by Gutenberg Press Ltd, printed in Malta
Digital conversion by www.dataworks.co.in

Paper used for this product comes from sustainably managed forests, and recycled and controlled sources.

AUTHOR

Emma Craig is a journalist who lives in the Isle of Man. She was born and raised on the island, spending her childhood hearing stories of her ancestors' exploits at sea and down the local mines. After moving to Paris to attend university, she was surprised to learn that not everyone grows up in a land dominated by fairies and shape-shifting ogres – and quickly realised that she came from somewhere quite special. Her lifelong love of words took her into a career in journalism and she spent over a decade working on national newspapers in London, while also finding time to write a little poetry on the side. She enjoys nothing more than telling willing listeners about her home – and the contents of this book are exactly what she would tell any visiting friend.

AUTHOR'S STORY

When I came to write this book, I expected to have the chance to explore my homeland again: take myself on days out to sites I hadn't visited since going on school trips, retrace beloved childhood walks and treat myself at my ever-growing list of favourite local restaurants. What I wasn't expecting was that this book would take me home again permanently.

I'd been living in London for over a decade when the opportunity arose to put together this guide. Like many young Manx people, I'd left the island at 18 to go to university and never really returned. There were reunions with family and friends at Christmas, and I always came back for the TT, but my life was in England. The Isle of Man stayed an important part of my identity but really, I was a Londoner.

A Londoner, that is, until I started doing the fieldwork for Bradt. With my walking shoes on and a map in my bag, I set out to traipse the lanes and footpaths I remembered so well. It was spring when I started – the hawthorn was blooming and daffodils nodded along the roadsides. I took myself round much-loved museums, absorbed information boards, and spoke to people brimming with knowledge and enthusiasm for this wonderful island. I stood on hilltops in the sunshine, lost in moments of stillness, and had quiet moments of reflection on the pews of innumerable little churches. And eventually it dawned on me: I want to come home.

So I did. Home for me is now a little cottage near the sea on this island that means the world to me. And while I can't quite promise that this guide will transform your life to the same extent, I hope you will agree that the Isle of Man is just a little bit magic.

ACKNOWLEDGEMENTS

No published work is the work of a single person, and I feel that is especially true of this guide. I am grateful beyond measure to all the wonderful people across the Isle of Man (and some further afield) who took the time to talk to me, answer my questions, show me round their favourite spot and share their expertise – I hope I have done their generosity justice. Special mentions go to John 'Dog' Callister for sharing his wonderful knowledge of Ballaugh Curragh; Matt Cain from the Association of Dunkirk Little Ships; James Franklin and Ruth Keggin at Culture Vannin; Dr Fiona Gell for being so generous and enthusiastic with her marine biology expertise; Anna Kerruish for being a fountain of knowledge about Maughold; Boris Kitching from the World Tin Bath Championships; Dario Leonetti for telling me about his ghostly encounters; Amanda Litherland for sharing her love of the Point of Ayre; Stephen Miller for his wonderful fairy knowledge; Peter Moore from Radio Caroline; Jacob O'Sullivan for his witchy knowledge; Vicky Quirk from Victory Café; Jenny Shepherd and Rawdon Hayne from Ballacosnahan Farm; John Woods from Laxey Woollen Mills; and the fabulous team running trips to the Calf of Man on the *Shona*. Thank you, all.

The team at Bradt also deserve bouquets for their patience, support and endless enthusiasm in bringing this book into the world. Claire Strange, Anna Moores and Emma Gibbs – thank you for taking my ideas and knocking them kindly and generously into shape. And of course, Sam Fletcher, without whom this would never have happened.

And last but by no means least, thank you to my friends and family, who contributed so much both in the way of support and with brilliant suggestions for places to include in the guide. I couldn't have done it without you.

This book has been written in memory of my Dad, Tim Craig, who loved this island and whose photos appear on these pages.

CONTENTS

GOING SLOW IN THE ISLE OF MAN 9
A brief history **11**, A Manx handbook **13**, The Manx & their motorsport **23**, Events calendar **26**, Food & drink **31**, Getting there **33**, Getting around the island **34**, Activities **38**, Accessibililty **41**, Further reading & listening **43**, How this book is arranged **44**

1 THE EAST 49
Getting there & around **50**, Douglas & around **51**, Laxey & around **80**

2 THE NORTHEAST 95
Getting there & around **96**, Ramsey & around **96**, Maughold & around **110**, South of Maughold & inland **117**

3 THE NORTHERN PLAIN 125
Getting there & around **126**, The northwest coast from Glen Mooar to Sulby **126**, The far north **136**

4 THE WEST 147
Getting there & around **148**, Peel **148**, South of Peel **161**, St John's & inland **169**

5 THE SOUTH 179
Getting there & around **180**, Castletown & around **180**, Port Erin & Port St Mary **214**, The far south **223**

INDEX 234

SUGGESTED PLACES TO BASE YOURSELF

These bases make ideal starting points for exploring the localities the Slow way.

RAMSEY page 97
The island's second biggest town, this working fishing port has charming indie boutiques on the high street.

PEEL page 148
Cosy fishermen's cottages abound in the shadow of Peel Castle. The sandy beach makes it a destination on sunny days.

CHAPTER 2 page 94

CHAPTER 3 page 124

Point of Ayre
The Ayres National Nature Reserve
Bride
Andreas
St Judes
Sulby
Jurby
Ballaugh Curragh
Ballaugh
Kirk Michael
Glen Mooar
Ramsey
Maughold
North Barrule 1,854ft
Cornaa Valley
The Dhoon
Agneash
Snaefell 2,036ft

IRISH SEA

0 — 6 miles
0 — 9km

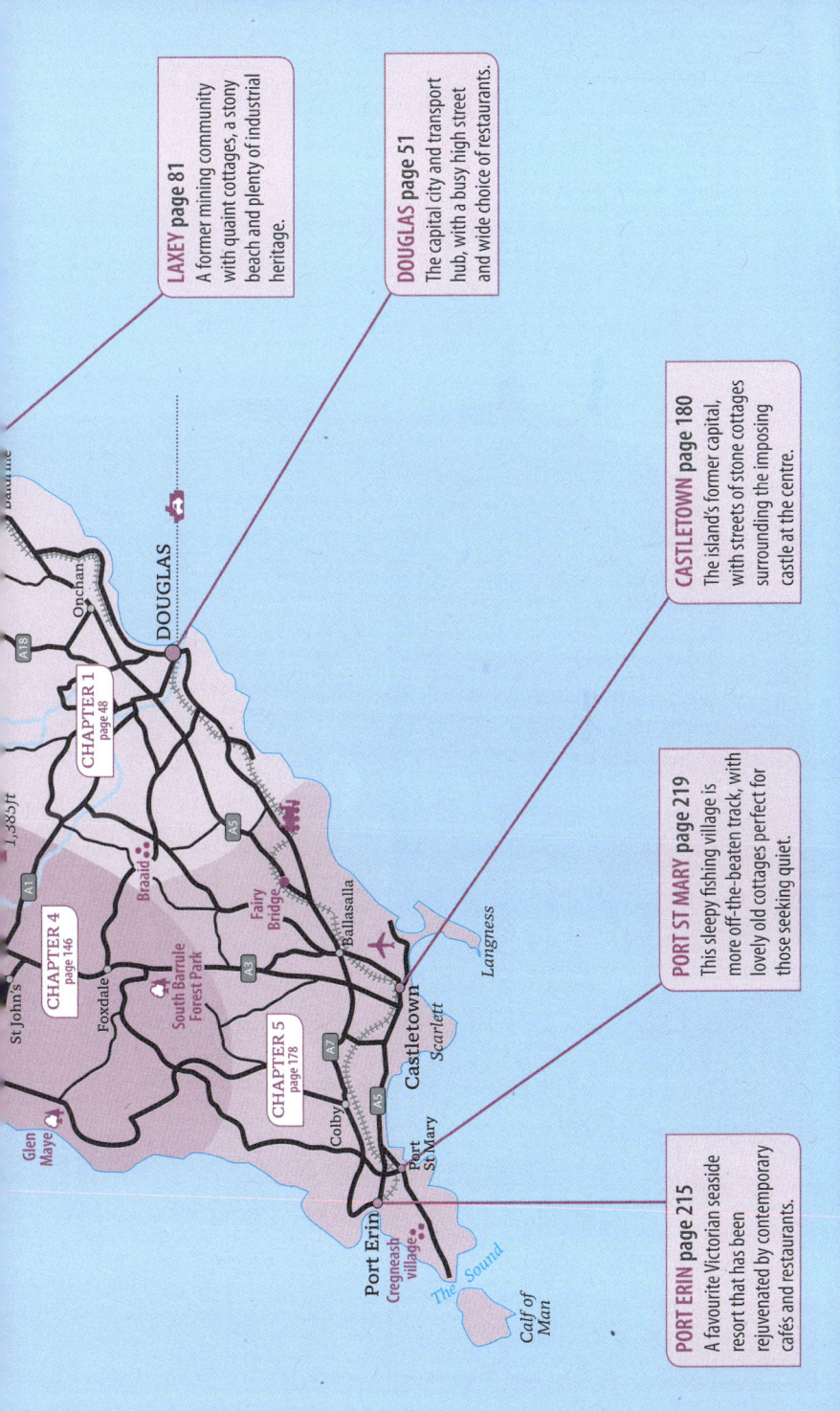

GOING SLOW IN
THE ISLE OF MAN

Walking along a Manx country road on a bright spring day – the sea in the distance, the coconut smell of gorse on the breeze and the sun on your face – it can feel as though time has stood still. There's no need to rush: the Neolithic tomb you're on your way to visit, tucked away in the corner of a farmer's field, has been there for thousands of years. What does it matter if you dawdle to stroke a tailless Manx cat that's hopped over a garden wall, or lean on a gate for a while to admire the view?

There is a saying in the Isle of Man that sums up this laid-back approach to life: *traa dy liooar*. It means 'time enough' in Manx Gaelic, and has long been adopted as the island's unofficial motto. Whether it's a relaxed chat with a shopkeeper, friendly greetings from a dog walker or tall tales in the pub, the Manx are generous with their time. There is enough of it, after all.

And who wouldn't wish to linger in a place like this? Its location in the heart of the Irish Sea means the Isle of Man has picked up characteristics of all the surrounding nations: it is often described as 'the British Isles in miniature'. Despite being just 33 miles long and 13 miles wide, it has flat plains in the north, rugged hills down the middle, beautiful sandy beaches on the west coast and craggy cliffs dimpled with rocky coves in the east and south. The capital city, Douglas, has all the mod cons – top-quality restaurants, major high-street shops and the gleaming offices of the island's finance sector. But travel a little further afield, maybe by steam train or the open-air Victorian tram, and a much older way of life is not hard to find.

Folklore and superstition are entwined with everyday life in a way that has largely been forgotten elsewhere – local children still celebrate Hop tu Naa instead of Halloween, bonfires are lit for Oie Voaldyn on 30

◀ Walking along the coast, with Bradda Head and Milner's Tower in the distance (page 219).

April and there won't be many among the 85,000 islanders who forget to say 'hello' to the fairies (or 'little people') on their way through the Fairy Bridge.

Wonders of a less mythical nature also abound. The Isle of Man is also the only entire jurisdiction in the world to have been declared a UNESCO Biosphere, in recognition of its unique mix of flora and fauna and efforts to maintain the natural environment. Dolphins, rare basking sharks and even the occasional minke whale can be seen off the coast during the summer months, while colonies of seabirds including gannets, Manx shearwater and puffins can be spotted at the national reserves. Further inland, the famous four-horned Manx Loaghtan sheep

THE SLOW MINDSET
Hilary Bradt, Founder, Bradt Guides

> **We shall not cease from exploration**
> **And the end of all our exploring**
> **Will be to arrive where we started**
> **And know the place for the first time.**
> T S Eliot, 'Little Gidding', *Four Quartets*

This series evolved, slowly, from a Bradt editorial meeting when we started to explore ideas for guides to our favourite part of the world – Great Britain. We wanted to get away from the usual 'top sights' formula and encourage our authors to bring out the nuances and local differences that make up a sense of place – such things as food, building styles, nature, geology, or local people and what makes them tick. Our aim was to create a series that celebrates the present, focusing on sustainable tourism, rather than taking a nostalgic wallow in the past.

So without our realising it at the time, we had defined 'Slow Travel', or at least our concept of it. For the beauty of the Slow movement is that there is no fixed definition; we adapt the philosophy to fit our individual needs and aspirations. Thus Carl Honoré, author of *In Praise of Slow*, writes: 'The Slow Movement is a cultural revolution against the notion that faster is always better. It's not about doing everything at a snail's pace, it's about seeking to do everything at the right speed. Savouring the hours and minutes rather than just counting them. Doing everything as well as possible, instead of as fast as possible. It's about quality over quantity in everything from work to food to parenting.' And travel.

So take time to explore. Don't rush it, get to know an area – and the people who live there – and you'll be as delighted as the authors by what you find.

is farmed around the island, and more than two dozen official 'dark sky' sites make stargazing extra special.

The blend of Celtic and Viking roots gives the island a distinct cultural flavour too. Manx Gaelic, incorrectly declared an extinct language by UNESCO in 2009, has flourished in recent years, while music and festivals throughout the year celebrate the island's status as one of the six Celtic nations. Tynwald, the Manx parliament – said to be the oldest continuous parliament in the world – was established by the Vikings, and Scandinavian place names (such as Snaefell, or 'snow mountain') are still scattered across the island centuries after the death of the last Norse king.

Perhaps the sense of magic on the island comes from the Bronze Age burial mounds that dot the landscape, where the fairies were once believed to live. Or maybe it comes from the Viking runes carved onto the medieval crosses that stand in ancient churchyards, keeping watch over land they have belonged to for 1,000 years. Or perhaps it comes from the simple joy of eating a really good ice cream on a sandy beach, fresh from a bracing paddle in the surf.

A BRIEF HISTORY

The story of the Isle of Man can arguably be traced back to a single point: when, around 8000BC, melting glaciers caused sea levels to rise and created the island. Humans set up home some time before 6500BC as the Ice Age retreated – and thus began the emergence of a nation that, while closely connected to the countries surrounding it, stands proudly apart. Today it is a British Crown Dependency: King Charles III is the head of state, but the island is not part of the United Kingdom.

Evidence of prehistoric communities can be seen in the numerous stone tombs and burial mounds scattered across the island, but the roots of what we now recognise as Manx culture arrived along with early Celts. The development of the distinct Manx Gaelic language is believed to be connected to Irish immigration beginning in the 5th century AD; one suggestion for the roots of the island's name is that it derives from Manannan, the Celtic god of the sea. The Celts also brought Christianity with them, with early monks leaving behind about 200 tiny *keeills*, or chapels.

Its strategic location made the Isle of Man a prime target for invaders, and it spent much of the Middle Ages caught in power struggles either among the Vikings, or between Scottish and English rulers. The Vikings first came ashore in the early 9th century to do some plundering and pillaging, but began to settle towards the end of that century, with the great conqueror Godred Crovan (known fondly by the Manx as King Orry) eventually aligning it with the Hebrides to form the Kingdom of Man and the Isles in the late 11th century. Along with the Celts, the Vikings are the other great pillar of Manx cultural influence – the parliament, Tynwald (page 61), can be traced back to their rule.

Following the death of the island's last Viking king, Magnus Olafsson, in 1265, Norway surrendered the islands to an increasingly powerful Scotland. It then passed back and forth between the Scottish and English throughout the 14th century, eventually landing in the control of Henry IV of England. In 1405 he gave it to Sir John Stanley – head of the family who would ultimately become the Earls of Derby – leading to a much-needed period of stability. Thirteen members of the family, who were based on Merseyside, ultimately ruled over the island. In the 16th century they changed their own title from 'King' to 'Lord', to avoid upsetting the newly established Tudor monarchy in England – King Charles III, who is now the island's head of state, is still known as the Lord of Man.

Control of the island passed to the Duke of Atholl in 1736, but was shortly returned to the British crown in an attempt to put a stop to smuggling. Growing calls for reform in the early part of the 19th century eventually led to the island's first public election in 1866 (members of the

THE THREE LEGS OF MAN

The origins of the three legs of Man, the symbol that appears on the island's flag, are a bit of a mystery. It appears to have been adopted as a coat of arms by the Kings of Man in the 13th century, and is depicted on the Manx Sword of State, which is believed to date from around AD 1300.

The roots of the three legs can be traced back to pagan times, when a triskelion was thought to represent the sun. There is also folklore suggesting that Manannan, the Celtic god of the sea, would transform himself into the three legs and run as fast as he could towards the invaders whenever the island was under threat. However, the reason for the symbol's adoption could be as mundane as the fact that it was simply quite distinctive.

island's parliament had previously selected new members themselves). It came amid a time of rapid social change, with the Industrial Revolution bringing mining to many areas of the island, as well as expansion of the fishing industry. The momentum continued towards to the end of the century – women were given the vote in 1881 (page 187), decades earlier than in the UK.

The Industrial Revolution also brought another new concept with it: that of the working-class holiday. Towards the end of the 19th century and in the early 20th century, the factory workers of northern England flocked to the Isle of Man for their annual getaway – at its peak, some 600,000 visitors arrived each year. For the first few decades of the 20th century the island was a destination to rival Blackpool, with all the deck chairs, donkey rides and cheeky postcards that entailed. However, the industry fell into steep decline after World War II, with the rise of cheap package holidays abroad.

This forced a shift in thinking that has shaped what the island has become today. In desperate need of an economic boost, Tynwald began cutting income taxes in the 1960s to attract incomers, and in the 1970s there was an influx of merchant and commercial banks. Offshore finance remains the backbone of the island's modern economy, supplemented by the newer e-gaming sector. The revival of the island's fortunes is a testament to the national motto, *Quocunque jeceris stabit* – or, 'whithersoever you throw it, it will stand'.

A MANX HANDBOOK

The distinct history and isolated geography of the Isle of Man mean it has developed an identity that is entirely its own – whether in the natural world or the cultural one, you will come across things you will never experience elsewhere. Here's a primer on what makes the Isle of Man truly unique.

GLORIOUS ISOLATION: THE BENEFIT TO WILDLIFE
The island's blend of very different landscapes makes for an exciting mixture of wildlife, which there has been a conscious effort to protect both by official means and through the actions of charities, landowners and farmers.

The Isle of Man first became an island around 8,000BC, when melting glaciers caused sea levels to rise and cut Britain off from the rest of mainland Europe. The island's geographic isolation means species that are commonplace in the UK simply never arrived in the Isle of Man: there are no squirrels or badgers, for example, and to import them would incur a hefty fine. Instead, unique fauna has been allowed to thrive – the tailless **Manx cat** is a result of genetic mutations within the local feline population, and has become a symbol of the island. Manx cats are described as either a 'rumpy', with no tail at all, or a 'stumpy', with just an inch or two of tail, and have longer back legs than regular moggies which give them a distinctive 'bunny hop' run. They are kept as pets and are a common sight perched on garden walls or slinking through cat flaps.

The famed **Manx Loaghtan sheep** (page 163) are descended from the hardy primitive animals once common across Scotland and the Scottish islands, and are easy to identify thanks to their four – often enormous – horns. The name 'Loaghtan' refers to the colour of their fleece and comes from the Manx for 'mouse brown' – the wool is used to make knitwear and tweeds. After almost dying out in the 1950s, the breed is now carefully managed and there are commercial flocks in the Isle of Man and across the UK.

The coastlines are a haven for marine creatures; clear waters and currents that sweep plenty of food past the island mean the sea teems with wildlife. Basking sharks, which grow up to 40ft in length, feed on plankton between May and August – the best area to spot their fins gliding through the water is along the coast between Peel and the Calf of Man. **Bottlenose dolphins** can be spotted off the east coast in the winter months, **common dolphins** are seen around the island in the summer months and **Risso's dolphins** move from the east to the south coast as spring turns into summer. **Minke whales** are visible off the west coast in summer and the east coast around Laxey in the winter, while Port St Mary has become a hotspot for **porpoises**.

A diverse range of habitats on land make the island great for spotting seabirds. **Guillemots**, **razorbills** and **kittiwakes** nest on the spectacular

---

1 The island has 26 official dark sky sites, perfect for stargazing. **2** Manx cats are a common sight perched on garden walls. **3 & 4** The Calf of Man (page 229) is an excellent place for spotting seals or birds such as guillemots. **5** Paddleboarders in Ramsey look on as a dolphin breaches. ▶

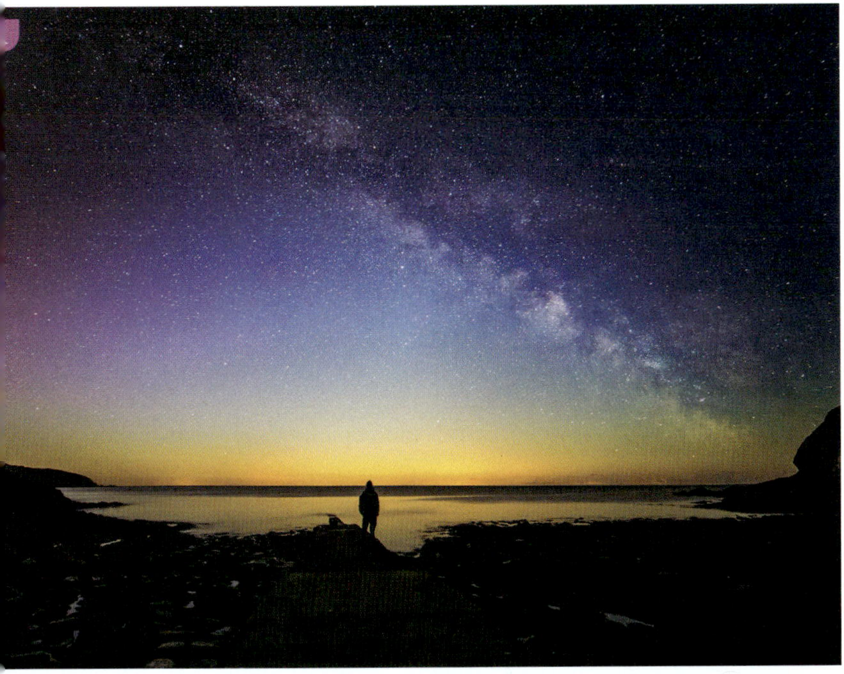

VISIT ISLE OF MAN

TIMOTHY CRAIG

VISIT ISLE OF MAN

VISIT ISLE OF MAN

VISIT ISLE OF MAN

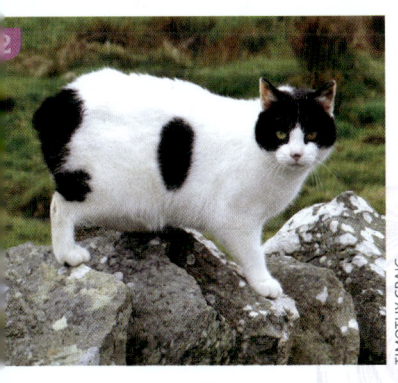

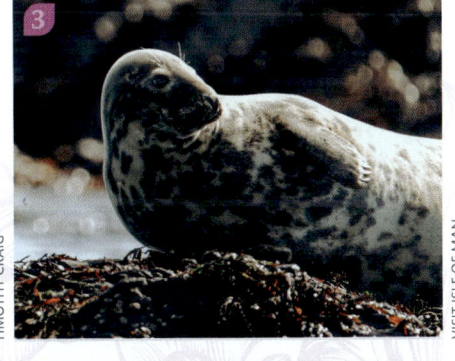

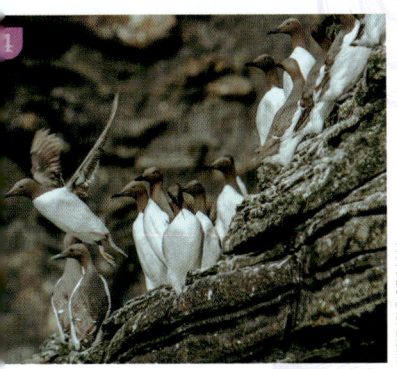

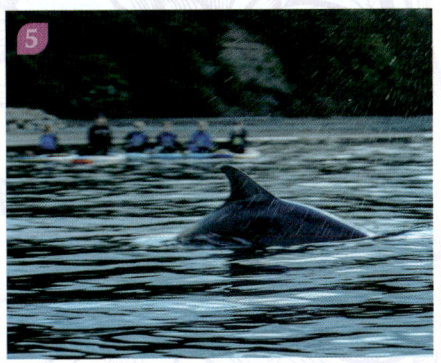

cliffs at the Chasms (page 226) near Cregneash, and **gannets** can be seen diving for fish around the island in the summer. The Ayres Nature Reserve (page 139) – one of 31 on the island – is home to **little**, **arctic** and **common terns**, while the bird observatory on the Calf of Man (page 229) monitors more than 30 species that breed on the tiny island each year. The ground-nesting **Manx shearwater** was first officially recorded on the Calf, hence its name, and hundreds of pairs return between March and July each year to breed.

The **Manx Wildlife Trust** looks after the nature reserves, of which six are Areas of Special Scientific Interest. A full list of locations can be found online at ⌘ mwt.im, or you can pop into their Wildlife Shop in Peel (page 160).

The abundant wildlife is testament to the island's efforts to protect it: the Isle of Man is the only entire nation in the world to have been declared a UNESCO Biosphere, in recognition of its focus on conservation, sustainable economic development and environmental education. The aim of the scheme is to connect residents with the world around them, and since its inauguration in 2016 more than 300 local organisations – encompassing everything from accountancy firms through to farms, the police force and art studios – have signed up to become Biosphere Partners. Those who sign up must detail the work they are doing to protect the natural environment and receive advice on improving their sustainability; the full list of partners can be found at ⌘ biosphere.im.

THE MANX LANGUAGE

As one of the Gaelic tongues, Manx is a close relation of Scottish and Irish Gaelic – but is different enough to be a language in its own right. Its roots are thought to go back to the arrival of Irish monks on the island in the early Middle Ages and it was commonly spoken for centuries. However, the language fell into rapid decline in the 19th century as commerce and tourism forced a more outward-looking stance and English became the medium for formal education. In 2009, UNESCO incorrectly declared the language 'extinct' – a blunder that they were forced to quickly retract, upon receiving letters in Manx from adults and children alike, including pupils of the Manx-language primary school, Bunscoill Ghaelgagh, based in the village of St John's.

AN EXPERT GUIDE TO MARINE WILDLIFE SPOTTING

By Dr Fiona Gell, marine conservation and climate policy specialist based in the Isle of Man, and the author of Spring Tides, *about her work protecting Manx waters.*

There is lots to see in the middle of the Isle of Man, but for marine life I'd strongly recommend the extremities – Ramsey up to the Point of Ayre in the north and Port Erin down to the Calf of Man in the south. The north and south have completely different landscapes, geology and habitats and associated marine and coastal life. Snorkelling and rock pooling are great, accessible options to explore the diverse shores and shallow waters and get a glimpse of what is so special about Manx marine life.

Port Lewaigue in the south of Ramsey Bay is the most highly protected zone of the Ramsey Bay Marine Nature Reserve and is my marine life highlight. At low tide you can snorkel out to the Carrick (a rock with a metal marker to show its location at high water) and see kelp beds and eelgrass meadows, spot spider crabs and little cuttlefish, sea hares and spotted catsharks. Port Lewaigue is a lovely rock-pooling site at low tide too – the rocky shore is home to diverse species of starfish, shore crabs and edible crabs and lobsters, all well-protected by the MNR. It's also the best place on the island to see seagrass on the shore – walk towards Ramsey from Lewaigue and you will see patches of it over a large area, on the sandy shore and in pools as the tides recedes. This is the same species of seagrass that grows underwater further out (*Zostera marina*) and it doesn't look quite as impressive lying in a puddle as it does swaying in the tide, but it certainly gives you a feel for its emerald-green loveliness.

Dedicated Manx speakers and learners had already been working for decades to keep the language alive. Today there are more than 2,000 speakers, with conversation groups meeting regularly in pubs, and classes available for children and adults. Bunscoill Ghaelgagh was established in 2001 and has links to playgroups that help children become familiar with the tongue from an early age – it can now be studied as far as A-level as a language (there are lessons available in schools across the island), and has also received considerable attention from academics.

There are some heroes in the story of Manx's survival. Ned Maddrell, a fisherman from Cregneash, was the last surviving native speaker when he died at the age of 97 in 1974. In 1947 he had met Eamonn de Valera, then Taoiseach of Ireland, during an official visit to the island – an encounter that left de Valera so alarmed at the parlous state of Manx that he dispatched the Irish Folklore Commission to the Isle of Man with a mobile recording unit. They made four hours of recordings of native speakers, which have now been remastered and digitised and provide a priceless link to the past for modern learners.

Where Manx has proved most resilient is in the island's place names. The common prefix *'balla-'* means 'farm' or 'homestead', *'beg'* or *'veg'* mean 'small', and *'mooar'* and *'vooar'* mean 'big'. The island itself is called *Ellan Vannin* (the Isle of Man) in Manx. Manx versions of human names have also survived, such as Breeshey (the Manx variant of Brigit), Voirrey (Mary) and Onnee (Annie).

An easy place to find contemporary spoken Manx is on Manx Radio (⌖ manxradio.com): its *Claare ny Gael* cultural magazine programme is presented in both English and Manx and is available as a podcast. Culture Vannin has a dedicated website for the language (⌖ learnmanx.com), including resources for independent learning. The Cooish Manx Language Festival takes place each November with taster sessions and talks – and in previous years has even included a vocab-themed sea-swimming session (*'feayr'* means 'cold') and cocktail-making workshops delivered through Manx.

FAIRIES, BUGGANES & FYNODEREES

On land, there is barely a clifftop, ruined cottage or sun-dappled glen that doesn't have its own story of fairies, bugganes or fynoderees attached. Keeping the fairies happy, or at least not displeasing them, is an overriding theme of Manx cultural beliefs. The 'little people' or 'themselves', as they are known (it is considered rude to call them 'fairies'), are not the sweet, sparkly creatures of Disney films – they are a mischievous, potentially dangerous, band whose attention it is best not to attract. They have been blamed for stealing babies (leaving behind a 'changeling' fairy child), leading walkers astray at night, or even punching people who forget to leave out food for them. The stories and beliefs were prevalent in the 18th and 19th centuries, but there is still a certain traditional respect for the 'little people' – just ask anyone crossing the Fairy Bridge (page 213) – and the tales are still fondly told.

Bugganes are an actively malevolent force: they are shapeshifters, but in their natural form are ogre-like with tusks, hooves, glowing red eyes and supernatural strength. The most famous is the buggane of St Trinian's, who lived on Greeba Mountain and was said to have repeatedly torn the roof off a church (page 172). The moddey dhoo ('black dog') is also one to watch out for; the most famous of these

CAUTION, FAIRIES!

By Stephen Miller, a folk-life scholar and researcher who has spent over four decades studying archives in the Manx Museum and beyond. In 2020 he was awarded the Reih Bleeaney Vanannan – the Isle of Man's most prestigious annual award for contribution to Manx culture. His work is available to read on his website, ⊘ chiollaghbooks.com.

George Waldron, who lived in the Isle of Man in the 1720s, was told that the fairies were the first inhabitants of the island and the Manx 'call them the good people'.

The fairies were believed to be everywhere… mortals lived in their world and not they in ours. The fairies set the rules to live by and when broken, harm followed. There were numerous ways in which one could fall foul of the fairies. A woman complained when the fairies helped themselves to her food and drink and was blinded in one eye. Cursing the fairies when drunk led one man to die. A mean farmer begrudged the fairies taking potatoes from his field and died soon after. Spying on the fairies through a keyhole caused a man to lose his eye from a poke with a fiddle stick. Complaining of the smell of the fairies caused one woman to lose her sense of smell. A drunk man threw a stick at the fairies who were crowding the road, only to have it thrown back at him with such force that he was lamed and bedridden.

Young or old, male or female, day or night, all were at risk from fairy abduction. Children before being baptised were often stolen by the fairies and a fairy changeling substituted in their place. Waldron related how the daughter of the family's butter seller was once abducted by the fairies when sent on an errand. A man from Kirk Andreas 'was absent from his people for four years, which he spent with the fairies'. It was three years for a woman who met two fairy armies at South Barrule before she managed to escape. A report from 1895 recorded: 'A superstition is still extant that fairies will take children who are out alone after sunset, unless they are marked on their faces with soot.'

Fairies misled at night, but sometimes it was simply bad luck – as recorded by the Manx Museum Folk Life Survey: 'The fairies took you if you lose your way over the mountains.' At night food and fresh water had to be left out for the fairies in the farmhouse after the household went to their beds. 'Mind the fairies don't get you,' was said to people going out alone at night.

How to avoid harm from the fairies today? According to William Cashen in 1912, 'the fairies had no power to hurt anyone who was on an errand of mercy or charity'. Otherwise, go to bed early, leave out food and fresh water, do not swear, cheat, or steal, and you (maybe) stand a chance…

> ### A FEW MANX PHRASES
> **Moghrey mie** [MORR-a MY] – good morning
> **Fastyr mie** [FASS-ter MY] – good afternoon
> **Kys t'ou** [kiss-TOW] – how are you?
> **Ta mee braew** [tamm-ee brow] – I am fine
> **Gura mie ayd** [gurr-a MY-edd] – thank you
> **Gaelg aboo** [gilg a-BOO] – hurrah for Manx

fearsome beasts haunts Peel Castle (page 156), but there are others said to prowl across the island.

The **fynoderee** is a much gentler soul – a fairy prince banished from his kingdom after falling in love with a human, condemned to take the form of a half-man, half-goat. The lonely fynoderee is a helpful presence who gladly assists the farmers and fishermen he befriends.

Many of the folk stories that are well known on the island today have survived thanks to the efforts of Sophia Morrison, a Manxwoman and passionate folklorist who collected the tales in the late 19th and early 20th centuries – often by going door to door, or talking to fishermen on the quay. Her book, *Manx Fairy Tales* (page 43), was first published in 1911 and is still the ultimate primer for anyone interested in Manx culture.

THE SOUND OF (MANX) MUSIC

The Isle of Man has a rich cultural scene, with its own distinct character that draws inspiration from its Celtic heritage and stunning landscape. Interest in Manx language, music and dance has undergone a revival in the 21st century and a new wave of performers have put their own twist on traditions to bring them bang up to date.

Current favourites among fans of contemporary 'trad' (short for 'traditional') music are **Ruth Keggin Gell**, a singer-songwriter who performs in Manx; **Mera Royle**, a harpist who won BBC Radio 2's Young Folk Musician Award in 2018; and **Mec Lir**, a Manx/Glaswegian band known for its lightning-fast fiddle playing against a background of electro synths and drums. Musicians from the island frequently appear at Celtic festivals further afield, such as the annual Celtic Connections in Glasgow and the Lorient Interceltic Festival in Brittany, and Manx Radio hosts a weekly *Folk Show* promoting some of the best new pieces. The week-long **Yn Chruinnaght** festival (⌀ ynchruinnaght.com) is held on the island each July in celebration of music from all the Celtic nations (its name translates as 'The Gathering'), and **Peel Centenary Centre** (⌁ centenarycentre.com) hosts folk-music performances – from local and visiting musicians – throughout the year.

PAINTINGS, PEWTER... & POSTAGE STAMPS

The first stop for anyone interested in Manx visual arts should be the **National Art Gallery** at the Manx Museum, which, as well as holding work by Manx artists, displays a collection of works by foreign internees who were kept at the island's camps during the First and Second World Wars. The **Hodgson Loom Gallery** in Laxey (Glen Rd, IM4 7AR, 🎏 ⊖ 10.00–17.00 Tue–Sat) is a showcase for artists of all genres, including craft and textile groups; the gallery occupies the first floor of Laxey Woollen Mills (page 82) so also offers the chance to see some weaving in action. **Studio 42** in Port St Mary (page 220) is also a great place to buy a piece to take home.

The influence of the Art-Nouveau designer **Archibald Knox** is still very much apparent in the island's visual identity. Born in Braddan on the outskirts of Douglas in 1864, Knox went on to be one of the guiding lights of the Arts and Crafts and Celtic Revival movements. His modern, elegant jewellery and pewter ware was heavily influenced by Celtic lore – giving it a distinctive look that ultimately led to him becoming the primary designer for Liberty & Co, the luxury London department store, in the early years of the 20th century. He died in 1933 and examples of his work can be seen in the Manx Museum (page 63). The V&A in London also holds a collection of his pieces, and credits Knox and his studio colleagues as moving 'the Arts and Crafts stylistic principles one stage further forward', therefore creating 'a distinctive British version of Art Nouveau'. Free maps for the **Archibald Knox Trail**, which highlights 27 sites around the island connected to his life and work, can be picked up at the Welcome Centre in Douglas (page 50) or downloaded from Visit Isle of Man (⌁ visitisleofman.com).

Other notable artists include **Bryan Kneale**, the internationally renowned sculptor and Royal Academician. Born in Douglas in 1930, Kneale studied in London and was already building a career as a portrait painter when he decided to return to the Isle of Man in 1959 to reconnect with his artistic roots – and began developing his signature metalwork sculptures. Kneale, who died in 2025, ultimately went back to London, but his circular *Yn Arreyder* ('The Watcher') is positioned outside the Manx Museum, and his giant *Three Legs of Man* is outside Isle of Man Airport. **Norman Sayle** – also born in Douglas, in 1926 – was a prolific watercolourist who studied at Goldsmiths College in London, but spent the vast majority of his career in the Isle of Man. With a clean, simple style inspired by the paintings of his predecessor Archibald Knox, Sayle – who died in 2007 – said his aim was 'to express my devotion to the Manx countryside, its grey churches, stone circles, [and] slate walls'.

Julia Ashby Smyth, who is based in Ramsey, is one of the most recognisable Manx artists working today. Influenced by the folklore and the enchanting landscape that surrounds her, she creates fantastical fairies and mythical creatures and has illustrated books, sets of stamps for the Isle of Man Post Office and labels for the likes of Okell's brewery (page 32) and Fynoderee gin (page 101).

THE WRITTEN WORD

The Victorian writer **TE Brown** is the Manx national poet; his works – written in English and the Anglo-Manx dialect – are described by Manx National Heritage as holding a 'mirror to the Manx'. Born the son of a schoolmaster and curate in 1830, Brown excelled at school and went on to graduate from Oxford University, ultimately moving home to become vice-principal of King William's College in Castletown. He maintained a love both of language and the Isle of Man, describing the Manx tongue as 'a fine old language, rich and musical; and full of meaning and expression'. Among his most famous lines are his reflections on childhood, from his 1870 poem *Betsy Lee*:

> Now the beauty of the thing when childher plays is
> The terrible wonderful length the days is [...]
> And the years do come and the years do go
> And when you look back it's all like a puff
> Happy and over and short enough.

There is still a vibrant poetry tradition on the island, with an official Manx Bard chosen each year to promote it within the community. Previous Bards have included **Annie Kissack**, **John 'Dog' Callister** (page 134) and **Michael Manning** – all of whose work has explored Manx identity, with many examples available online. Other Manx poets worthy of note are **David Callin**, whose book *Poems from the Nab* was released in 2024, and **Jacob O'Sullivan** (page 194), who is from

THE BESTSELLER WHO FELL INTO OBSCURITY

Despite being largely unheard of today, the novelist Hall Caine was a bestseller in the final years of the 19th century and was hugely popular both in the UK and the US. His melodramatic and moralistic novels, including *The Deemster* and *The Manxman*, addressed Victorian concerns such as social hierarchies and the dangers of giving in to passion.

Born in Cheshire in 1853 to a Manx father and English mother, Caine spent his impoverished early life in Liverpool before moving in with relatives in the village of Maughold in the Isle of Man. A journalistic career took him back to England, where he ended up working as a secretary for the Pre-Raphaelite painter and poet Dante Gabriel Rossetti. He also developed a close friendship with Bram Stoker – so much so that Stoker dedicated his masterpiece *Dracula* to Caine (the 'Hommy Beg', meaning 'Little Tommy', on the dedication page was Caine's childhood nickname).

Caine lived at the gothic Greeba Castle (page 174), near St John's village, from the 1890s until his death in 1931 – he is buried in Maughold churchyard, where there is a monument designed by Archibald Knox in his memory (page 111). Although Caine's style of writing fell out of fashion with the arrival of the 20th century, *The Manxman* was given a new lease of life when it was adapted into a film by Alfred Hitchcock – the film, released in 1929, was Hitchcock's last silent movie.

---

the island but now lives in Edinburgh and is a trustee of Scotland's International Poetry Festival.

Other writers of note include the Victorian novelist **Hall Caine** (page 23) – little known today, but he was a bestseller in his day. The screenwriter **Nigel Kneale**, creator of the *Quatermass* sci-fi series that first aired on the BBC in the 1950s, also grew up in Douglas.

THE MANX & THEIR MOTORSPORT

The smell of racing oil on the air is as much a part of the Manx summer as gorse hedgerows or picnics on the beach. The island has been hosting international motorsport events for well over a century and each year attracts tens of thousands of visitors to soak up the excitement.

By far the biggest race in the calendar is the **TT** (iomttraces.com). The Tourist Trophy, as it was originally called, began in 1904 with a road race for motorcars – a sister event for motorcycles was launched in 1907 and it is this that is still with us today. For two weeks over the end of May and the start of June (with a week of practices followed by a

CULTURE VANNIN

VISIT ISLE OF MAN

CULTURE VANNIN

CULTURE VANNIN

VISIT ISLE OF MAN

DANIEL SZTORK/S

THE MANX & THEIR MOTORSPORT

week of racing), the island transforms into the centre of the motorbiking universe: the streets are lined with leather-clad fans, rock music blares out of pubs and upstairs windows, and the smell of ale and bacon baps mingles with that of burnt rubber.

The 37-mile course begins at the Grandstand in Douglas, before sweeping down through Braddan and along the main road towards Peel, then heading north through Kirk Michael and Ramsey and returning to Douglas over the famous mountain section via Snaefell. Each race (there are ten over the main week of racing, catering to different classes) is run as a time trial, with riders setting off at ten-second intervals. The whole event culminates with the blue ribband Senior TT, which sees the best riders wrestle the most powerful bikes around six laps of the course.

It is one of the greatest spectacles in motorsport, and winners are recognised the world over as being the best of the best. It also brings about £40 million into the island's economy. However, it is not universally loved – largely because of the disruption, but also because of the risks. It is rare a year goes by without a death during racing, but accidents also happen on the open roads among spectators and visitors – the combination of overexcitement and unfamiliarity with the roads can prove dangerous.

If you do wish to visit during the TT, it is worth booking as far in advance as possible. Travel operators often start advertising for the following year during the event itself, and accommodation is always vastly oversubscribed (there is a government homestay scheme in recognition of the fact that the hotels simply don't have room, and many of the island's sports fields and football pitches are turned into campsites for the fortnight). Flights and ferries cost considerably more than usual, and often sell out entirely.

If you want to get a taste of motorbike racing without all the hullaballoo, there are quieter events throughout the summer. The **Manx Grand Prix** (⌗ manxgrandprix.co.uk) takes place over nine days at the

---

◀ **1** Turnips are carved for Hop tu Naa, which marks the start of the ancient new year. **2** The TT motorbike races are one of the greatest spectacles in motorsport. **3** Shennaghys Jiu is a festival of Manx music and dance. **4** Yn Chruinnaght ('The Gathering') celebrates music from all the Celtic nations. **5** Sample local produce such as tiny scallops known as 'queenies'. **6** A fairy door near Peel; keeping the fairies happy is an overriding theme of Manx cultural beliefs.

HOW THE MANX CAT LOST ITS TAIL

The first recordings of Manx cats not having tails come from the early 18th century and, while science insists that it is simply a genetic mutation that has spread among an isolated population, there are plenty more interesting stories to explain how it came about.

Probably the best known is that the Manx cat was late boarding Noah's ark: impatient to get going, Noah shut the boat door just as the cat was slipping on board, catching its tail and cutting it off. Another theory is that a tailless cat swam ashore from a wrecked ship that was part of the Spanish Armada. A third is that it is the result of crossbreeding between cats and rabbits (hence the animal's rabbit-like long back legs).

With their loyal temperament and unusual appearance, the cats have long had fans off-island too. The Romantic painter JMW Turner had a home in London where his housekeeper kept her collection of up to 30 Manx cats – one of his paintings was even said to have been used as a cat flap for them.

---

end of August, and is widely seen as a training ground for riders who hope to graduate on to the TT later in their career – it follows the same course and can be just as thrilling. The **Southern 100** (⌀ southern100.com), meanwhile, is raced on the Billown course – a small loop just outside Castletown – over four days in July; it is more akin to grassroots Irish road racing, with a mass start and much jostling for space on the tarmac. Travel and accommodation will be busier during both events, but nothing like the scale of the TT.

The bikes have very much become embedded in Manx life, and there are museums and cafés paying homage to them year-round. Some of the most iconic are **Murray's Motorcycle Museum** (page 214), the **Leece Museum** (page 149), the **TT gallery at the Manx Museum** (page 63), the **Isle of Man Motor Museum** (page 138) and the **Victory Cafe** (page 92).

There are also car rallies split into multiple stages across the island, notably the **Manx Rally** (⌀ manxautosport.org) in the spring – heading out to watch a night stage with warm clothing and a flask of tea is one of the secret joys of being a Manx motorsport fan.

EVENTS CALENDAR

Rarely a weekend goes by when there isn't something special to see or do, particularly in the summer months. Even if you're not joining in, it's worth making a note if there's anything big – such as a motorsport event or music festival – taking place during your visit, as it could mean road closures or diversions and accommodation being busier than usual.

JANUARY

New Year's Dip Grab your swimming costume and woolly hat and join hundreds of dippers as they welcome the new year with a dunk in the Irish Sea. The events take place around the island at around lunchtime, and spectators are welcome. A full list of locations is published on ⊘ manxradio.com each year, though the main ones are at Douglas, Laxey, Ramsey and Peel.

MARCH

Darts Festival ⊘ isleofmandartsfestival.com. A four-day annual extravaganza held over a weekend in early March at the Villa Marina in Douglas. Big names in the darts world have added their names to the silverware, including Luke Littler, who in 2025 became the youngest world champion at the age of just 17.

EASTER

Easter Festival of Running ⊘ easterfestival.info. Three races over three days of Easter weekend, including a 10k, a hill race and a 5k.

Egg rolling at Cregneash ⊘ manxnationalheritage.im. On Easter Monday, decorate your eggs and try some Easter crafts in the crofts of the island's open-air folk museum (page 223) in the morning, then take part in the egg rolling after lunch.

Isle of Man Art Society Easter Exhibition ⊘ isleofmanartsociety.com. An annual exhibition from the local art society held over Easter weekend at the Villa Marina Arcade in Douglas. It is free to visit, standards for the hundreds of entries are high, and it's a great place to pick up a bargain.

APRIL

Beer and Cider Festival ⊘ iombeerfestival.com. A hugely popular event held over three days at the Villa Marina in Douglas, with more than 100 beers, ciders, perries and fruit wines to try, plus food and musical entertainment.

Manx Music Festival ⊘ manxmusicfestival.org. The biggest event of the year for Manx music, speech and dance, known locally as The Guild. A week-long programme of competitions for choirs, solo singers, Manx speakers, stand-up comedians, tap dancers, brass bands and many more. It's been going since 1892 and is held at the Villa Marina.

Manx Rally ⊘ manxautosport.org. Going for more than 60 years, the Manx is one of the longest-established closed-road rallies in the UK. Expect two days of motor mayhem over more than a dozen stages around the island.

Shennaghys Jiu ⌖ shennaghysjiu.com. A four-day youth festival celebrating traditional Manx music and dance, with events at various locations in Ramsey.

MAY

Oie Voaldyn: the Manx May Fire Festival ⌖ oievoaldyn.com. Held on the beach at Peel during the first weekend in May, this folk festival is a reinterpretation of the old Manx May Day custom of lighting fires to cast off the winter darkness and welcome summer. There are fire performers, bonfires and music, culminating in a grand battle between winter and summer.

Race the Sun ⌖ thechildrenscentre.org.im. A popular team relay race to raise money for the local Children's Centre. Beginning at sunrise, teams must complete a lap of the 100-mile Raad ny Foillan coastal footpath before sunset.

JUNE

Parish Walk ⌖ parishwalk.com. A walking race that usually takes place on the weekend nearest the summer solstice. It covers 85 miles, passes through all 17 of the island's parishes and attracts about 1,000 competitors (though few make it all the way to the finish line).

TT races ⌖ iomttraces.com (page 23)

World Championship Viking Longboat Races ▮ PeelVikingLongboats. Held in June or July, depending on tides, teams draw the crowds by rowing replica Viking longboats across Peel bay.

JULY

Round the Island Race ⌖ msandcc.org. A round-island yacht race organised annually by the Manx Sailing and Cruising Club. It starts in Ramsey and takes up to 27 hours to complete.

Southern 100 ⌖ southern100.com (page 26)

Tynwald Day ⌖ tynwald.org.im. Usually held on 5 July (check website as it can move), the Tynwald Day ceremony takes place at St John's (page 170) and is the grand centrepiece of the island's political year. There's music, stalls, speeches and lots of smart hats.

Yn Chruinnaght ⌖ ynchruinnaght.com. Literally translated as 'The Gathering', Yn Chruinnaght is a week-long Celtic music and dance festival, with performers coming from across the Celtic nations. Events are based in Peel, and include concerts, ceilis (visitors may be more familiar with the Scottish spelling, ceilidh), workshops and lectures.

AUGUST

Isle of Man Marathon ⌖ isleofmanmarathon.com. The island's own version of the classic 26-mile running event, with a route that starts in Ramsey and takes in the surrounding countryside.

HOP TU NAA

Halloween is not Halloween in the Isle of Man – it is Hop tu Naa. Closely connected to the Celtic festival of Samhain, it is thought to be the oldest unbroken Manx tradition and marks the beginning of winter and start of the ancient new year.

Pronounced 'hop-choo-nay', the name is a corruption of *shogh ta'n oie* meaning 'this is the night' in Manx. Songs are sung, there is traditional dancing, and turnips – or 'moots', as they are called – are carved into fearsome lanterns to scare off the spirits. There is also much talk of Jinny the Witch: a character entwined with Hop tu Naa, thought to have been inspired by a local woman tried for witchcraft in the early 18th century.

Look out for events around the island, particularly at Manx National Heritage sites and on the heritage railways. Children also go round the houses singing for sweets or a few coins; there are many variations of the song sung, but this is the one I grew up with in the east of the island:

> Hop tu Naa, my mother's gone away,
> And she won't be back until the morning.
>
> Jinny the Witch flew over the house
> To catch a stick to lather the mouse.
>
> Hop tu Naa, my mother's gone away,
> And she won't be back until the morning.

Manx Grand Prix manxgrandprix.co.uk (page 25)
Royal Manx Agricultural Show royalmanx.com. A highlight of the summer calendar, this vast agricultural show has all the prize cows and sheep you would expect, along with craft and trade stalls, fantastic food, and entertainment from the likes of motorbike stunt riders. Held over two days at Knockaloe, just outside Peel.

SEPTEMBER

End to End Walk endtoendwalk.org. A 39-mile walking race from the island's northern tip at the Point of Ayre to the Sound in the south. Nearly 300 competitors take part.
Manx Litfest manxlitfest.com. A six-day celebration of reading, writing, poetry and storytelling held across multiple venues. Past guests have included *Chocolat* author Joanne Harris and crime writer Ann Cleeves.

OCTOBER

Hop tu Naa The island's version of Halloween (see above), look out for events around the island including trips on the Steam Railway 'ghost train' (page 58), turnip-carving and crafts at Cregneash folk village (page 223) and groups of children singing about Jinny the Witch.

Isle of Man Festival of Choirs festivalofchoirs.im. A three-day competition for choirs from around the UK and Ireland. The friendly event at the Villa Marina in Douglas attracts big audiences.

NOVEMBER

Cooish Manx Language Festival learnmanx.com. An annual five-day festival celebrating the Manx language, with dozens of events across the island including lessons, games nights and concerts.

Douglas fireworks display douglas.gov.im The biggest and best Bonfire Night display on the island, with thousands coming to watching the free event over Douglas Bay.

DECEMBER

Hunt the Wren A major part of the Manx festive calendar, Hunt the Wren (see below) is a singing and dancing tradition on Boxing Day that encourages everyone to get involved. Simply turn up at the event you want to attend (there are several around the island), then make your way to St John's for the annual cammag match in the afternoon (page 171), when the North takes on the South in a uniquely Manx game that has been described as 'killer hockey'.

Young Farmers' Tractor Run Tractor-Run-IOM. The island's young farmers decorate their tractors up to the nines with fairy lights, antlers and waving Santas for a nighttime parade around the island. It takes place over two nights – one north, one south – and is a joyous hoot.

HUNT THE WREN

Boxing Day, or St Stephen's Day, is a big one for Manx culture enthusiasts as it is the annual chance to Hunt the Wren. Events take place across the island, but they all follow the same pattern: everyone joins in to either dance around a festively decorated pole to which a stuffed wren is attached or they provide the music by singing the dedicated song. The whole carnival moves from place to place around a neighbourhood, knocking on doors and collecting donations for charity as they go.

Records of the custom go back at least 300 years, when men and boys would traditionally hunt and catch a wren – known as 'the king of all birds' – for good luck (the feathers were said to be particularly protective at sea). It has undergone a revival since the late 20th century, and everyone is now welcome to take part.

The song sung on the day tells the tale of catching a wren, and lovely renditions can be found on Spotify and YouTube, or the Culture Vannin website (culturevannin.im).

FOOD & DRINK

The Manx food scene has truly blossomed in recent years. While the traditional kippers still retain pride of place on Manx menus, today there is also a vibrant array of craft bakeries, delis and specialist producers who go to great lengths to ensure other top-quality ingredients make it onto Manx tables (with the benefit of having zero air miles).

'There's been a big focus in recent years on great quality local produce,' says Georgia Moorley, from the **Woodbourne Deli** (2 Dalton St, Douglas IM1 3JU ⌀ woodbournedeli.im). 'There's a lot of enthusiasm about buying local and supporting Manx-owned businesses, which we see firsthand.'

The deli, which was inspired by farm shops in the UK and is just across the road from the Manx Museum, is a foodie heaven. 'Over half the stock in here is Manx,' Georgia says, as she points out delicacies in the fridge such as charcuterie made from local loaghtan sheep. There are shelves of Manx honey, ale and hand-harvested sea salt that more than hold their own alongside the international treats like Italian cannoli. Particular favourites include **Red Mie's Duck and Hen Eggs** from a farm in Ballaugh, and natural yoghurt from **The Dairy Shed** (⌀ thedairyshed.com), which uses milk from its own herd in Andreas.

And the Manx stock isn't just for the benefit of tourists – far from it. 'Locals are really passionate about Manx produce,' Georgia adds. 'We have a solid base of customers who come in weekly.'

It's this growing local interest that has spurred the boom in quirky, high-quality cafés and restaurants around the island, catering to a broad range of tastes. The best at each location are highlighted in each chapter, and they draw on a culinary heritage that goes back generations.

The island's deep-rooted fishing industry puts seafood at the heart of local cuisine, with crabs and scallops the main modern harvests. However, in 2023, crews hauled in the first Manx herring catch for 25 years thanks to a post-Brexit deal with the UK government. The restarting of herring fishing has been a boon to the Manx kipper industry, which for years had to rely on imported fish. The fishmonger and smoker **Devereau's** (page 160) has been going since 1884 and is once again able to use locally caught herring in its smokehouse in Peel. Manx kippers are traditionally more heavily smoked than those produced elsewhere, gaining them legions of dedicated fans.

The tiny scallops known as 'queenies' are also a speciality of the Irish Sea – the name comes from 'queen scallops', thanks to their size relative to the more widely known king scallops, and has been used fondly by the Manx for well over a century. They are on menus across the island, though the queenies with bacon and sourdough at **Little Fish Cafe** in Douglas (page 67) are particularly superb and **The Fish Bar** van in Peel has excellent take-away options (page 158).

The island's climate makes it ideal for good grass growing, so local farms often have a leaning towards dairy and meat production. The old-fashioned, family-run butchers (there is one in most towns) are the best place to find the island's high-quality lamb, beef and pork – the best are highlighted in the following chapters. Manx cheddar – a product of the **Isle of Man Creamery** – is also a delicacy. The creamery is a co-operative of more than 30 local farms, and its range of hard cheeses have taken medals at the likes of the Global Cheese Awards and British Cheese Awards; you can find the range in local supermarkets.

For those with a sweeter tooth, a piece of Manx **bonnag** is the perfect teatime treat. An evolution of the flatter griddle cakes made in homes for centuries, the modern bonnag is usually a sweet fruit bread made with currants and buttermilk, though recipes for savoury versions also exist. Look out for it on café menus across the island.

There are plenty of local drinks to sample, with the stalwarts **Okell's** and **Bushy's** ales joined in recent years by numerous craft breweries and distilleries. Okell's is the grandfather of Manx beer: the brewery was founded by Dr William Okell, a surgeon from Cheshire, in 1850 – weekly brewery tours take place at its modern site just outside Douglas (Okell's Brewery, Old Castletown Rd, Kewaigue IM2 1QG, ⌀ okells. co.uk ⊙ 19.00–22.00 Wed) and end at its in-house bar. Bushy's (which sells itself as the 'Ale of Man') began life as a bar and micro-brewery in Douglas in the 1980s, and is now synonymous with the TT (page 23) thanks to the hugely popular beer tent it hosts each year in Douglas. The most recent addition to Manx beer, the independent **Kerroo Brewing Company** (page 218), was set up in 2024 and has quickly gained a foothold, with its own taproom in a former depot in Port Erin.

While the island doesn't have an established history of distilling (with the involvement in smuggling, there was historically no need for the Manx to make their own spirits), a small but thriving sector has emerged in recent years. Ones to watch out for are **Fynoderee** gin (page 101);

CHIPS, CHEESE & GRAVY

Despite 'spuds and herring' being the traditional national dish, there is a young contender for the crown: chips, cheese and gravy. Served at all local chip shops, this unofficial national dish took off in the 1990s and has drawn comparisons with the Canadian *poutine* – though with grated Manx cheddar replacing the Quebecois curds. A dedicated Chips, Cheese and Gravy Day was proposed in 2018 and is now held on the last Monday of January each year, with local chippies marking it by reducing prices. Salty, gloopy and gloriously fatty, it's the ultimate comfort food.

Seven Kingdom gin (⌀ 7kd.im); **Outlier** rum (⌀ outlierdistilling.com), which has been stocked by Harrods; and **Manx Spirit** (⌀ manxspirit.com), an unusual clear drink redistilled from Scotch whisky.

GETTING THERE

The Isle of Man is easy to get to from the UK and Ireland. There is a year-round ferry service operated by the Isle of Man Steam Packet Company (⌀ 08722 992 992 ⌀ steam-packet.com), which takes both foot passengers and vehicles – you can also take your bicycle (though be sure to add it on the 'extras' page when making your booking). It operates up to 12 sailings a week out of Heysham in Lancashire, with this route covered year-round; there are also daily sailings out of Liverpool from April to October and on weekends throughout winter. There are twice-weekly sailings from Belfast from April to August, and a roughly once a week service from Dublin between May and August. Sailings take approximately three to four hours on all routes, depending on the weather and which vessel is being used, and end at the Sea Terminal in the heart of Douglas.

Joint 'sail and rail' tickets, which cover the ferry and UK rail travel, are sold at discounted rates and can be booked via ⌀ raileurope.com – though you will need to contact the reservations team at the Steam Packet (✉ IOM.Reservations@steam-packet.com) separately to confirm your ferry booking.

There are regular flights into Ronaldsway Airport, near Castletown in the south of the island, from many major hubs including London Gatwick, London City, Manchester, Liverpool, Edinburgh and Dublin. The flight from London takes just over an hour.

It is worth noting that air and ferry ticket prices are considerably higher around Christmas and the TT fortnight in June (page 23). Travel can also be severely impacted by the weather, with flights cancelled in strong winds and ferries either cancelled or taking considerably longer than usual.

GETTING AROUND THE ISLAND

The island has an extensive, reliable public-transport system that is split into three main prongs, **Bus Vannin** (which operates year-round), the **Isle of Man Steam Railway** (⊙ late Mar–early Nov), and the **Manx Electric Railway**, also known as the MER (⊙ late Mar–early Nov). The bus fleet is modern with free onboard Wi-Fi and covers routes island-wide; the Steam Railway and Manx Electric Railway are heritage lines running beautiful old stock – the steam route going south from Douglas to Port Erin and the electric route travelling north from Douglas to Ramsey.

If travelling by bus, single fares can be paid when boarding using cash or contactless. Individual rail tickets can be bought at any manned station, using cash or contactless. The most cost-effective option for visitors, however, is likely to be one of the 'Go' cards – a physical card that allows unlimited travel across the network for either one, three, five or seven days. The **Go Saver** covers travel on the buses, while the **Go Explore** covers both bus and rail services. The **Go Explore Heritage** card provides unlimited travel and unlimited access to Manx National Heritage sites for five days.

Go cards can be purchased at ⊘ iombusandrail.im or by visiting the Welcome Centre at the Sea Terminal in Douglas (page 50); both of these provide timetables and ticket information for all three services. Single-day Go Explore tickets are also available to buy on board any bus, train or tram on the day of travel.

As good as the public-transport system is, some places are still only accessible by car, bicycle or walking. There are several **car-hire** companies, most of which are based at Ronaldsway airport. Athol (branches at the Sea Terminal in Douglas and Ronaldsway Airport ⊘ athol.co.im) includes electric-vehicle options, for those wishing for a bit of independence while limiting environmental impact. By early 2025, there were 39 electric-vehicle charging points on the island, including at the Sea Terminal and on the promenade in Douglas; in Tesco car parks in Port Erin, Peel and Ramsey; and at the Bungalow tram stop on the Snaefell mountain road. A map showing the location of all the charging points can be found at charge.pod-point.com.

WALKING

The island is an excellent place to explore on foot, with the long-distance **Raad ny Foillan** footpath ('Way of the Gull' in Manx) tracing a loop 95 miles around the entire coast. It can be broken down into easy chunks for a pleasurable way of getting from town to town – with views that are unbeatable – or dedicated hikers can tackle the whole thing in a

PEAT RESTORATION

Head out for some hillwalking in the Isle of Man and it will quickly become apparent that this is peat country. A spongy, springy squelch underfoot is the giveaway – much of the Manx uplands are covered by a 'blanket bog' of peat up to 10ft deep. Formed over thousands of years from vegetation that has failed to fully decompose in the wet, acidic conditions, the peat – or 'turf' as it is known locally – was used for generations of Manx as fuel; families would be given a licence to head up to the hills and cut blocks from a particular patch. Once dried, the peat, which has a high carbon content, could be used on the fire instead of coal or wood.

Attitudes have changed in recent decades, and the peat bogs are now seen as habitat that desperately needs preserving and restoring. Peatlands cover just 3% of the world's surface yet hold 42% of all soil carbon, so they are an important battleground in the fight to limit carbon emissions. They can lose carbon through erosion, or from drying out entirely due to drainage channels and fuel cutting, which lowers the water table.

The **Manx Peatland Project** (manxpeat.org) was established in 2023 to survey the extent of peat coverage, identify areas of damage and work out a recovery plan. Within a year it had surveyed 6,500 hectares, holding 2½ million tonnes of carbon, and carried out restoration work on 100 hectares. The work is still ongoing, and can involve installing boardwalks to prevent erosion by hikers, laying coconut matting to protect any exposed peat and help vegetation to re-establish, and managing water flow through the area.

As well as carbon storage, Manx peatlands are important habitats for species such as the mountain hare, hen harrier, red grouse and short-eared owl. The Manx Peatland Project welcomes volunteers who wish to help with restoration work; details can be found on its website.

four-day march. The route is marked by blue signposts with the white silhouette of a gull.

An alternative long-distance route is the **Millennium Way**, which takes walkers 23 miles across the central hill range from Ramsey to Castletown. Formally established in 1979 to mark the 1,000th anniversary of Tynwald, it is said to follow the route taken by early medieval kings who needed to get from the port in the north to the seat of power in the south. A good level of experience and appropriate clothing is highly advised for this one, particularly for the northerly section, which crosses heather moorland and reaches an altitude of 1,500ft on some rough terrain.

A slightly shorter – but still strenuous – walk is the **Bayr ny Skeddan** (Herring Road) from Castletown to Peel, a 14-mile hike following the old route taken by fishermen between the two ports. Downloadable guides, maps and further details about each of the long-distance routes can be found on the Visit Isle of Man website (⊘ visitisleofman.com).

For a much shorter – but still very pretty – stroll, there are 18 national glens dotted around the island that are maintained in a semi-natural state by the Manx government. Many are listed individually in this book – they are open to the public throughout the year, and a full list can be found on the Visit Isle of Man website (⊘ visitisleofman.com).

CYCLING

Having produced an Olympic medallist in Peter Kennaugh and the most successful Tour de France rider in history in Sir Mark Cavendish, it's fair to say the Isle of Man treats cycling as a big deal – both on and off road. For anyone bringing their own bike on the ferry, a good first stop is **Bikestyle** (Peveril Sq, Douglas IM1 2BS ⊘ bikestyle.im) – directly opposite the Sea Terminal. This much-loved bike shop has been running for over 30 years and is the place to pick up any last-minute bits of kit and advice.

The coastal roads provide a glorious backdrop for cyclists who prefer to stay on tarmac, while the flat country roads of the northern plain have some of the easiest cycling to be found on the island. More challenging road routes can be found further south – a guide containing four routes of varying difficulty, and including plenty of sightseeing, is available to download from the Visit Isle of Man website (visitisleofman.com). The **Heritage Trail** that runs ten miles along the old railway line from Douglas to Peel is also a lovely option – though unsurfaced, it is well maintained and is a flat, pretty route that's ideal for families.

For those who want something a bit more extreme, many of the island's plantations have dedicated mountain-bike trails, including **Archallagan** in Foxdale, **Conrhenny** just outside Onchan and **South Barrule**. A selection of dedicated forest and cross-country routes can be found on the Visit Isle of Man website. The company **Adventureology** (2A Waterstreet, Ramsey IM8 1JP adventureology.im) offers half-day and full-day treks using e-bikes.

WHERE CYCLING SUPERSTARS ARE BORN

On 3 July 2024, in Saint Vulbas in eastern France, **Sir Mark Cavendish** cycled into the history books. With his arms outstretched in his signature victory pose, he crossed the finishing line and took his 35th stage win in the Tour de France – beating a record that had been held for 49 years.

It had been a long time coming for the 39-year-old sprinter. His previous stage win had been in 2021 – bringing him into line with the previous record holder, the Belgian Eddy Merckx – and in 2023 he had crashed out of the race entirely with a broken collar bone. In theory that had signalled his retirement from racing, but with the outright record so close he decided to give it one last go. And nowhere was more ecstatic about his triumph than the Isle of Man.

The 'Manx Missile', as he is known in cycling circles, was born and grew up in Douglas, and discovered his love of cycling when he joined a BMX club at the age of nine. He has always been proud of his roots, and after his 35th stage win at the Tour he returned to the island to do a lap of honour at the National Sports Centre – the first track he used as a child – flanked by children from local cycling clubs and cheered on by flag-waving fans.

'It was beautiful, it was really nice, a wall of noise the whole way round the race circuit,' he told the BBC. 'It makes me proud that I get to call this place home.'

And Cavendish is not the only cycling star to come from the island. His friend and compatriot **Peter Kennaugh**, who grew up in Onchan and who has also taken part in the Tour de France, raced to a gold medal in the London 2012 Olympic Games in the men's team pursuit. He was the first Manxman to win an Olympic gold since 1912, when Sidney Swann from Sulby was part of the victorious men's eights rowing team.

'The Isle of Man is a small place and it has been incredible the response and good wishes I have received from people,' Kennaugh told the BBC after his win in 2012. 'It means a lot to me.'

A day in the saddle wouldn't be complete without breakfast or lunch at **Cycle360** (Isle of Man Business Park, Douglas IM2 2QZ ⌀ cycle360. com). This combined café and bike shop has a classic, brunch-style menu (think a zhuzhed-up full English or avocado on toast), and also offers cycle hire.

BIKE HIRE

Cycle360 See above
Erin Bike Hut The Showroom, Station Rd, Port Erin IM9 6AE ⌀ erinbikehut.im
Outdoors Ramsey Queens Promenade, Ramsey IM8 1ET ⌀ outdoorsramsey.co.uk

ACTIVITIES

Unsurprisingly, outdoor fun on the Isle of Man often centres around the water – whether it's kayaking round the coastline or fishing on a reservoir, there are plenty of options. The wide open spaces mean golfers are also well served, as are amateur astronomers.

WATERSPORTS

With its varied marine life, craggy coastline and plenty of wrecks, the Isle of Man has plenty to offer those looking for an adventurous day out on (or under) the water. Snorkellers, scuba divers and kayakers are all well catered to, especially in the warmer months – and even novice paddlers have the chance to experience the incredible coastline from a whole new angle. Here are a few companies to get you on to the water – just don't be surprised if a curious seal pops up its head to say hello.

Adventurous Experiences The Shack, Ballabrooie, Patrick Rd, St John's IM4 3BR ⌀ adventurousexperiences.com. Going for over 20 years, the friendly and knowledgeable team here offers sea-kayaking experiences suitable for all levels, as well as coasteering and gorge scrambling for those seeking an adrenaline kick. They provide all the kit, so all you have to do is turn up and have fun.

---

1 The Steam Railway still runs some beautiful heritage trains (page 34). **2 & 3** Sea kayakers have no shortage of cliffs and coves to explore (see above) and this craggy coastline is ripe for exploration for scuba divers. **4** Cycling is not only a pastime in the Isle of Man – it's a source of national pride (page 36). ▶

VISIT ISLE OF MAN

VISIT ISLE OF MAN

DR BEN HOUGHTON

VISIT ISLE OF MAN

SPOTS FOR STARGAZING

A lack of light pollution makes the Isle of Man an ideal place for stargazing, either with a telescope or just the naked eye. There are 26 official **'dark sky' sites** dotted around the island (there is a full list at ⌀ visitiom.co.uk), from where the band of the Milky Way can be clearly seen on a cloudless night – the experience is particularly spectacular in winter when the air is cold and crisp. The northern lights have also been known to put on a show, and are best viewed from the north of the island.

Discover Diving Marina House, Bay View Rd, Port St Mary IM9 5AQ ⌀ discoverdiving.im ⊙ 09.30–15.30 Sat, other times by arrangement. The island's only scuba and snorkel dive centre, run by a team with decades of experience. As well as stocking equipment, it offers testing services and runs regular try dives and training courses. It also does four-day charter trips, with low-cost accommodation available at the centre's self-catering guest flat.

Happy Explorer ⌀ happyexplorer.co.uk. An outdoor-adventure company with a focus on the benefits nature brings to mental wellbeing. As well as paddleboarding, wildlife watching, walks and foraging, it offers trips in glass-bottomed kayaks – allowing everyone from beginners upwards a unique view of life below the waves.

Isle of Man Diving Charters Port St Mary harbour ⌀ isleofmandivingcharters.com. Trips on offer here vary in length from one day to a week, with accommodation nearby and breakfast provided. Skipper Mike Keggen – who is joined at the helm by his son – was part of the Port St Mary lifeboat crew for 51 years before stepping down as coxswain in 2024.

Sea Kayaking Isle of Man Port Erin beach ⌀ seakayakingisleofman.com. Offering everything from family trips up to adventures for experienced kayakers, which involve exploring coves, caves and cliffs that would otherwise be inaccessible.

GOLF & FISHING

There are **eight golf courses** around the island, with all the major towns having at least one. Castletown Golf Links (⌀ castletowngolflinks.com) features in the Rolex world rankings of top golf courses, with its location on Langness peninsula (page 195) giving it superb views out to sea. Ramsey Golf Club (⌀ ramseygolfclub.im) in the north of the island boasts a course designed by the five-time Open Championship winner James Braid. Douglas Golf Course (⌀ douglasgolfclub.com) was designed by the renowned Alister MacKenzie, who also created the Augusta National course in Georgia, US – the home of the Masters.

There are tour operators who offer dedicated golf packages, including **Isle of Man Golf Holidays** (⌀ isleofmangolfholidays.com) and **IOM Event Services** (⌀ iomevents.com).

The Isle of Man also has an abundance of **fishing** opportunities. The reservoirs are stocked with rainbow trout from March to October, with the fishing season continuing until the end of January. Reservoir anglers must have a valid fishing licence, which can be acquired at ⌀ services.gov.im/fishing-licences. The island's rivers offer the opportunity to catch wild brown trout, sea trout and even Atlantic salmon; river fishing requires an 'other waters' licence, bought at the website listed above. No licence is required for seawater fishing; the best time of year for sea fishing is between April and October when blooms of plankton attract shoals of mackerel, grey mullet, pollack and cod, but even in winter the likes of coalfish and dogfish can be caught.

ACCESSIBILITY

Visit Isle of Man has a dedicated page listing **accommodation** (⌀ visitisleofman.com/accommodation/accessible-accommodation) that has been rated against the UK-wide National Accessible Scheme, which accredits places to stay based on a ranking of four levels of accessibility.

If you require **accessibility aids**, such as a wheelchair, while visiting the island, contact the British Red Cross (⌀ redcross.org.uk) or the Douglas-based Disability Networks (⌀ disabilitynetworks.info/equipment-and-aids), who can assist.

All **Bus Vannin** (page 34) vehicles are fully wheelchair accessible, with kneeling suspension and fold-out ramps. The **Steam Railway** (page 34) has a limited number of wheelchair spaces and each train carries a ramp to allow access – call ahead on ☏ 01624 673623 to arrange a space in advance. Note that ramp access is not available at Santon, Ronaldsway, Ballabeg or Colby Level stops. The **Manx Electric Railway** (page 34) has a modified trailer for wheelchair access, which requires 48 hours' notice by phoning Laxey Station on ☏ 01624 861226. There is no wheelchair access on the Snaefell branch line.

The website for **Manx National Heritage** (⌀ manxnationalheritage.im) has detailed accessibility guides, including photographs, for all its sites – by their nature, some of the historic sites are less accessible than

others, though efforts have been made to make them as inclusive as possible. MNH also has detailed access guides for many of the unmanned heritage sites around the island, such as stone circles or burial mounds.

FURTHER READING & LISTENING

The first port of call for any local-interest books is one of the two branches of the Bridge Bookshop (⊘ bridge-bookshop.com), located in Ramsey and Port Erin. They stock a plethora of publications covering Manx language, culture, folklore and the great outdoors. The gift shops at the Manx Museum in Douglas (page 63) and House of Manannan in Peel (page 150) are also well stocked with books.

However, here are a few to get you started. For anyone interested in folklore, *Manx Fairy Tales* by Sophia Morrison is the Bible, and has been keeping children scared and awake for well over a century. For a comprehensive list of every interaction with the paranormal recorded on the island – complete with precise location and description of the event – there is no better than *A Guide to the Folklore Sites of the Isle of Man* by James Franklin, Sam Hudson and Katie Newton. James also gave a fascinating hour-long interview on the subject with the podcast *Some Other Sphere* in 2020, which can be listened to on the Culture Vannin website (⊘ culturevannin.im).

For Manx history, an excellent primer is *A Brief History of the Isle of Man* by Sara Goodwins. For a deeper dive into the archaeological sites, along with directions of how to visit them, *A Guide to the Archaeological Sites of the Isle of Man* by Andrew Johnson and Allison Fox is superb. *Manx Crosses* by David M Wilson goes into detail on the carved stone crosses found in churches around the island.

If you're looking for something about the great outdoors, *Spring Tides* by Dr Fiona Gell is a gorgeous memoir of working to preserve Manx marine life (she also offers her expertise in this guide, pages 17 and 218). Clare Balding's two episodes of *Ramblings* recorded on the Isle of Man for Radio 4 are also well worth looking up on BBC Sounds.

Meanwhile *That Near Death Thing* by the Times sports writer Rick Broadbent gets right under the leathers of the adrenaline-fuelled TT.

◀ Niarbyl is a remote promontory curving out into the Irish Sea about four miles south of Peel (page 167).

ISLAND PRACTICALITIES

While the Isle of Man is British, being both quite small and outside the UK means there are a few administrative quirks that could trip up the unsuspecting visitor. Ones to watch out for are listed below:

Currency Most high-street banks have branches in the Isle of Man. However, the Isle of Man issues its own currency (which has the same denominations as the UK). While UK cash can be spent in the Isle of Man, Manx money is not accepted in the UK – although it can be exchanged at UK banks.

In or on? This is a slightly heated topic, however, the Isle of Man is its own jurisdiction, so this guide describes things as being '*in* the Isle of Man' rather than 'on' it. That said, as 'island' is a geographical description, things are described as being '*on* the island'.

Parking discs If you are driving, be sure to pick up a parking disc from the Welcome Centre at the Sea Terminal, or police stations or local authority offices. This will allow you to display your time of arrival when parking at one of the free 'disc zones' – these are clearly marked with signposts and allow free parking for a certain length of time (usually two hours). Simply toggle the disc to show the correct time, and leave it face-up on the dashboard.

Place names Manx place names do not always have consistent spellings across government websites, maps, road signs, Google, etc. A good example is the village of Cregneash/Cregneish. For the sake of

HOW THIS BOOK IS ARRANGED

Despite its small size, the geography of the Isle of Man allows it to be split fairly naturally into distinct areas – the hills down the middle divide east and west, while the flat north and flat-ish south are nicely self-contained. With this in mind, the chapters are divided into The East, The Northeast, The Northern Plain, The West and The South, starting with The East because it is home to the island's capital, Douglas.

Each region has its own personality, but it is easy to travel between them to cover sites within different chapters in the same day – the only hindrance will be any awkward connections in the bus timetable.

All businesses mentioned have been selected entirely on merit; there have been no charges made for inclusion. While every effort has been made to ensure opening times and days are correct, the nature of small businesses means these can easily change – I highly recommend double checking online or by phone if there's somewhere you have set your heart on visiting.

consistency, this guide follows the spellings used by Ordnance Survey.

Reciprocal health agreement There is a reciprocal health agreement in place with the UK, meaning UK residents will receive free NHS treatment if they fall ill while visiting. However, visitors should ensure they have any necessary insurance in place in the event of repatriation being required.

Telephone numbers If you are using a UK mobile phone while travelling in the Isle of Man, you will be charged roaming fees; the only two mobile networks on the island are Sure and Manx Telecom.

The island also falls within a single area code, so residents and businesses often only list the final six digits when giving out phone numbers. If you are using a UK mobile, you will need to add the area code: 01624 for landlines, or 07624 for mobiles (the last six digits of a landline number will start with 6 or 8, a mobile number will start with 2, 3 or 4).

What3words There are places mentioned in this book that don't have a precise address (a remote beach car park, say, or an ancient tomb in a field), so the What3words app has been used to give the exact location (indicated by the /// symbol). It works by dividing the entire world into 10ft squares and giving each one a unique identifier of three words (eg filed.palms.salads) – you can enter these words on its website (what3words.com) or use the app, which will show you the exact spot on the map.

MAPS

Each chapter begins with a map with numbered stopping points that correspond to numbered headings in the text. The featured walks also have maps accompanying them, and there is a more detailed map of Douglas city centre highlighting the main sights.

The whole island is covered by the OS Landranger 95 – sticking a copy in your backpack is highly recommended as footpaths can sometimes be hard to make out, especially in the hills.

ACCOMMODATION

There is an acknowledged shortage of visitor accommodation on the island, with efforts currently under way to improve what's on offer. There are some smart business hotels in Douglas, but the places I have chosen to include are all either self-catering or B&B – they have been selected because they embrace the Slow philosophy of friendliness, local character and taking life at a gentler pace.

Places naturally book up quicker during the summer months, and if you plan to visit during late May or early June it's a good idea to start looking up to a year in advance – the TT races (page 23) mean every bed is taken way ahead of time.

TOURIST INFORMATION

Details of tourist offices can be found at the start of each chapter. The island's main tourist-information point is at Douglas Sea Terminal (page 50) and has knowledgeable staff and every leaflet you could need, plus the option to purchase travel tickets.

> ### FEEDBACK REQUEST
>
> At Bradt Guides we're aware that guidebooks start to go out of date on the day they're published – and that you, our readers, are out there in the field doing research of your own. You'll find out before us when a fine new family-run hotel opens or a favourite restaurant changes hands and goes downhill. So why not tell us about your experiences? Contact us on 01753 893444 or info@bradtguides.com. We will forward emails to the author who may post updates on the Bradt website at bradtguides.com/updates. Alternatively, you can add a review of the book to Amazon, or share your adventures with us on Facebook, or Instagram (@BradtGuides).

JOIN
THE TRAVEL CLUB

THE MEMBERSHIP CLUB FOR SERIOUS TRAVELLERS FROM BRADT GUIDES

Be inspired
Free books and exclusive insider travel tips and inspiration

Save money
Special offers and discounts from our favourite travel brands

Plan the trip of a lifetime
Access our exclusive concierge service and have a bespoke itinerary created for you by a Bradt author

Join here:
bradtguides.com/travelclub

Membership levels to suit all budgets

Bradt GUIDES

TRAVEL TAKEN SERIOUSLY

THE EAST

1
THE EAST

For those arriving by ferry, the wide sweep of Douglas Bay and the craggy greyish-brown cliffs stretching up and down the eastern coastline will be their first glimpse of the island. Shiny new office buildings and old hotels jumble together in the compact little capital city of Douglas, which quickly gives way to the dark-green patchwork of farmland and heather-strewn hills beyond. Seagulls swirl noisily overhead, the main coast road running north to Ramsey is busy all day with cars zipping to and from the capital, and the tooting trams of the **Manx Electric Railway (MER)** rattle back and forth along the clifftops. The area is lively, has all the mod cons and, on a clear morning, boasts unbeatable views of the sunrise over the Irish Sea.

The maritime connection with Liverpool, which lies directly southeast across the Irish Sea and was the first destination served by Isle of Man Steam Packet Company ferry in 1830, has long pumped money and tourism into the east of the Isle of Man like a financial umbilical cord. **Douglas** has boomed since the mid-19th century into a bustling little city comparable in size to the likes of Sevenoaks or Stroud, and is in the process of shedding its former identity as a slightly run-down seaside resort in favour of its bright future as a financial hub. The village of **Laxey**, six miles north up the coast, is no longer the industrial powerhouse it was when its mining industry was in full swing, but with a population of 1,600 it still carries weight and in the summer months is busy with coachloads of happy tourists.

It makes the area a great base for exploring further afield, whether on foot, bicycle or the several options of public transport. The **Raad ny Foillan footpath** links the towns and villages along the coast, providing plenty of vantage points for spotting **whales and dolphins** out to sea, while the trams follow a similar route for those who would rather take the weight off their feet. The beaches along this side of the island are

THE EAST

largely pebbly, with Laxey in particular a fun location to look for the sparkling white quartz, and the cliffs are steep and rugged, leaving the coastline dotted with numerous small coves.

Inland, the area is hilly, culminating in the island's only true mountain: **Snaefell**. But even this part of the island is by no means remote – a branch line of the electric railway winds its way up to the summit for the most expansive views on the Isle of Man, with cafés providing options for lunch once you get there.

Despite the relatively modern feel of the island's east, its ancient history still pokes through the 21st-century veneer. A bungalow in the village of **Baldrine** (page 77) has a Neolithic tomb for a front garden (the 6ft standing stones line the brick driveway nicely), while a Neolithic chambered tomb known as **King Orry's Grave** (page 86) sits immediately behind a housing estate in Laxey. Venturing into the countryside, the foundations of a **Viking longhouse** are still visible at the Braaid (page 69), while early Christians left their mark at the ancient chapel of **Lonan Old Church** (page 79). There are things to do and see at every turn, and most of it within walking distance of somewhere to get a cup of tea.

GETTING THERE & AROUND

As the island's capital, Douglas is also its transport hub. The **main bus interchange** is at Lord Street, just 200yds west of the Sea Terminal, with connections to all the island's main towns and villages year-round.

The terminus for the **Isle of Man Steam Railway** (⌀ iombusandrail.im ⊙ late Mar–early Nov approx 10.00–17.00 daily with a few exceptions, check timetables) is at the north end of the harbour; it runs down the east coast, stopping off at Port Soderick before continuing south to Ballasalla, Castletown, Port St Mary and Port Erin.

> **TOURIST INFORMATION**
>
> **Welcome Centre, Douglas Sea Terminal** Loch Promenade, Douglas IM1 2RF ⌀ 01624 686801 ⊙ mid May–Sep 08.00–18.30 Mon–Sat; Sep–Nov 08.00–18.00 Mon–Sat.
> **Laxey and Lonan Heritage Trust** Mines Road, Laxey IM4 7NH ⊙ mid May–Sep 10.30–16.30 daily

The **Manx Electric Railway** (⌀ iombusandrail.im ⊙ late Mar–early Nov approx 10.00–18.00 daily with a few exceptions, check timetables) begins at the north end of the promenade, and heads northwards along the east coast through Onchan, Baldrine and Laxey.

DOUGLAS & AROUND

The capital is a great place to start your trip, with the island's flagship Manx Museum (page 63) offering a solid grounding in its unique history and culture, and remnants of Victorian grandeur dotted throughout the city. There is a good choice of restaurants and cafés down on North Quay (page 65), while the villages and hamlets outside the city contain historic gems dating as far back as the Neolithic.

1 DOUGLAS
 Sail Lofts

The beating heart of the Manx economy, Douglas's fortunes have risen and fallen (and risen again) fairly dramatically over the past 300 years. Evidence of this can be seen from the deck of the Steam Packet ship as you pull into the harbour: the promenade is lined with the old hotels left over from the tourism boom of the late 19th and early 20th centuries, while the gleaming headquarters of one of the island's many e-gaming companies sits on Onchan Head on the north side of the bay. The financial sands have shifted as much as those that swirl around in the seaweedy surf of Douglas beach.

After stepping out of the **Sea Terminal** (which houses the island's main visitor-information centre), a two-minute walk down the main road to the left takes you to the island's main bus terminal at Lord Street. The high street, or **Strand Street**, is a five-minute walk northwest of the terminal and has most of the chain stores you would expect to find in a small British city.

Douglas has by far the largest population of any settlement in the Isle of Man at about 26,000 (roughly a third of the island's inhabitants) – and celebrated a major milestone in 2022 with its promotion from a town to a city as part of the Queen's Platinum Jubilee celebrations. Initially a small settlement, with records of harbour infrastructure dating from the 17th century, Douglas began its rapid ascent during the 18th century thanks to its easy maritime connection with the great port

THE EAST

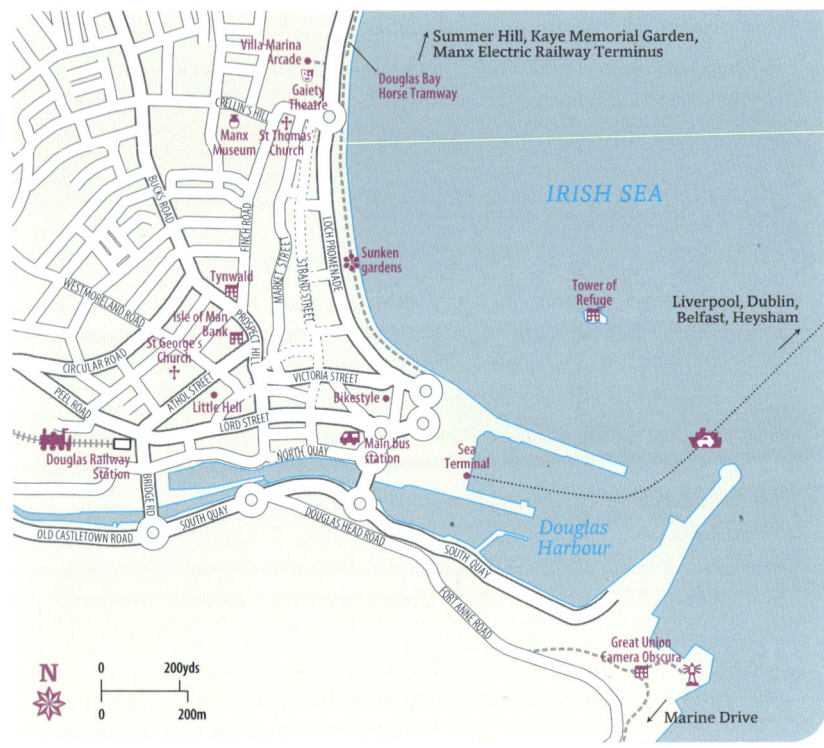

of Liverpool. Before the Revestment Act was imposed by Westminster in 1765, which brought the island under the British customs system, goods such as brandy, wine, rum, tobacco and tea could be shipped to the island – where duties were relatively low – before being smuggled into UK ports. The landing of cheap goods also led to connections with the slave trade: some products brought into Douglas were then collected by ships on their way out of Liverpool, so they could be traded for slaves in Africa.

The growing importance of trade over military strength – which in earlier centuries had meant the seat of power was based in Peel (page 148) and later Castletown (page 180), thanks to their dominating castles – eventually led, in the 19th century, to the island's political centre shifting from Castletown to Douglas. The port officially became the island's new capital in 1869 with the arrival of **Tynwald** (page 61), which had upped sticks from its base in the south. Grand Victorian banks, such as the **Isle of Man Bank** (page 58), sprang up along Prospect Hill in the centre of town to cater for the wealthy merchants and mining companies, which had been established across the island as the Industrial Revolution gathered pace. Official investment in the harbour was a boon for passenger ships as well as trade, and the construction of the promenade in 1876 helped turn the town into a 19th-century tourist hot spot. (The arrival of the promenade pushed the shoreline about 100yds further east than it had been previously; a section of the **old sea wall** can still be seen on the side of WH Smith on the main high street.)

As British tourism declined in the middle of the 20th century, finance came to the fore – later joined, at the turn of the millennium, by the e-gaming industry. Today Douglas is largely about shiny glass buildings and office workers grabbing a Marks and Spencer sandwich on their lunch break, but there are still pockets of Victorian grandeur for those who know where to look.

A tour of Victorian Douglas

For all its glossy accountancy firms and glass-fronted e-gaming offices, much of Douglas is still built on the foundations laid down by 19th-century town planners and investors. Credit for many of the city's sites can be attributed to the money that began pouring in with the arrival of industry and, later, tourism – and knowing where to look can reveal some of the glamour and excitement that greeted Victorian visitors stepping off the steam ships.

Roughly a third of the way north along the promenade from the Sea Terminal stands the **Gaiety Theatre** (Harris Promenade, IM1 2HP villagaiety.com), which is undoubtedly the jewel in the city's architectural crown. Opened in 1900 at the height of the tourism boom, the opera house and theatre was designed by the renowned Frank Matcham – who also conceived the Hackney Empire, Coliseum and Palladium theatres in London. It had fallen into disrepair by the mid-20th century, but was bought by the government in 1971 and work began in 1976 to restore it to as close to its original appearance as possible. Today it compares in decadence to anything that can be found in the West End: angelic cherubs fly high above the audience in a grand mural adorning the domed ceiling, and ornate plasterwork and lush velvet cover every available surface. Hosting everything from the Christmas pantomime through to local am-dram societies and

TOWER OF REFUGE & THE CREATION OF THE RNLI

With its dinky turrets and RNLI flag flying proudly in the breeze, the Tower of Refuge – a miniature castle perched on the small reef known as Conister Rock in the middle of Douglas Bay – can look rather toylike on a nice day. Its sweetness belies the catastrophes that led to its construction, and the creation of the Royal National Lifeboat Institution (RNLI) itself.

The Irish Sea is a treacherous place with a long history of shipwrecks: there have been more than 2,000 recorded in Manx waters. Wrecks could sometimes bring riches as the cargo of foundered ships washed ashore: in one case in 1890, revellers had to be hauled off the beach below Onchan Head in carts after drinking themselves into a stupor when a ship carrying 10,000 gallons of spirits hit the rocks (customs officers attempted to halt the party by spilling the barrels onto the sand; the locals simply scooped up the liquid with their shoes). But wrecks frequently had tragic consequences, and by the early 19th century there were unofficial teams of local seamen who would row out in an effort to save those onboard stricken vessels.

It was among these teams of rescuers that **Sir William Hillary**, who went on to set up the RNLI, found himself after moving to Douglas in 1808. Born to a merchant family in Yorkshire in 1771, he had moved to the island after facing money troubles and set up home on Douglas Head, where he became intensely aware of the risks of the sea. Hillary himself is estimated to have helped save 500 lives in Manx waters. Determined to do something to alleviate the dangers faced by mariners, in 1823 he published a pamphlet calling for a lifeboat service to be set up around the whole coast of the British Isles, to be manned by trained crew. He insisted on the need for 'a large body of men... in constant readiness

---

world-famous ballet companies, an evening at the Gaiety is worth getting dressed up for.

The treasures continue backstage too, including the only surviving example of a Victorian device known as the Corsican Trap – a mechanism that allowed an actor to rise up on to the stage from below while simultaneously gliding sideways across it, as if a ghost. And as with all good theatres, there are plenty of allegedly real phantoms to keep an eye out for, the most famous being the elderly lady who sits in seat B14. Some believe she lost her husband during World War II, and her favourite seat is often left empty in case she fancies popping in to catch a show. Cast members also report coming across the ghost known as 'helping hands': an unseen presence that lingers in the wings, where it hands props to actors or nudges them onstage. A lady in black is said to

to risk their own lives for the preservation of those whom they have never known or seen, perhaps of another nation, merely because they are fellow creatures in extreme peril'.

After an unpromising start, his campaign began to catch the eye of London society figures and on 4 March 1824, a group of philanthropists put their name to the fledgling organisation at the City of London Tavern, Bishopsgate. King George IV also offered his support, allowing it to be called the Royal National Institution for the Preservation of Life from Shipwreck. It became the Royal National Lifeboat Institution in 1854 and today has 238 lifeboat stations around the British Isles. By its 200th anniversary in 2024, the charity had recorded saving more than 146,000 lives.

The Tower of Refuge was built in 1832 on the instruction of Hillary, for use by sailors shipwrecked on the perilous reef. It was stocked with provisions such as bread and fresh water to sustain the seamen until they could summon help, and rapidly became an attraction in itself. The tower is sometimes accessible on foot from Douglas beach during exceptionally low tides – a guided group walk is usually organised by Douglas City Centre Management (douglastowncentremanagement) during the summer months to raise money for the RNLI. The timing of the walk varies enormously from year to year, as it is dependent on the conditions; trying to go it alone is not advised.

A statue of Hillary now stands on Douglas Head, looking proudly out over the Tower of Refuge and the bay. A further lifeboat memorial – a bronze sculpture capturing the drama of crews attending a wreck on Conister Rock in 1830 – can also be found in the sunken gardens of Loch Promenade, Douglas.

walk the corridors and staircases, while a man has been known to sit in one of the boxes before exiting via the wall. Tours taking in the stunning front of house, backstage secrets and unique historical artefacts run from April to October, and last just over two hours – the tours often fill up in advance, so booking ahead is highly advised.

Back out on the promenade, the **Douglas Bay Horse Tramway** was established in 1876 and runs for 1½ miles from the middle of the promenade to the Manx Electric Railway terminus at the northern end of the bay. It is one of the last surviving horse tramways in the world, and still uses many of its original cars (the roofless car that runs in sunny weather is known as the 'toast rack'). It operates from April to October and, as pleasing as the old tramcars are, the horses are really the stars of the show – known as 'trammers', the enormous creatures are mostly

THE MIGHTY WURLITZER

Not from the 19th century but still a charming relic of the heyday of seaside holidays, Douglas's prized Wurlitzer now has pride of place in the Villa Marina Arcade, a covered arcade that runs alongside the Gaiety Theatre.

A sister instrument to the one originally played by Reginald Dixon in Blackpool's Tower Ballroom, the Wurlitzer was built in the US in 1929 and was originally used by a cinema in Leicester. It was bought for a now-demolished Manx entertainment complex in 1989 and has been fully restored.

The organ weighs ten tonnes and has 754 pipes. Free concerts run throughout July and August, with special events at Christmas. Details can be found at wurlitzeriom.

---

shires and Clydesdales, and each has its own name badge proudly on show while working. The horses have a working life of about 15 years, before being retired to the **Home of Rest for Old Horses** sanctuary (Richmond Hill, IM4 2HJ ☉ 10.00–16.00 Wed–Sun) just outside Douglas. A trip to see the older animals is a lovely afternoon out, with the sanctuary having a coffee shop and a gift shop, plus opportunities for visitors to feed the horses by hand. Younger animals can sometimes be spotted being trained on Douglas beach, harnessed up to a frame that they pull along the foreshore.

From the theatre, head 50yds south down the promenade and turn right on to Finch Road, where you'll find **St Thomas' Church** (Finch Rd, IM1 2PL ⌂ stthomaschurch.im) towering over the road. Though made of rather unassuming grey stonework on the outside, the inside of the church – built in the Gothic style in the 1840s – is an explosion of candy colours and patterns more akin to the façades of Italian duomos. The eye-popping combination of green, yellow and red murals covers the walls as high as the raftered ceiling, stretching more than 600 square yards. The murals were begun in the 1890s after the presiding vicar decided that the Gothic architecture lent itself to the sort of wall paintings often found in medieval churches, with his chosen theme for the artworks being 'the Christian life'. The church is not generally open to

---

VICTORIAN DOUGLAS: **1** The city stretches around a sweeping promenade. **2** The Gaiety Theatre is the jewel in the city's architectural crown. **3** The Douglas Bay Horse Tramway is one of the last surviving horse tramways in the world. **4** Electric trams rattle along the coastline. **5** The interior of St Thomas' Church looks like something out of an Italian duomo. ▶

HENRYK SADURA/S

VISIT ISLE OF MAN

PETER G LAWSON/S

VISIT ISLE OF MAN

CHARLES GUARD

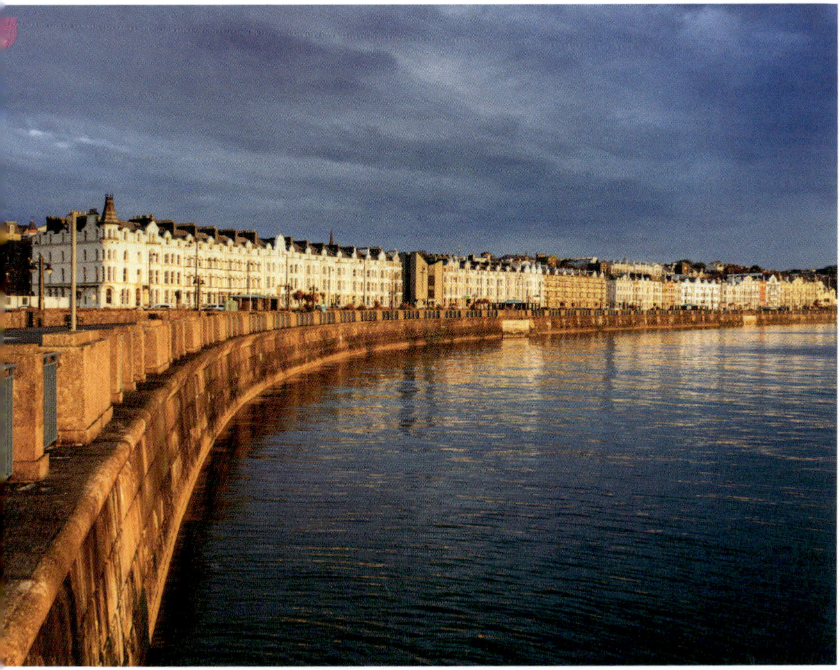

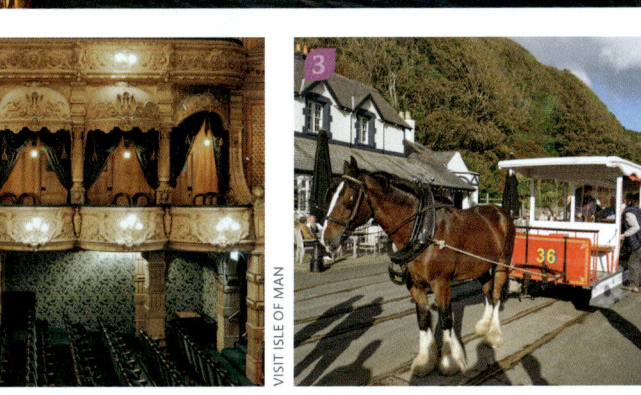

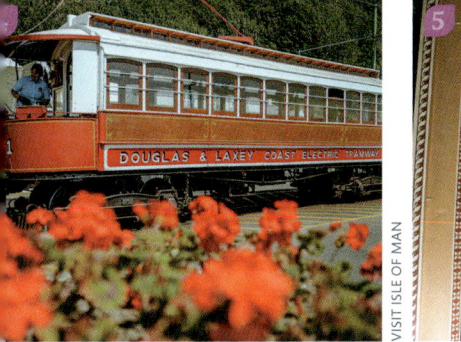

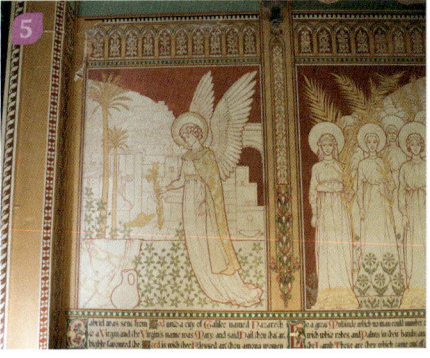

the public, but it hosts a coffee morning on Fridays from 10.30 to noon, when visitors can look around (contributions are gratefully received).

The church itself came about because the rapid expansion of Douglas meant there were too few places of worship to accommodate the growing population. Part of the funding for its construction came from the sale of a 'floating chapel' in the harbour: a former navy frigate had been installed at the top end of the harbour to provide space for 200 worshippers, but was closed in 1845 because it needed repairs and the materials were subsequently sold off.

Directly across the road from St Thomas' is the exceptionally steep Crellin's Hill, which leads straight up to the Manx Museum (page 63). (For anyone daunted by Crellin's Hill, the museum can also be reached by taking the lift to the top level of the multi-storey car park on Finch Road and crossing the footbridge.) The older part of the building was initially built as the town's hospital, opening in 1888. Mysterious noises, spectral sightings and sudden drops in temperature have all been reported, particularly in the basement that now contains the TT display.

Moving from robust Victorian public duty to an ostentatious display of wealth, continue heading south down to the end of Finch Road and go across the street into the **headquarters of the Isle of Man Bank** (2 Athol Str, IM99 1AN ⊙ 10.00–16.30 Mon–Fri). The building is a breathtaking tribute to mahogany and swirling white and pink marble, all topped off with a vast, exquisite, stained-glass ceiling dome depicting the seven locations of the bank's branches when it was created. The bank was set up in 1865 to cope with the growing demand for financial services from Victorian industrialists, and moved into its current opulent premises in 1902. A small but entertaining display inside the branch charts the ups and downs of the island's economy since the mid 19th century, including the dramatic collapse of another local bank in 1900.

Of course, it wasn't all marble and mahogany during the 19th century; the streets immediately south of the bank were home to the city's slums (see opposite), where cramped, badly maintained housing allowed disease to spread and poverty to flourish.

From the bank, Athol Street leads southwest to the golden-turreted gateway of **Douglas Railway Station**. The red-brick building is an imposing presence at the top end of the harbour, and is home to the **Isle of Man Steam Railway** (Bank Hill, IM1 5PT ⊘ iombusandrail.im ⊙ late Mar–early Nov approx 10.00–17.00 daily with a few exceptions,

THE SLUMS OF LITTLE HELL

As with the rest of Britain, for plenty of Manx the 19th century meant a life of poverty and overcrowding as town populations grew. The slums of Douglas – by 1851 the city had a population of 10,000 – clustered around North Quay in what was known as 'Old Douglas'. Even by the late 1870s, conditions in the area were leaving inspectors appalled.

A special report in the *Mona's Herald* newspaper in 1879 lamented the 'absolute absence of any sort of record' of sanitation efforts. It singled out a neighbourhood aptly called *Little Hell* – between Athol and Lord streets, where the modern Shaw's Brow multi-storey car park now stands – as being in a 'disgraceful' state. The reporter wrote:

> I walked up a slope called Shaw's Brow, and, turning to the left, entered a yard where the excrement from a privy... formed a mound of reeking filth right in front of one's eyes and nose. Beneath was one of the old streets of the town, with its narrow and cramped back yards. Each had its own little repository of filth, the oozings from which were lying about the imperfectly paved surface.

The slum houses, built higgledy-piggledy along dark, narrow streets and poorly maintained by landlords, could be home to up to 30 people. With open drains and little in the way of street cleaning, it is perhaps unsurprising that these areas were hotbeds of disease. The arrival of cholera in 1832 caused devastation over the following year. It spread so quickly that bodies were wrapped in tarred sheets and buried at night in an attempt to contain it; a mass grave for 120 victims of the outbreak can be found just up the hill at *St George's Church* (Upper Church St, IM1 1EE). The slums of Old Douglas began being demolished in the 1930s, with Little Hell dismantled in the 1950s.

check timetables) – the station's red-painted verandah and colourful hanging baskets are a gaudy invitation to adventure. The first steam train left Douglas in 1873, with the network eventually spreading to all corners of the island. Today this has been trimmed to a 15-mile route from Douglas to Castletown and Port Erin – but it is still the longest narrow-gauge steam line in Britain running with its original locomotives and carriages.

And what carriages they are: panelled in polished wood, with leather straps to hold the windows open. Each compartment is entirely self-contained – the line's 3ft gauge leaves no room for a connecting corridor. It means departure time is often accompanied by cheerful whoops and waving as friends lean out of windows to ensure the rest of their party joins them in the right compartment, before the train begins chuffing its way through the countryside. As well as the regular travel service, the railway hosts special events in its restored 1905 dining car, with a menu focusing on Manx produce. The **Tickethall Café and Restaurant** (⌂ tickethall.im ⊙ 09.00–15.00 Tue–Sat) inside the station building also serves up classic breakfasts and light lunches, including its famous 'fireman's breakfast', a fry-up served on a coal shovel.

Another example of 19th-century ingenuity can be found at the opposite end of the harbour on Douglas Head, hidden inside a wooden structure that looks remarkably like a white and green circus tent. This is the **Great Union Camera Obscura** (f cameraobscuraiom ⊙ Easter–Sep 13.00–16.00 Sat, 11.00–16.00 Sun), an attraction built in 1892 to entertain the Victorian masses arriving on the passenger ships below. Inside, 11 lenses project various views from around the bay onto a circular table in a darkened room in real time, allowing visitors to marvel at the moving colour images. The novelty of such a thing may not be quite the same for modern tourists, but it is an engaging curiosity for fans of Victoriana. Note that there is a nominal fee for entry, and it is closed if poor weather interferes with viewing.

About 300yds along the main road that leads around the headland from the obscura stands the grand, turreted stone archway that marks the start of **Marine Drive**, a four-mile flat promenade built into the cliffs

THOMAS THE TANK ENGINE

For anyone who spent their childhood in Britain, the sight of a steam train almost inevitably leads to comparisons with the fictional Thomas the Tank Engine. But in the case of the Isle of Man, the connection with the children's stories runs far deeper than just the visual similarities: the island's rail network directly inspired the character's creator.

The Rev Wilbert Awdry, an English cleric, was visiting the island when his attention was caught by the name of the local diocese: the Diocese of Sodor and Man. He noted that while there was an Isle of Man, there was no Island of Sodor – and so his fictional island off the coast of Cumbria was born. (The word 'Sodor' in the name of the diocese actually comes from when the island was part of the Viking Kingdom that included the Hebrides, or 'Sudereys'.)

The first of Awdry's *Railway Series* was published in 1945, with the collection eventually reaching 42 books – the final 16 were written by his son, Christopher. The character's connection with the Isle of Man has been retained well into the modern day: the 2000 film *Thomas and the Magic Railroad* was filmed on the island, with Castletown railway station used as one of the locations.

in the 1890s to make the most of the spectacular views out over the Irish Sea. Hugely popular with walkers and cyclists (it is part of the long-distance Raad ny Foillan route, page 35), the sweeping vista stretches down the coast as far as Port Soderick, and offers plenty of opportunities for wildlife spotting, including bottlenose and Risso's dolphins, basking sharks and even minke whales.

Tynwald

Legislative Buildings, Finch Rd, IM1 3PW ⌀ tynwald.org.im ⊙ free tours 14.00 Mon, 10.00 Fri, plus May–Sep 14.00 Wed

As national parliaments go, Tynwald is an unusual one. It claims to be the oldest continuous parliament in the world, having been established more than 1,000 years ago (Iceland claims to have an older parliament – however, it has been interrupted). It has no party political system, with members instead standing as independents. And you can wander into the building directly off the street, to be met by a smiling receptionist who points you in the direction of the coat cupboard with the friendly suggestion that you needn't carry yours round with you.

The lack of police, scanners or even security guards makes the tiered white building – which, with its delicate icing-like façade, is known as the Wedding Cake – on a corner in central Douglas a welcoming place to find out about the functioning of the island's democracy. The pride taken by the Manx in their political independence can be felt in every carefully draped flag and polished handrail.

Tours are free and open to anyone. Simply present yourself at reception at the allotted time for a fascinating walk through the three legislative chambers, up and down dark wood-panelled staircases, across mosaic floors and past stained-glass windows showing figures from Manx political history. Take a leather-bound seat in the lower chamber, the House of Keys (theories vary on where the name comes from, whether it is a reference to the 24 members or the fact that they hold the 'keys' to power), and hear about the hollow ram's horns that were once used to pass snuff to wilting politicians during sittings. A visit to the upper chamber, or Legislative Council, reveals the story behind the grand chair upholstered with kangaroo skin. The Tynwald Court – the name given

"The pride taken by the Manx in their political independence can be felt in every carefully draped flag."

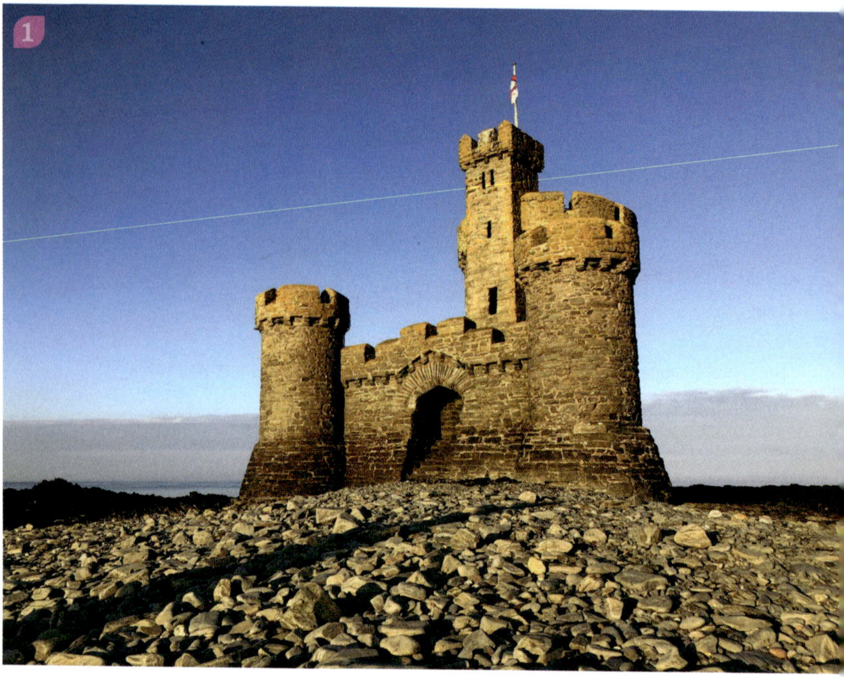

ERNIE372/S

VISIT ISLE OF MAN

MRSBAIN/S

ROGERMECHAN/S

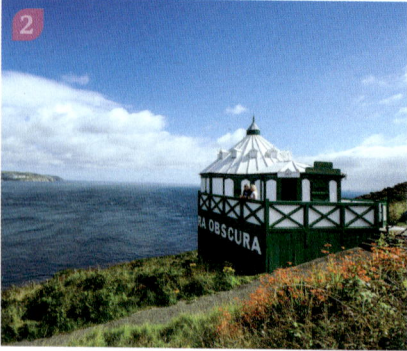

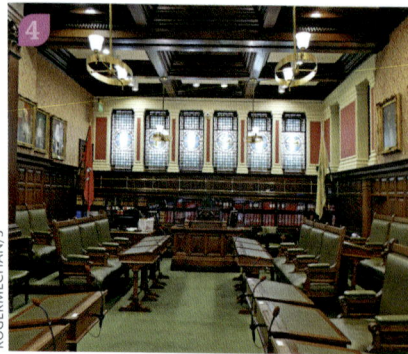

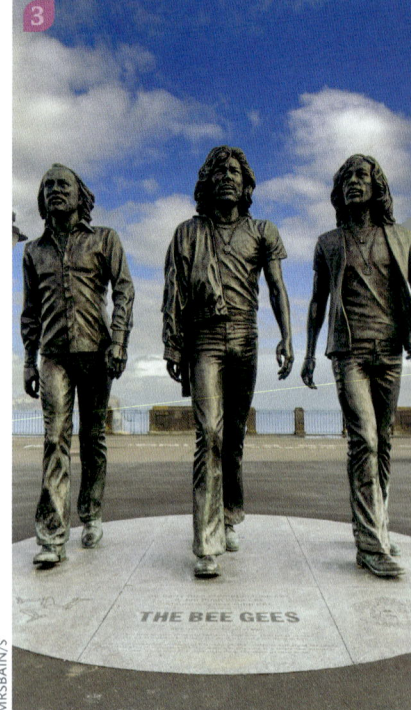

when the two chambers sit together – is home to a hollowed-out stone which may have been an ancient swearing-in stone or may have just been a poultry feeder (the jury is still out, but Manx National Heritage has loaned it to Tynwald just in case).

The imposing building is a treasure in its own right. Built in 1855 as a bank, it was purchased by the government for £3,700 in 1879 after the bank failed. The Keys had previously sat in Castle Rushen (page 183), before spending a chunk of the 19th century shuffling around various buildings in Castletown – including a pub – and Douglas. Today the main political chambers are obviously the main attractions, but just moving between them is a delight for the visitor with the green-tinged wallpaper and twisting staircases harking back to the days of top hats and waxed moustaches.

It is also the place to ask about some of the laws that stuck around on Manx statute books long after they were repealed elsewhere. For example, the use of birching (beating with a birch rod) as a punishment is one older visitors may have heard of, with the practice last carried out 1976.

The Manx Museum
1 Kingswood Grove, IM1 3LY ⌂ manxnationalheritage.im ⊙ 09.30–16.30 daily; free admission

The flagship of Manx National Heritage, this grand Victorian museum contains galleries and exhibits covering the whole sweep of Manx history – from the skeleton of an Ice Age giant deer through to Bronze Age farmers, the Vikings and 19th-century crofters – as well as geology and wildlife. It also houses the island's national art gallery.

The museum opened at the site in 1922 and has become an outstanding introduction to the island's story. Whether you're sitting beside the fire of a croft being told about peat cutting, lazing in a deckchair learning about the island's tourism boom or marvelling at the vast taxidermy collection, it will be an engaging, informative visit.

◀ DOUGLAS: **1** The Tower of Refuge was built in 1832 on the orders of Sir William Hillary, founder of the RNLI. **2** The 19th-century Great Union Camera Obscura offers views across the bay. **3** Visit the life-size statue of the Bee Gees, who were born on the island. **4** The House of Keys, the lower chamber of the Manx government, claims to be the oldest continuous parliament in the world.

SPOT THE STARS

There might not be much Saturday night fever along Douglas promenade these days (outside TT week, at least) but the spirit of disco is stayin' alive in one small way. A swaggering, life-size bronze statue of the **Bee Gees**, complete with 1970s flares, was installed opposite the Admiral House hotel at the southern end of the promenade in 2021 in honour of the band's Manx roots. The sculpture has proved a popular spot for a photo opportunity with locals and visitors alike.

Barry Gibb and his twin brothers, Maurice and Robin, were born on the island in the 1940s – there is a blue plaque on their old home at 50 St Catherine's Drive, near Ballakermeen High School on the western side of the city centre. The family later moved to Manchester, before emigrating to Australia. The brothers went on to become one of the biggest pop acts of all time, but retained their Manx connections: in the 1990s they did a cover of the Manx hymn *Ellan Vannin*, and in 2009 they were made freemen of Douglas (Maurice, who died in 2003, was given the honour posthumously). Following the death of Robin in 2012, his son, Robin-John, told the BBC: 'The Isle of Man was a very special place for my father throughout his career – he loved the folklore of the island, he loved its strong sense of independence and he had a great affinity for the place.'

The Bee Gees are not the only stars remembered on the seafront. A bronze **Norman Wisdom** sits on the bench beside the entrance to the Gaiety Theatre, outside the aptly named Sir Norman's bar. The actor and comedian – whose statue sits with arm outstretched as though in conversation with whoever sits beside him – first visited the island in 1978 to do a run at the Gaiety; he fell in love with the place and had moved here permanently by 1980. He lived on the island until his death in 2010 at the age of 95, and is buried in the north of the island (page 139).

George Formby can be found leaning on a lamppost outside Douglas Town Hall near the harbour, strumming his famous ukulele. The comic film star is dressed as his motor-racing character from the 1935 musical *No Limit*, in which a chimney sweep from Wigan dreams of winning the TT. His song from the film, *Riding in the TT Races*, is still played on local radio during race fortnight.

And there may not be a statue, but other famous feet have walked Douglas promenade – long before they were household names. There is a black-and-white photo taken in 1951 of a group of primary schoolboys from Liverpool enjoying a school trip to the Isle of Man: their arms around each other's shoulders, they lark about for the camera while paddling on Douglas beach. The boys in the image turned out to be Peter Sissons, the former BBC News presenter; John Lennon from the Beatles; the comedian Jimmy Tarbuck; and the future Everton captain Brian Labone. The photo was believed to have been taken by their teacher at Dovedale Junior School, Fred Bolt, and emerged after the death of Sissons in 2019.

The latest additions to its displays are the 'Mann at War' gallery, covering the island's military role since the 1700s, and the rip-roaring TT gallery covering the thrills and sometimes tragic spills of the great race (page 23). Fans of the bikes will have their nose pressed against the glass of the cabinet containing the genuine trophies, while those less familiar with the sport will get a sense of the risks riders take from a sidecar that was involved in a crash – and still gives off the strong smell of burnt rubber.

North Quay

The gleaming yachts of inner Douglas harbour and the stylish restaurants that now line the quay are an inescapable symbol of the island's economic shift from traditional industry to finance in recent decades. The first written record of harbour infrastructure dates from 1660, and the basin has evolved and expanded over the centuries to accommodate a growing fishing industry, trade, the arrival of steamships in the 1800s (and the thousands of tourists they brought with them), and ultimately the weekend sailors who now need somewhere to keep their craft.

"Despite the 21st-century overhaul, the outer harbour still has space for a few working vessels."

Where once rows of colourful fishing vessels were roped together, since 2001 private hobby boats with names such as *White Gold* and *Pegasus* have jostled for space along the floating boardwalk of the newly created marina, their rigging clinking in the breeze as flocks of herring gulls cry out overhead.

The revamp of the early 2000s extended beyond the water, too. The thoroughfare along North Quay is now largely pedestrianised, offering a broad, paved space to amble in front of the 18th-century warehouses, which still stand proudly in the sunshine that peeks over the headland to the south at the height of the day. At the far west end, the harbour is fed by a convergence of the rivers Dhoo and Glass (meaning 'black' and 'green' in Manx) – the combination of the two words being one of the theories as to how the city gained its name.

Despite the 21st-century overhaul, the outer harbour still has space for a few working vessels. The smell of a fresh catch might tempt you to try one of the bustling restaurants that have sprung up along North Quay, which is rapidly becoming the heart of the island's food scene. On warm summer evenings, patrons of the pubs and restaurants often spill out onto the walkway, creating a relaxed, jovial atmosphere.

At the mouth of the harbour, a modern blue lifting bridge acts as the gateway for vessels heading back to their mooring in the marina – watching their leisurely comings and goings can be a fine way to pass a gentle afternoon. The views from the bridge capture the two sides of the modern-day harbour: inland sits the marina, where leisure is king, and seawards are the remaining fishing boats, lifeboat station and Steam Packet berths that speak of the practical role it still has to play in island life.

And if this all seems a little too serene, pop into The British pub (North Quay, IM1 4LB) for a chat with the barman. When asked if the pub has any good stories, he replied that the chef had seen a ghostly child walk through the door of the function room upstairs. 'The hanging tree used to be out the back so we think it might be something to do with that,' he said. Pressed if he has seen anything paranormal himself, he replied cheerfully: 'Not yet – but I only started in October.'

SPECIAL STAYS

Sail Lofts 15 North Quay, IM1 4LE 01624 625005 saillofts.im. A collection of four stylish, self-contained guest rooms on Douglas harbourside, three with en suite bathrooms and kitchenettes and one a fully fledged apartment. Converted from a former merchant's house, the rooms are bright and airy with a modern nautical theme, and are just a stone's throw from the main bus station, Sea Terminal and Steam Railway Station. A continental breakfast is included and is placed in the room daily, while some of the island's best restaurants are right on the doorstep. Each room comes with a 42in smart TV and a Nespresso coffee machine, and there are snuggly bathrobes for relaxing after a day's exploring.

FOOD & DRINK

Kiki Lounge 32 North Quay, IM1 4LB kikis.im 16.00–01.00 Mon–Fri, noon–01.00 Sat. Inspired by tropical tiki bars, this cocktail lounge has taken the hospitality business by storm, winning Bar of the Year at the 2024 Spirits Business Awards and named one of the 2025 Top 50 Cocktail Bars in Britain by Franklin & Sons. The wide-ranging menu is peppered with local brews and spirits, and it hosts pop-ups from visiting UK cocktail bars. Mixing masterclasses are available for those who want to recreate the flavoursome magic at home.
La Nuova Isola 10–12 Prospect Hill, IM1 1EJ (down the steps opposite the Isle of Man Bank) 01624 623764 lanuovaisola.com noon–14.00 & 17.00–21.00 Wed, noon–14.00 & 17.00–21.30 Thu– & Fri, 18.00–21.30 Sat. A brilliant little Italian that's a favourite with

locals. Situated down a quiet flight of steps in the city centre, Isola serves heartfelt, generous dishes in a cosy setting and has a wine list curated to complement the menu. Ideal for a smart lunch or grown-up dinner. Booking highly recommended.

Little Fish Cafe 30 North Quay, IM1 4LB ⌀ 01624 622518 ⌀ littlefishcafe.com ⌀ noon–14.00 & 17.00–21.00 Mon–Fri, 11.00–14.30 & 17.00–21.00 Sat. This snug, beautifully tiled little seafood restaurant sits on a corner overlooking the marina, with ceiling-height windows offering a panoramic view across to the headland. The place to linger over a sophisticated cocktail and indulge in the local catch, lovingly prepared in the tiny kitchen. It is hugely popular; booking is essential.

THE SCAR OF SUMMERLAND

At the northern end of Douglas promenade, next to the Manx Electric Railway (MER) shed, is a scar in the landscape that is hard to ignore. It is the site of the former Summerland entertainment complex, now razed but with fragments of the old swimming pool still fused to the exposed cliff face – and is the scene of the island's most deadly disaster of modern times.

Summerland was opened in 1971 in an effort to entice the tourists who were increasingly turning to cheap package holidays in the Med. One of the biggest indoor leisure complexes in Europe at the time, the five-storey venue boasted attractions including restaurants and bars, a heated swimming pool, amusement arcades and a theatre. There were 3,000 people inside on the evening of 2 August 1973, when a discarded match from smokers outside set a small outbuilding alight.

The blaze spread rapidly, soon igniting the modern cladding that had been used to coat the building and spreading up to the roof. Those inside rushed for the exits, but locked fire doors meant they ran in the same direction towards the main entrance. The flames first became visible inside the building at around 20.00 and the first fire engine was on the scene by 20.07. By the time the brigade arrived, however, the whole building was ablaze. Fifty people died, 11 of whom were under the age of 20, and 80 more were seriously injured.

The complex was subsequently reconstructed on a smaller scale and reopened in 1978. It closed for good in 2004 after the building was deemed unsafe, and demolished in 2006. There have been various plans and suggestions to regenerate the site, none of which have thus far got off the ground.

A memorial to those who died was erected by Douglas council in 2013, and stands in the small **Kaye Memorial Garden** at the bottom of Summer Hill at the north end of the promenade. However, there has been a push for a more substantial memorial to be placed on the site itself, and in 2024 a campaign group, made up of survivors and relatives of victims of the blaze, set out plans to ask for a fresh inquest. Summerland is a wound that has not yet healed.

THE EAST

Noa Bakehouse Peveril Square, IM1 2BS ⌀ noa.im ⊙ 08.00–14.30 Mon–Fri, 09.00–noon Sat; **Noa Market Hall** Old Market Hall, IM1 2BH ⊙ 08.00–14.30 Mon–Sat, 09.00–14.30 Sun. Part of the ever-expanding, family-run Manx bakery Noa, these are the ideal spots for a delicious brunch or coffee-and-doughnut pitstop. The bakery itself is situated on Peveril Square opposite the Sea Terminal – it specialises in sourdough and has enormous windows separating the working area from the relaxed, on-site café. Watch the bakers at work while sipping on coffee that was roasted just yards away. The branch at the Old Market Hall on the quay makes the most of the high ceilings, tall windows and red-bricked robustness of the Victorian municipal building.

Vibe 9 Ridgeway St, IM1 1EW ⌀ 01624 612355 ⌀ vibeplantbasedcafe.com ⊙ 11.00–14.00 & 17.30–20.00 Wed–Sat, 11.00–15.00 Sun. An entirely vegan café offering a full, flavoursome menu from brunch to dinner in a plant-filled, tropical-inspired setting. The flavoured lattes and kombucha range are particularly delicious. The building wasn't always so pure in its intentions: the trapdoor in the café floor leads down to a basement that was once an illegal gambling den for sailors.

2 PORT SODERICK

Three miles south of Douglas sits the secluded bay of Port Soderick. In its heyday a thriving destination for day-trippers, it has now returned to a state of tranquility – the hotel on the promenade has long since closed down and the old electric tram route from Douglas no longer operates. It can be reached by bus (the 29 from the main Douglas bus station), which runs twice a day on school days only, or the Port Soderick stop on the Isle of Man Steam Railway line, which is a short walk inland.

The sense of forgotten-about seclusion is very much part of the charm. The old promenade is still paved but now has hungry vegetation eating away at its edges. Whether wished for or not, the scene gives rise to reflective thoughts about the passage of time and the inevitability of decay. The beach itself is a mixture of sand and shingle, enclosed by rocky headlands on both sides – three large caves at the southern end are whispered to have been used by smugglers. An island in the bay was said to have been cursed by a magician and sunk below the waves; it is now said to reappear only once every seven years, at the end of September – though you would struggle to find any basis for this in fact.

Port Soderick Glen is a narrow, peaceful corridor of lush greenery that covers 15 acres starting near the Old Castletown Road and following the River Crogga down to the beach – it is known for its excellent display of bluebells in the spring. Some 30 species of native wildflowers have been added to the meadow at its centre. The bay and glen can also be reached on foot from Douglas via the Raad ny Foillan route that follows Marine Drive around the coast.

3 THE BRAAID VIKING FARMSTEAD
/// wrinkle.divisions.reforming

About 1½ miles to the west of Douglas, sitting unobtrusively in the fenced-off corner of a sheep field, three groups of lichen-covered standing stones hint at the everyday lives of the early Manx. They are the remains of an Iron Age roundhouse and two Viking longhouses, the 2ft-high rocks and earthen banks clearly demarcating the shape of each.

On a bright, fresh day with the occasional fluffy cloud scudding overhead, it is not hard to see why past farmers would have wanted to set up home here. The broad vistas up towards the central hills and down to South Barrule (page 174) are sublime, with the rolling farmland stretching out in all directions.

While archaeologists haven't been able to pin down a construction date for the roundhouse (almost no artefacts have been found to assist), it is thought to have been a dwelling before becoming an animal shelter once the longhouses were built. The longhouses, both pushing 20yds in length, are large and suggest the occupier had a high status, with construction techniques similar to those found in Scandinavia.

Visitors are free to walk around the site and explore the stones up-close, and there are information boards explaining its history. It is not the easiest place to reach without a car – buses 4 and 4b from the main Douglas bus station drop off at Braaid roundabout at the bottom of the hill, from where it is an 800yd walk back up the hill along a fast road without pavements. A clear signpost on the western side of the road points down the short path to the site, which involves clambering over wooden stiles. However, it is a tranquil spot with stunning views, and is a curious insight into the evolution of a farm over centuries.

4 OLD KIRK BRADDAN
Braddan Bridge, Peel Rd, IM4 4LB ⊖ 10.00–16.00 daily

Standing on the western outskirts of Douglas in the suburb of Braddan, beside the main road to Peel, Old Kirk Braddan is an easy one to miss – especially as it is dwarfed by its later 19th-century replacement directly across the road. But, set back from the traffic behind a screen of mature trees, this plain, rectangular little church and its compact graveyard hold some precious nuggets of Manx history.

The simple church building that stands today is as it was after a series of extensions and the addition of the bell tower in the 18th century – changes made to accommodate a growing population. Much of the interior, including the pulpit, is also from this era. However, the main body of the church is thought to be part of the original structure built in the 12th or 13th century, and it now houses a superb little collection of stone **Manx Crosses** from around the 10th century.

One of the stones, which is 5ft tall and had previously stood out in the churchyard, is known as **Thorleif's Cross**, and alongside the swirling carvings of dragon-like creatures carries a clear runic inscription that translates as: 'Thorleif Hnakki raised this cross in memory of Fiac, his son, Hafr's nephew'. It is a personal memorial that hints at the broader shifts of the era: while Fiac's father and uncle have Norse names, Fiac is a Celtic name meaning 'raven', leading to suggestions he may have had a Celtic mother and been a first-generation Manxman.

"This plain, rectangular little church and its compact graveyard hold some precious nuggets of Manx history."

Outside, one of the headstones carries a story thousands of miles in the making. The unobtrusive grey marker beside the wall is the headstone of Samuel Ally, who died in 1822 at the age of 18, and is known as the **Slave's Grave**. Ally had been born into slavery on the island of St Helena, a British Overseas Territory in the South Atlantic, which was governed by the Manxman Colonel Mark Wilks from 1813 to 1815. Wilks departed shortly before the arrival of the exiled Napoleon Bonaparte, bringing his manservant, Ally, to whom he had granted freedom, with him back to the Isle of Man. A small modern plaque beside the headstone carries a copy of the stone inscription, now much weathered, which describes Ally as 'an African and native of St Helena' who was 'born a slave' and praises him as a 'model of truth and probity'.

---

1 The Braaid Viking farmstead. **2** Baldwin offers plenty of fresh air and hilltop views just three miles from Douglas. **3** Molly Carrooin's Cottage is thought to be the oldest building in Onchan. **4** Caves on secluded Port Soderick beach are said to have been used by smugglers. ▶

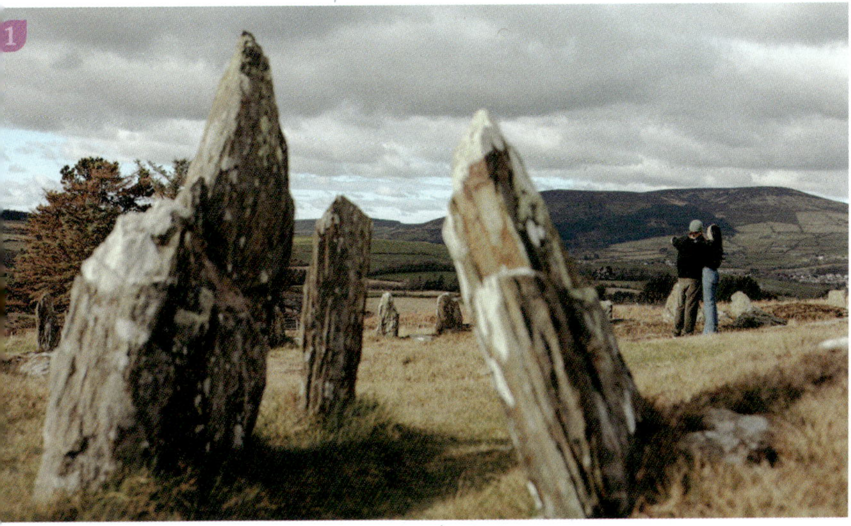

VISIT ISLE OF MAN

SS

ADRIANPOPESCU/S

ROGERMECHAN/S

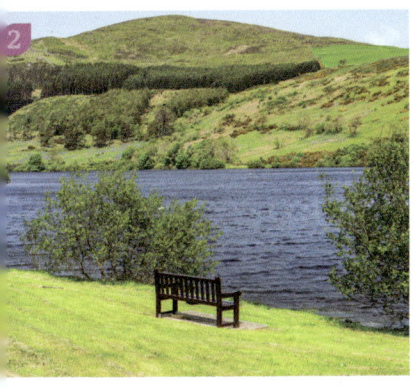

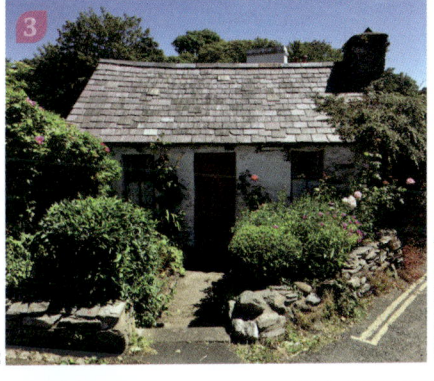

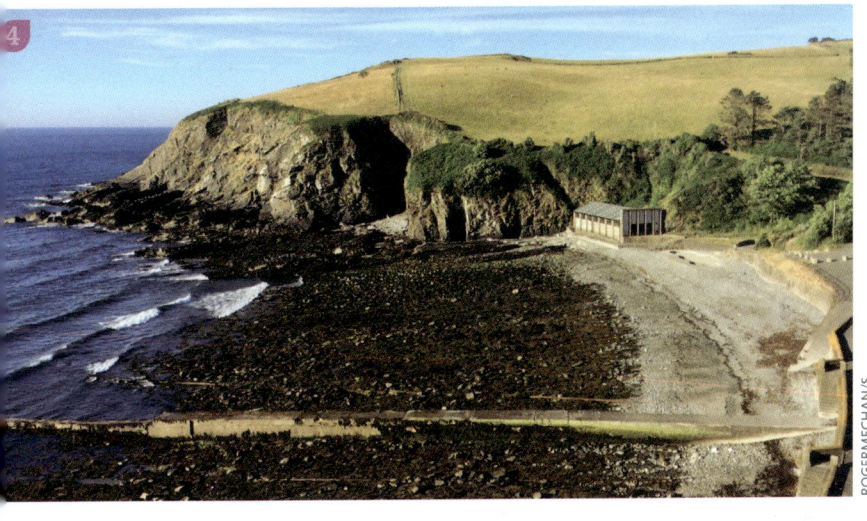

THE SADDLESTONE

/// intelligible.grin.figure

Poking out of the wall beside the pavement, about 500yds up the hill from Old Kirk Braddan, is the saddlestone: a saddle-shaped rock sticking out of the stonework. One story behind it links it to a former vicar of Kirk Braddan, who caught a fairy borrowing his horse for a bit of joyriding in a nearby field – when the fairy was spotted, he vanished, but his saddle turned to stone and was installed in the wall where it was used to grant wishes. This can allegedly be achieved by sitting astride the stone, making a wish with closed eyes and attempting to spit into the small hole at the front. It is said to be particularly good for women who wish to have a baby.

5 BALDWIN

For great lungfuls of fresh air, hilltop views as far as Anglesey and a solid workout for the glutes, head to Baldwin, about three miles northwest of Douglas. A pair of valleys created by the rivers Glass and Baldwin, divided by **Carraghan** with its summit of 1,650ft, this area of steep, heather-strewn grazing land offers truly panoramic vistas southeast over the capital and north across the peaks of Snaefell and the island's central spine of hills, with the West Baldwin reservoir glistening in the valley below.

It is remote and barely populated, with the few roads here often single-track (though they are navigable by car). For this reason it is inaccessible by public transport: the nearest bus stop is at Strang, on the 5, 5C or 6A routes out of the main Douglas bus station. From here it is a further three-mile walk along pretty, tree-lined country roads to **St Luke's church** (StLukesBaldwin) on the lower slopes of Carraghan – follow the road northeast from the Strang crossroads, keeping the hospital to the right, then take the first left where the road forks. Follow the road for about 1½ miles, then turn left uphill at the white signpost for West Baldwin. After 400yds, turn right, following the sign for Injebreck. After 500yds, bear right at the fork where St Luke's sits on the corner. It is a fairly gentle, sun-dappled walk as far as the church, but bear in mind that there are no pavements so road safety is paramount. For those with their own wheels, there is limited parking on the road outside the church.

St Luke's, standing proud on the hillside, is believed to be the highest church on the island at about 550ft above sea level. The current building, a single-storey, grey-stone construction from 1836, is on the site of an ancient keeill and is always open for those in need of a quiet place to reflect, with services held on Sunday evenings. The interior is bright, airy and pared back, with the plain latticed windows letting the sun stream in on a bright day. It is also one of the few graveyards recorded by Victorian folklorists as having had a wren buried in the corner during the Manx 'Hunt the Wren' celebrations on Boxing Day (page 30).

One story connected with the church is that of the **'cursed stone'**, which is now part of the external wall above the window on the eastern side of the building. It was said to have been taken from the old keeill by a farmer, who used it to build his house. However, his family were then kept awake at nights by loud noises such as distressed animals or falling rocks – with the disturbance only stopping when the stone was taken away to become part of the church.

Hidden at the edge of a field about 200yds further up the same road, which becomes an unsurfaced track shortly past the church, is a spot known as the **Old Tynwald Site**. Accessed via a stone stile on the left, it is one of four recorded Viking assembly sites on the island, with the others being at Kirk Michael, Castle Rushen and Tynwald Hill in St John's. The earliest written record for this particular site dates from 1429, and while the precise location of the meeting point isn't known, a round stone enclosure was built to commemorate its existence in 1929 – it is this monument that is still visible on the site today.

If you intend to head up to the top of Carraghan, about a three-mile walk from St Luke's, this is where the real work starts. Carry on up the rough track as it curves up and around to the north side of the hill. Once on the northern flank, turn left off the main footpath on to the flattened grass path that leads to the summit – the route is steep for the final section, but the sensational views from the top are worth it. Head back down via the same route. It is uneven under foot and the weather in the hills can change quickly, so suitable clothing is a must.

6 ONCHAN

It would be easy to overlook the village of Onchan as just somewhere to pass through on the way between Douglas and Laxey. The sugared-almond-coloured cottages along the main road are halted rather abruptly by the modern brickwork of the Co-op and post office, and the distinguished old bank sits cheek-by-jowl with a modern block of flats.

However, the village – which, with a population of about 9,000, is now really more of a northern suburb of Douglas – has deep roots that are determined to poke through the modern trappings, if you know where to look.

The bus stop outside the Manx Arms pub in the centre of the village, on the number 3 bus route, is a good place to begin an exploration. The **golden post box** directly across the road stands in honour of the Olympic cyclist Peter Kennaugh, who hails from the village and won gold in the men's team pursuit at the London Games in 2012.

Head north along the main road and you will see the first point of interest on your right, at the top of Royal Avenue. Squat and white, with a tall roof, the **parish hall** opened in 1898 and is one of 11 buildings on the island designed by Mackay Hugh Baillie Scott, an architect associated with the Arts and Crafts Movement who was a contemporary of Charles Rennie Mackintosh – the Scottish influence can be seen in the elegant, pared-back heart designs in the stained glass windows.

"The village has deep roots that are determined to poke through the modern trappings, if you know where to look."

Back on the main road, take the second right turning, immediately after the old-fashioned antiques shop, and head down steep Church Road to the little white-and-red cottage at the bottom. This area is known as **The Butt** and is the most historic part of the village – the name Onchan is thought to come from *Kiondroghad*, Manx for 'Bridge End', after the crossing over the stream that ran through this part. Built as a weaving shed in the 18th century, possibly as early as 1740, the tiny, whitewashed house with red window frames is thought to be the oldest building in the village and is now known as **Molly Carrooin's Cottage** after the washerwoman who lived there with her daughter at the turn of the 20th century. It was presented to the local community for preservation in the late 1960s and is now a much-loved emblem of the village. It is open for visits on irregular days throughout the year, announced in the Friends of Onchan's Heritage Facebook group.

Directly across the road is another curiosity: an unusually ornate streetlight. The cream and burgundy post, decorated with an entwined 1897, was actually erected in the 1980s along with four others. The lamps had originally been installed around the village to celebrate Queen Victoria's jubilee, with the local tram company offering to provide the necessary electricity. When the company went bust a few years later, the

Jubilee Lamps fell out of use – but were salvaged and resurrected as part of celebrations of the island's heritage in 1986.

Following the road as it rises on the other side of the dip leads to the wall of **St Peter's churchyard**. The boundary itself contains a little piece of local folklore: about halfway up the hill, where the road curves round to the right, a lichen-covered triangular monolith juts out of the otherwise regular stone wall. Known by locals as the **whipping post** as it was thought to be where punishments were meted out, more recent suggestions for its existence include its use as a tethering post for the vicar's horse (it is opposite the vicarage), or that it could be the last remaining element of an ancient stone circle.

St Peter's church (⌂ stpeterschurch.org.im ⊙ 10.00–16.00 daily) itself is a repository for a millennium of history. The current building dates from the 1830s but a footprint from an early church – built in the 1100s and dedicated to St Christopher – can still be found in the grounds, to the north of the modern construction. The previous building on the site, St Catherine's, was the location of the marriage of Captain Bligh – who was mutinied on the *Bounty* in 1789 – to his wife, Elizabeth Betham, the daughter of the local customs officer (page 78).

A collection of Viking-age **carved stone crosses** from as early as the 10th century can be found inside the church, with various examples of intricate, interlaced designs, images of beasts and runic inscriptions. The carving officially labelled as Onchan 85 – a broad Celtic cross decorated with five small circles that originally stood near the original church of St Christopher – was colloquially known as **the betrothal cross**, as engaged couples would place their hands on top of it and pledge their dedication to one another, thereby ensuring a long and happy marriage.

At the north end of the village, separated by the Whitebridge (the name becomes obvious when you see the white stone walls) on the A2 main road, are two glens: Molly Quirk's and Groudle (page 77). **Molly Quirk's Glen**, on the western side of the road, is said to be named after a local woman who was murdered for her money centuries ago; the thudding blows of the attack and the moans of the victim can still allegedly be heard by those passing along the road late at night. Today it is a tranquil spot popular with dog walkers, and the path can be followed as far as Little Mill Road, which leads up to the **Clypse Reservoir and Conrhenny Community Woodland** (page 79) for those looking for a longer day out on foot.

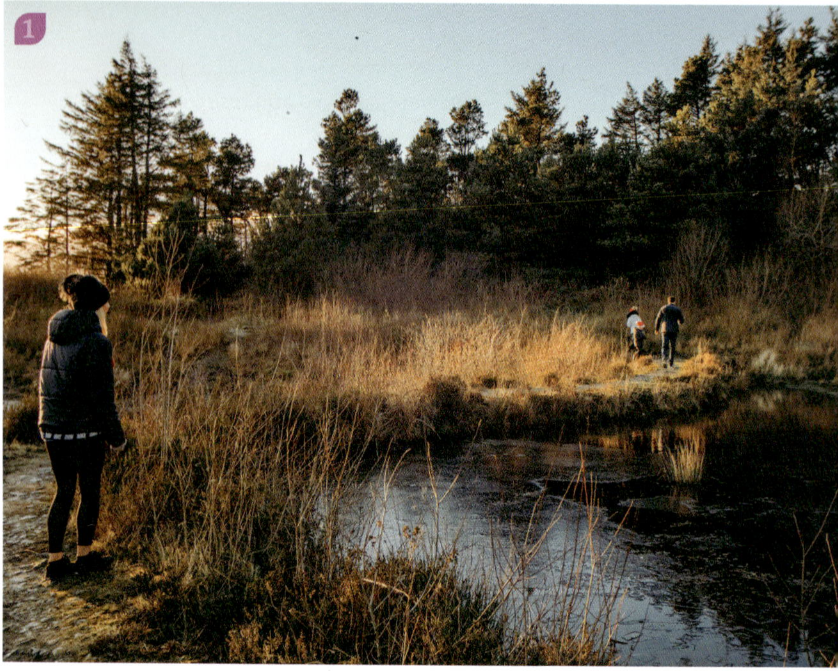

VISIT ISLE OF MAN

CULTURE VANNIN

TIMOTHY CRAIG

VISIT ISLE OF MAN

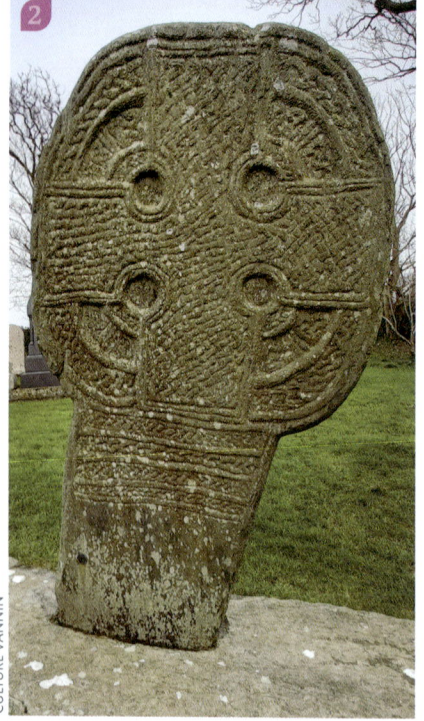

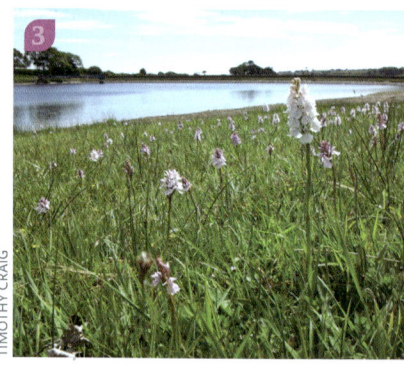

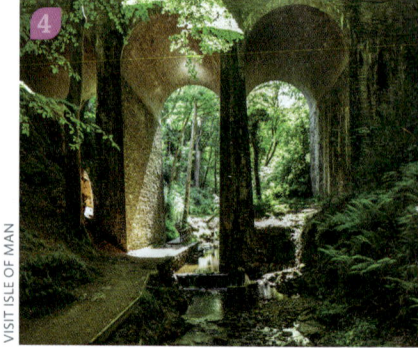

DOUGLAS & AROUND

Groudle Glen & railway

Groudle Glen, on the eastern side of the road, is a narrow corridor of woodland following the Groudle River as far as the pebbly **Groudle Beach**. Largely planted in the late 19th century to attract Victorian visitors, the glen is home to a distinctly Arts and Crafts working waterwheel called the Little Isabella, with its black and white wheelhouse.

Tucked away among the serenity of the trees, not far from the beach, is a dinky little Victorian railway station. With its slatted wooden ticket office and scalloped platform canopy, it looks remarkably like somewhere Hansel and Gretel might disembark on their way to finding a witch in the woods.

But this fairytale has a rather happier ending – one that takes the form of tea and cake. The line, which was originally set up as a tourist attraction in 1896 and saved by volunteers in the 1980s, carries miniature steam trains (⌂ ggr.org.uk ⊙ May–Oct 11.00–16.30 Sun) and is the only way to reach the Sea Lion Rocks tea rooms, ¾ mile away on the headland (there is only one other request stop, at a footpath about halfway along the route). There is no mains power this far out, so visitors can enjoy the novel collision of the 19th and 21st centuries by travelling by steam to reach a café that runs entirely on solar power.

And the café's name? Well, it seems the expansive, uninterrupted views out across the Irish Sea weren't enough to entice Victorian visitors onto the cliffs, so a small zoo was also established featuring sea lions, brown bears and, slightly staggeringly, a pair of polar bears. The remains of the enclosures, now mercifully empty after the attraction closed during World War II, can still be seen from the headland.

7 BALDRINE

A blink-and-you'll-miss it village about four miles north of Douglas, the main road through Baldrine is busy with cars moving at a fair clip between Laxey and the capital. The arterial route is overhung with mature trees and lined with a jumble of architectural styles from the old corn mill on the corner to 1930s semis and mid-century bungalows,

◀ **1** Enjoy a bracing walk up from Baldrine into the Conrhenny Community Woodland. **2** One of the medieval carved crosses at Lonan Old Church. **3** Orchids growing beside tranquil Clypse Reservoir. **4** A viaduct carries the MER and main road over the river in Groudle Glen.

THE MANX & THE MUTINY ON THE BOUNTY

The Mutiny on HMS *Bounty* took place on 28 April 1789, in the South Pacific Ocean, and has gone down as one of the most notorious events in British maritime history. Captain Bligh and 18 of his loyal crew were set adrift in an open boat – leaving Bligh to navigate them 4,000 miles to safety in a feat of naval brilliance. Twenty-five men remained on board the *Bounty*; Bligh's acting lieutenant, Fletcher Christian, had led the uprising of disaffected crew, eventually taking them and the ship to the tiny island of Pitcairn in the southern Pacific.

The tumultuous tale may have ended in the South Pacific, but its early shoots could be found 9,000 miles away in the Isle of Man. Captain Bligh was from Plymouth and had joined the Royal Navy as a boy, and in the 1770s was a midshipman on a vessel that operated in the Irish Sea. He visited Douglas often, eventually marrying the daughter of the local customs officer, Elizabeth Betham, at Onchan Parish Church (page 75) in 1781.

The graves of Elizabeth's parents, Richard and Mary, are in Onchan churchyard.

Peter Heywood, a midshipman who stayed on board the *Bounty* during the mutiny (whether willingly or not is disputed), was born in Douglas and knew the Betham family, who helped him to secure the commission to join Bligh's *Bounty* voyage.

Fletcher Christian was born in Cumberland in the northwest of England, but was descended from the Christians of Milntown (page 108), near Ramsey, through his father, who died when Christian was a child. After his father's death, the family moved to be with their relatives at Milntown, and Christian was said to have frequented The Mitre pub in Kirk Michael (page 132). He joined the Royal Navy at the age of 17 – briefly serving on the same frigate as Bligh. He later joined Bligh's ship, the Britannia, in the merchant navy, before Bligh approached him in 1987 to be in his crew for the two-year voyage on the *Bounty*.

which are also spread further up and down the valley. The whole village can have the slight feeling of being caught in a thoroughfare.

Yet one of the bungalows – or rather, its garden – contains something quite extraordinary. Turning east down Packhorse Lane (at the base of the dip in the main road), the second house on the right has what remains of a **Neolithic tomb** on its front lawn. Alongside the neat brick driveway and potted shrubs, and easily visible from the road, two upright slabs of stone about 6ft tall mark what would have been the tomb's forecourt, leading to a small chamber (now in the middle of the lawn) enclosed by smaller slabs. One of the larger standing stones has at some point split in two, giving rise to the site's name: **the Cloven Stones**. A group of miners dug into the site in the early 19th century and found human bones – these have since been lost, but flint tools found nearby have been used as evidence of the tomb's age.

According to local legend, the stones are said to clap when there is thunder. There are also tales of the stones having been seen to move at night – though there is speculation as to whether this was the result of the supernatural or the effect of spirits of a more liquid variety.

Baldrine sits within a small valley that provides some lovely opportunities to explore on foot. **Garwick beach**, a pebbly cove at the eastern mouth of the valley, can be reached via the footpath through Garwick Glen (find the footpath by turning east off the main road on to Clay Head Road, about halfway up the hill on the south side of Baldrine – the path is marked by a blue Raad ny Foillan signpost, on the left about 100yds along the road). This secluded bay, with clear waters and trees overhanging the beach, is popular with swimmers and anglers. It's also a favourite spot among local photographers who want to catch the perfect shot of the sunrise – though on misty days things take a turn for the spooky, as a ghost ship is said to move silently in and out of the fog.

A bracing walk can be taken from Baldrine up into the foothills as far as **Conrhenny Community Woodland**. Turn west up Baldrine Road (about 50yds downhill of the Millennium Clock on the main road), cross over the tram lines at the MER halt and follow the road uphill for about a mile until an unsurfaced trail leads into the trees on the left, by the wooden gate marked with a green footpath sign. The woodland, established as a plantation of mostly pine and spruce in the 1960s, has since been diversified and is now crisscrossed by a network of paths and mountain-bike tracks. The views on the way up are glorious, stretching back down the valley to Garwick Bay. You can turn it into a longer route by following the roads and footpaths south from the plantation to the Clypse Reservoir, a tranquil fishing spot about a mile away on foot.

Lonan Old Church
Ballmenaugh Rd, IM4 6AH stadamnanslonan

For big skies, gorse-lined hedgerows and the companionable mooing of livestock, head for the farmland to the southeast of Baldrine. At the southern end of the village, turn east uphill next to the Millennium Clock (an ornate, free-standing green clock tower erected to mark the year 2000) and follow the road behind the houses. Keep going as it becomes a track, then turn left as it rejoins the road – this will take you between the fields towards the dinky former parish church.

The entrancingly pretty St Adamnan's Church is known to locals as Lonan Old Church, Lonan being the name of the parish. The site itself – a compact, square little churchyard surrounded by trees – goes back to the earliest days of Manx Christianity, with **eight medieval carved crosses** in the churchyard dating from the 7th to the 10th centuries. A church is believed to have stood here since the 12th century; the door in the south wall is of a style from this era. The simple, rectangular stone building here today is a blend of past and present: the east end has been re-roofed and is still opened up for services, while the rest of it has been left as the ruins it became after a church was opened elsewhere in the parish in the 1830s. Wildflowers now sprout from the stones along the derelict old roofline, and patches of bluebells and daffodils pop up around the neat and tranquil graveyard in spring.

"Patches of bluebells and daffodils pop up around the neat and tranquil graveyard in spring."

Most of the stone crosses are housed in a shelter in the southwest corner, with information panels for visitors. However, one monumental slab from the early 10th century still stands in its original position on the south side of the churchyard. Despite batterings from the weather and its rather drunken lean, the broad, 5ft-high cross still carries its highly intricate, interlaced Celtic carvings – the woven design covers the entire face of the cross, which is a monument to craftsmanship as much as faith.

The site's connection to the deepest roots of Celtic Christianity – it sits beside the old route from Douglas to the north and had a well nearby, making it a convenient spot for worship – is also highlighted by the dedication: St Adamnan was the abbot of Iona, the holy island in the Inner Hebrides, who died in AD704.

LAXEY & AROUND

An industrial powerhouse during the 19th century, today the village of Laxey and the surrounding valley offer a much more sedate day out. The stony beach is popular with families in summer and wild swimmers year-round, while heritage enthusiasts will enjoy discovering the feats of engineering that kept the local mines clanging during the Industrial Revolution.

8 LAXEY

Hunkered in the steep, narrow valley that leads from Snaefell mountain down to the sea, the rows of old miners' cottages and the large, double-fronted homes of the Victorian middle classes are the first hint that the village of Laxey – seven miles north of Douglas – may once have had more to it than immediately meets the eye. Today, it is a small but lively community of about 1,600 people, with cheerful dog walkers chatting on the promenade, rows of well-looked-after old cottages and an annual rubber-duck race on the river. Yet at the turn of the 20th century it was a roaring industrial centre and a powerhouse of the island's economy.

This history starts to reveal itself as you follow the main A2 road around the valley, through the centre of the modern village. Passing over the castellated Laxey Bridge that joins the two sides of the valley, the towering **Laxey Glen Mills** (laxeyglenmills.com) beside it speaks to the scale of operations that once took place. Four storeys high, twice as wide as it is tall and with a striking green and red logo on its roof, the mill has been producing Laxey Flour using local wheat since 1860. Its products, which can be ordered online for collection on site, have deservedly held Great Taste awards since 2016 – but the enormity of the building does feel a little out of place.

Then, rounding the corner, the pillar-box red titan that is the **Great Laxey Wheel** (page 84) roars into view, standing proudly above the village. A wonder of Victorian engineering, the 72ft-wide waterwheel has been in motion since 1854 and is the largest working waterwheel in the world. It was constructed to pump floodwater from the lucrative mines that burrowed deep into the surrounding hillside and today stands as a highly visible reminder of the village's good economic fortune.

The village is thought to have originated as a favourite fishing spot for the Vikings (the name Laxey comes from 'Laksaa', derived from the Old Norse for 'salmon river'), and by the late 1700s had evolved into a small fishing community clustered around the seafront, where the herring boats would launch straight from the beach. Now known as **Old Laxey**, this area can be reached via the extremely steep, narrow roads that wind down from the main road to the valley floor – where tiny traditional cottages can still be found dotted among the later Victorian terraces.

The **beach** consists of banks of pebbles at high tide, with a stretch of flat sand revealed at low tide – the dramatic rock formations jutting out of the sand at the southern end are a beacon for older children wishing to clamber, though can be very slippery. A raft is anchored in the bay during the summer months for the use of swimmers. The breakwater can be reached via a short footpath that leads over the headland; simply follow the lane that runs behind the house on the northern side of New Laxey Bridge, which crosses the river at the top of the harbour.

With the arrival of the Industrial Revolution, the focus shifted inland to the village's other natural resources: lead and zinc. The area was rich in both and by the 1830s the local mining company had a workforce of 200; by the end of the 19th century the whole valley had been transformed into the industrial landscape that is still visible today. The modern harbour with its muscular breakwater was built not for the

MANX TARTAN AT LAXEY WOOLLEN MILLS
Glen Rd, IM4 7AR ⌀ laxeywoollenmills.com ⊙ 10.00–17.00 Tue–Sat

'The beauty of the Manx tartan is it's distinctive,' says John Woods, master weaver and the owner of Laxey Woollen Mills. 'There's hardly a tartan out there that's anything like it, so when you see it you know where it came from. You can be anywhere in the world, and if you see a bloke in a Manx tartan kilt, you know he comes from the Isle of Man.'

The tartan he's referring to is the blue, green, yellow, purple and white design that his mill has been weaving since the late 1970s. The colours represent the sky, hills, gorse, heather and whitewashed cottages of the island – and John uses it for a range of products, from travel rugs to ties and scarves. The design has become an emblem for the island, with expats just as keen to take some away with them as locals are to wear it out and about in Douglas.

'The people who keep Manx tartan alive and buoyant… it's the young men in Douglas that buy the wool ties,' John adds. 'We make lambswool scarves in it, and again, half the young people walking down the street have got a Manx scarf on. It's a badge of honour.'

John has been working in the mill since 1974, when he joined his father as an apprentice. The long stone building with eye-catching blue window frames sits beside the river at the base of Laxey Valley – as much a part of the village's industrial heritage as the Great Laxey Wheel (page 84) up the road. Inside, it is set up as a shop, with John pedalling on his loom at the far end. The machine clatters away behind stacks of tweed bolts woven from Loaghtan, Shetland and Herdwick wool. Coats, hats and mittens line the shelves and rails, and the air has the comforting smell of fleece.

fishing fleet, but to ship out the ore; the open lawns in the centre of the village, now called the **Valley Gardens**, were the mines' washing floors; rows of miners' cottages sprang up; and, of course, the Great Wheel came to stand watch over it all. A conscious effort to diversify the local economy came with the establishment in the 1880s of **Laxey Woollen Mills** (see opposite), which now produces Manx tartan, but mining still dominated.

A useful little introduction to the village can be found at **Christ Church** (⊙ 10.00–16.00 daily), behind the substantial MER station in the centre of the village (the charming wooden ticket office houses a kiosk that's handy for a refreshing cup of tea and piece of cake, which can be eaten on the benches outside). The church was built for the miners in the 19th century and welcomes visitors, who can sit among the pews and watch a 20-minute film about the area's history. From here, make like a Victorian

---

The space hasn't always been so tranquil. The mill was set up in 1881 by a friend of the art critic John Ruskin, in an attempt to create an alternative form of employment for villagers when the local mining industry was at the height of its dominance. Business had its ups and downs, but even in the 1960s there were 12 looms running and 30 members of staff. Then the arrival of cheap products from the Far East in the late 20th century meant British-made woollens went from being a staple to a luxury product, and a new market was needed.

Today that market is younger people who are willing to spend a bit more for something sustainable and ethically made. Ruskin was against the rampant commercialism of the Industrial Revolution, and his ideology was one of wanting to strip things back to using as few processes as possible – industrial dyeing was one element that he particularly disliked. John points out that this ethos is still being followed at the mill, as he runs his hand over a stack of beautiful bolts of cloth woven from undyed wool. 'That to us is going back to what the history is,' he says.

The main mill shop is a pleasure to browse, with everything from gorgeous tweed glasses cases at souvenir prices up to investment jumpers and tailored coats. The upper floor of the mill has been transformed into the **Hodgson Loom Art Gallery** (same opening hours), which hosts exhibitions by local artists, and there is a dedicated **Manx Tartan Shop** (⌂ presenceofmann.com ⊙ 11.00–16.30 Mon–Sat) on site too.

And if all this creativity is inspiring a bit of a career change, bear in mind it won't happen overnight. 'About 25 years' experience is what you need,' says John. 'After 25 years you might be able to call yourself a master weaver.'

industrialist and head to **The Mines Tavern** (3 Captain's Hill, IM4 7AY f) on the other side of the station to enjoy a drink in the former home of the captain of the mine – the bar decked out to look exactly like one of the electric trams is a sight worth seeing in itself.

Dumbells Terrace, directly across the main road from the pub, has led a double life that is revealed by its alternative name. The row of two-up, two-downs is still known to locals as 'Ham and Egg Terrace', thanks to the enterprising ladies who once lived there. The cottages were built for miners and their families in the 1860s when the industry was in full swing – a period that overlapped with the tourist boom of the late 19th century. Many visitors to the island were keen to see the spectacular Laxey Wheel for themselves, creating a handy business opportunity for the women living on Dumbells Terrace, which leads directly to the wheel. They began serving up teas and lunches for the tourists for a little extra cash, and the street's nickname stuck.

The Great Laxey Wheel

Wheel Hill, Mines Rd, IM4 7NL ⊘ manxnationalheritage.im ⊙ Apr–Oct 09.30–16.30 daily

It appears on the Manx £20 note, is the subject of the best-known local folk song and it even had a starring role in the 2016 comedy film *Mindhorn*. It's fair to say the Great Laxey Wheel has a cultural presence that equals its towering physical one.

The **72ft waterwheel**, an absolute triumph of Victorian engineering and today the largest working waterwheel in the world, was built in 1854 to pump water from the mines that burrowed into the hills above Laxey village. Despite the closure of the mines in 1929 – ending 150 years of industry in the valley – the wheel still gleams and the white stonework of its base, complete with large, circled relief of the three legs of Man, is pristine. A major restoration project was completed in 2022 to keep the Lady Isabella, as the wheel is fondly known, turning for years to come. Visitors can climb the 96 spiral steps to the viewing platform at the top, and enjoy the slightly giddy feeling of seeing the slats of the moving wheel thunder past just inches below their feet. Those feeling intrepid can don hard hats and head a short way underground to see some of the workings of the mine itself; the thick smell of damp, constant sound

"Those feeling intrepid can don hard hats and head a short way underground to see some of the workings of the mine."

of dripping and glistening wet walls make it perfectly clear why the powerful pump of the waterwheel was needed in the first place.

Information boards are dotted around the site and there is a scattering of picnic tables (note that there is no café on site, so visitors should bring their own refreshments). The relative tranquillity of enjoying a sandwich beside the rhythmically sloshing wheel is a stark contrast to the heft and effort that went into its construction; some of the castings were so large that they had to be brought into Laxey Bay by cargo ship, dropped overboard at high tide, then hauled up the beach at low water.

The Great Laxey Mine Railway & Snaefell Wheel

At the western end of Laxey Valley Gardens, directly across the river from the Mines Tavern at the top of Captain's Hill, IM4 7AY ⌁ laxeyminerailway.im ⊙ Railway: Easter–Sep 11.00–16.30 Sat

To further explore the valley's industrial heritage, take a trip on the **Great Laxey Mine Railway**, which is now run as a separate attraction but was once an integral part of the valley's mining ecosystem. The train, propelled by a chuffing little locomotive that is a replica of the original steam engine, takes passengers on a short trip up the valley through a low, narrow 76yd tunnel that runs under the main road – the narrow gauge and tight dimensions of the tunnel mean the passenger carriage is

THE LAXEY WHEEL SONG

In 1958 the Isle of Man sent its first team of cyclists to compete at the Commonwealth Games in Cardiff. It proved to be a rewarding decision – the 23-year-old rider Stuart Slack, from Douglas, clinched a bronze medal for the island in a nail-biting 120-mile road race.

But sporting prowess is not the only reason Slack, who died in 1998, is remembered today. For he was also a musician and wrote a song that has entered the canon of Manx music. Written in 1957, *The Laxey Wheel* was performed and made (relatively) famous by the band Mannin Folk in the 1960s. Over three verses and a stomping chorus, it charts the rise and fall of the mining industry, and the wheel's stoic persistence throughout the economic ups and downs. Various renditions can be seen on YouTube – or, for a live performance, simply ask anyone who attended primary school on the island, as they are likely to know it off by heart.

Slack's other folk song about the village, *Laxey Girls*, was banned by Manx Radio for being too risqué. Containing humour that was very much of its time, this tune has always been kept well away from the ears of primary pupils. There is a version on YouTube for those who would like a listen.

very snug. What is now the boarding point at the western end of Valley Gardens was where ore was offloaded from the railway wagons to be washed after being transported from the pits.

There is also another, lesser known, red waterwheel in the Valley Gardens. The Snaefell Wheel measures 50ft in diameter and originally powered the pump for the Snaefell mine shafts at the top of the valley, where it was built in 1865. It was taken to Cornwall after the mine closed in 1908, before falling into disuse in the 1950s – eventually making its way back to Laxey with the help of heritage enthusiasts, where it was rebuilt in its new position in 2006.

King Orry's Grave & the triskelion
Ballaragh Rd /// curious.pans.inferior

A monument that harks back to the days long before Laxey was a hive of Victorian industry can be found just off the main road heading north out of the village. Squeezed between a 19th-century house and a later housing estate, King Orry's Grave is a fantastic and easily accessible example of a **Neolithic chambered tomb** . It can be viewed from the road or reached via a short set of steps – the site is completely open access.

To find the tomb, travel north along the main road out of Laxey towards Ramsey until you reach the crossroads about half a mile from the MER station. Turn left up the Ballaragh Road, following the brown sign for King Orry's Grave, and the site is 75yds directly ahead – the site is split in two, with one half on each side of the road. The most obvious section is on the **eastern side**: a cluster of standing stones roughly 5ft high form a curved portal that once would have been the entrance to the tomb, leading to the burial chambers (the back section of the cairn was chopped off when the house was built in the 1800s). Excavations have found fragments of bone, flint tools and pottery inside the chambers, while evidence of fires outside the entrance suggest it was a revered place of ritual. The site is thought to have been constructed around 4000BC but radiocarbon dating has revealed it was still in use a thousand years

---

1 & 2 Laxey today might be a small, quaint place, but the towering Laxey Glen Mills are one of the reminders of its industrial past. **3** The 72ft Great Laxey Wheel is the largest working waterwheel in the world. **4** Enjoy sweeping views from the top of Snaefell, the island's only mountain. ▶

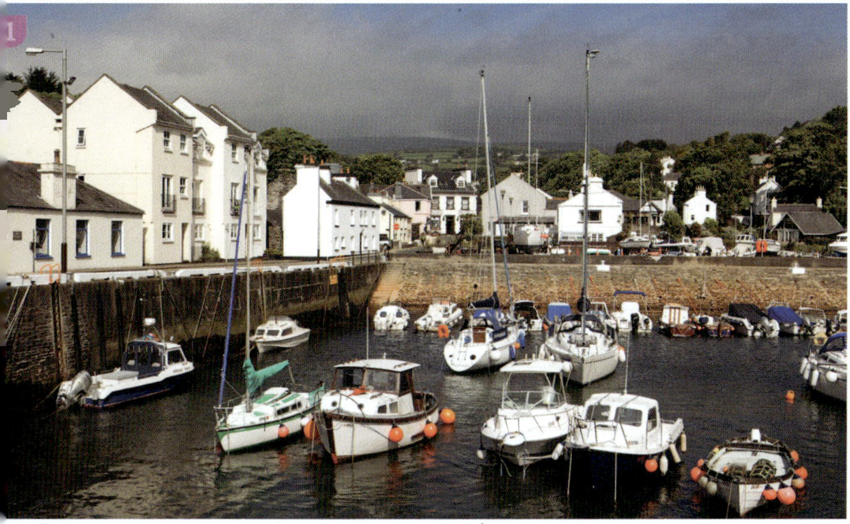

TRAVELIB PRIME/A

EVE HARDING/S

GRAHAM TAYLOR/DT

SAMANTHA FLETCHER

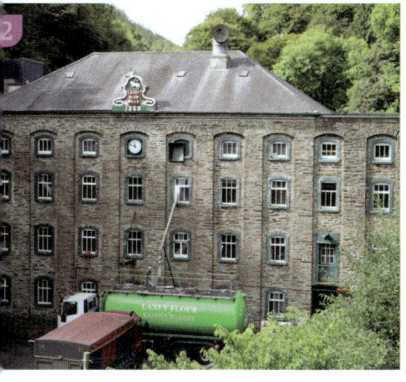

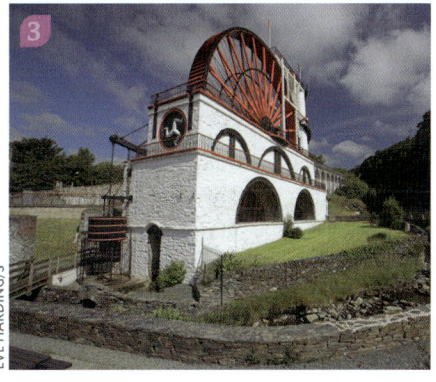

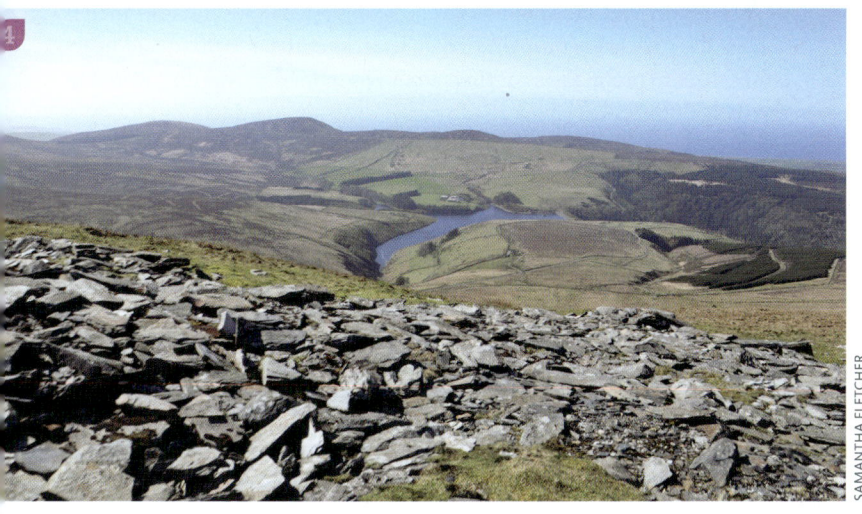

later. The covering for the chambers has long since disappeared, but the structural stones remain and can be explored up-close.

Across the road, the **western side** of the site takes a little finding via a path round the back of another private house. The structure is similar to the eastern side, with a small curved forecourt leading to burial chambers that would have been covered by earth – the strikingly narrow, 10ft-high obelisk known as King Orry's Stone would have formed part of the entrance.

Despite being Neolithic, there were claims during the 19th century that evidence of a Viking burial had been found at the site – though these were disputed, and the story may have been invented by entrepreneurial Victorians to attract tourists. It does seem, however, to be a potential explanation for the site's name, which links it to the Viking king.

"People were once thought to have attempted to cure sickness by passing through the entry portal on the eastern side."

Myths about the spot have abounded, with suggestions that King Orry was in fact murdered at the site, or that it was the burial ground of giants. People were once thought to have attempted to cure sickness by passing through the entry portal on the eastern side, while the Victorians were said to fear travelling past the dark and brooding stones after midnight.

While the looming King Orry's Grave is hard to miss, there is a much more subtle memento from the ancient ancestors of the Manx just over a mile further up the Ballaragh Road. Ensconced in the western hedge is a lichen-covered boulder that carries a faint carving of a triple spiral, or **triskelion** (compounds.runners.requested). Just a few inches across, the rock art is thought to date from as early as 2000BC and bears similarities to prehistoric carvings found in Ireland. It was discovered in the early 20th century by a road worker clearing the ditch, but today is marked by a metal plaque from Manx National Heritage poking out the top of the hedge, making it easier to spot.

FOOD & DRINK

The Laxey Glen Glen Gardens, New Rd, IM4 7BE ⌀ thelaxeyglen.com ⊙ 10.00–16.00 Wed–Sun. Treat yourself to an affordable lunch from one of the contestants on *MasterChef: The Professionals*. Pippa Lovell, who appeared on the BBC show in 2024, has taken over this old Victorian pavilion to offer decadent takes on classic dishes while celebrating the best of local produce. Try a Manx crab roll with elderflower mayo or pollack baked in lemon verbena and rock salt, or just pop in for a coffee and a scoop of bonnag (page 32) ice cream.

The Shed Laxey Promenade, IM4 7DD ⌀ theshed.im ⊙ 09.00–17.00 Tue–Sun. A quirky coffee and cake spot adored by locals. Based on the concept of bringing the indoors outside, the bunting-strewn café – which does pies, pasties, paninis and soups – is based in an old deckchair storehouse at the quiet, southern end of the promenade. Gaggles of happy customers (known as 'shedders') spill out onto the pavement, staying cosy under thick blankets that are kept on the racks by the door. When the weather turns too cold, head to the old swimmers' changing cubicles next door, which have been converted into a snuggly seating space. There is a focus on Manx produce, with more than 90 of the café's ingredients locally sourced.

 SHOPPING

Ginger Giraffe Whitehouse Building, New Road, IM4 7BE 📷 gingergiraffe_iom. Ostensibly a furniture upcycler, but also stocks interior décor pieces and artworks that are a mix of locally made and brought in from further afield. The team here also blends essential oils and pours its own scented candles on site – the luscious smells wafting out of the shop alone are enough to pull in the passing trade.

9 AGNEASH

High above Laxey, about a mile west up the valley from the Laxey Wheel, sits the hamlet of Agneash. It is made up of a scant handful of traditional white Manx cottages and farmhouses snuggled together on the hillside, reached via an extremely steep, single-lane road leading up from Laxey MER station. A place long associated with fairies (they were once said to be as common as rabbits up here), it has also been a place of deep Christian faith – and its tiny, charming primitive methodist chapel sits at its heart in more ways than one.

The plain, square, cream-coloured **chapel** (⊙ 10.00–16.00 daily) sits in the centre of the hamlet; to lift the latch and let yourself in through the narrow wooden door is to step back in time to the turn of the 20th century. The warm glow of the old lamps spills over just half a dozen rows of dark wooden pews; an old-fashioned spinning wheel in the corner is a reminder of how women spent their days while their men were down the pits. The pulpit at the centre rises above a harmonium that was installed in the 1920s,

> "It is made up of a scant handful of traditional white Manx cottages and farmhouses snuggled together on the hillside."

replacing an earlier instrument from the 1870s. Coat hooks run around the walls, as a reminder to worshippers that they are to feel 'at home' in God's house.

The chapel is the only place on the island that is part of the Small Pilgrim Places Network – a network of simple, reflective spaces across England and Wales that are relatively unknown but welcome those of all faiths and none, who wish to ponder, pray or meditate. The air might

SNAEFELL MINES DISASTER

On Monday 10 May 1897, workers began arriving at the lead mine at the base of Snaefell – a short walk across the hillside from Agneash – for the start of the 06.00 shift. It was a bright, clear spring morning and as the bell rang out to signal the start of the working day, the men clambered down the ladders that would take them deep into the earth.

Within a few minutes, several of the miners had scrambled back to the surface. Gasping for breath, they signalled that something was very wrong far underground. The alarm was raised. A rescue mission was scrambled – but it was too late. Twenty of the men would not emerge alive.

What unfolded that morning became the worst mining disaster in Manx history. A candle left burning underground on the Saturday had set ablaze the wooden timbers propping up the shaft; as the rock collapsed it had cut off the oxygen supply, leaving the fire to fill the tunnels with odourless carbon monoxide. As the workers descended, they had breathed in the gas, fallen unconscious and ultimately suffocated.

'The effect of the air... was to render powerless their limbs and to cause dizziness of the head and laborious breathing,' reported the **Peel City Guardian** newspaper on 15 May, adding that the miners 'had met and succumbed to death in one of its most horrible forms'. It described the 'terror-stricken face' of the first of the men to return to the surface: 'On being helped from the ladder, the almost unconscious man told a horrible tale... to the effect that the mine was either on fire, or that the air was so foul and poisonous it could not be breathed.'

Attempts to save the workers were heroic, with the captain of the mine himself joining the teams risking their lives to retrieve those taken unwell underground. But the impact on the small community was devastating. It took weeks to retrieve all the bodies; when the first was hauled out on the Monday evening, the newspaper reported that the reaction of the gathered crowd was 'painful in the extreme'.

The shells of the stone buildings at the entrance of the mine still stand and can be seen from the Snaefell Mountain Railway (page 91) as it ascends the valley, though the site is out of bounds for those on foot due to collapsed and unstable masonry. More details can be found in the 2022 book *The Snaefell Mine Disaster* by local historian Andrew Scarffe.

be chilly – the building dates from 1857 and double glazing has yet to arrive – but the welcome is warm. Visitors can help themselves to tea and biscuits while they read the history of the chapel on display around the walls.

The site has a history of worship going back 1,300 years. A keeill was built in AD690 where the chapel's boundary wall now stands, which was inhabited by a monk who tended to the spiritual needs of the community and offered hospitality to those passing through. Primitive methodist services began in the area in the 1840s, when they were conducted in people's homes. They proved so popular that money was raised for a chapel.

Old newspaper cuttings on display around the chapel walls and black-and-white photographs of horse-drawn milk carts and flat-capped workers hint at a life that could be riven with hardship. The eastern windows of the chapel look out over the entrance to one of the mine shafts. One local family, many members of which were preachers at the chapel, lost both a father and son in the Snaefell mines disaster of 1897, while a younger brother was later imprisoned as a conscientious objector during World War I. There is the sense that this chapel has held all these memories and wants to share them with anyone new who comes its way.

10 SNAEFELL MOUNTAIN

There are few places in the world where you can see seven kingdoms at once, but that is precisely what the Manx will tell you is possible from the summit of Snaefell. The Isle of Man's only mountain reaches a height of 2,036ft, just breaching the 2,000ft threshold to be declared as such. On a clear day, the summit offers views over the rest of the island and as far as England, Ireland, Wales and Scotland. The final two 'kingdoms' in the sales pitch are those of the sea and the heavens.

It is a bracing, blustery place amid the stark, wind-scoured hill range. Its name comes from the Norse for 'snow mountain', as in winter it is often the only part of the island to receive a dusting. Grazing sheep dot the mountainside, and the occasional hare can be spotted darting for cover as walkers approach.

The **Snaefell Mountain Railway** (manxelectricrailway.co.uk/snaefell Mar–Oct 10.00–16.00 daily), a branch line of the MER, provides a regular public-transport link to the summit during the tourist

VICTORY CAFE

31st Milestone, Mountain Rd, Snaefell IM4 5AF ⌀ victory-cafe.com
⏲ 09.30–16.30 Wed–Sun

The Victory Cafe describes itself as a 'British canteen café in a Cold War radar station on the side of a mountain'. Can it get much cooler? Well, yes actually, it can. Because the café, sitting by the roadside at the highest point of the TT course (page 23), is also a year-round destination for motorbike fans.

The building itself is unmissable: a charcoal-grey bunker next to the Snaefell Mountain Railway Bungalow stop with 'Victory Cafe' emblazoned on the side in 8ft-high letters. There are ships out at sea that could probably spot it with a decent pair of binoculars. It is the perfect spot for a hearty lunch to prepare for a breezy day of hillwalking (or perhaps as a reward for making it down from Snaefell summit).

'It can be extreme up here,' says Vicky Quirk, who opened the café along with her husband Benn in 2021. 'Definitely a "push your way through the wind to get to the front door" kind of thing. But actually, that's something that brings people to the café.'

Stepping inside, it becomes clear that this is not just a café, it's a mini community. Leather armchairs sit either side of wood-burning stoves, the black walls have been signed by visitors from all over the world and a cosy cinema room – kitted out with the moss-green seats of a former Japanese airline – shows biking films throughout the day. A well-stocked shop sells biker gear and branded souvenirs, while the canteen itself is a vast space lit by strings of bare bulbs, with spectacular picture windows that look up the mountain.

'It is utterly, utterly beautiful,' says Vicky, when asked about the benefits of working

season. The only halt on the way up is a request stop at the Bungalow, where the line crosses the main Mountain Road about half a mile from the summit and where the **Victory Cafe** canteen and motorcycle hub (see above) can be found. It is possible to disembark here to finish the ascent on the well-trodden footpath, which is steep in places and very uneven. For those with their own wheels, there is car-parking space next to the Victory Cafe, which is on the main A18 mountain road.

The tram route is a triumph of Victorian ingenuity – built in 1895, it runs up the valley from the Laxey MER station before spiralling up the mountain, and still carries much of the original rolling stock. The tram, all polished wooden panels and brass fittings, takes 30 minutes to rattle up to the summit, with a piped commentary about the landmarks that can be seen out of the window. There is a small, no-frills café at the summit offering snacks and cups of tea.

somewhere so exposed to the elements. 'The weather is so changeable. One day the cloud is so low you can hardly see 10yds in front of you. Other days, you can see for miles and the air is so clear and pure.' And it's not just bikers who make the trek up to Victory café. 'The beautiful countryside brings walkers, bikers, cyclists, fell runners, people on the tram and folk out for a pootle in the car.'

Much of the menu, which comes in generous portions, is locally sourced. The steak and ale pie – made using Manx beef and the local Bushy's brew – is arguably the best on the island, and the steamed sponge puddings are giant spoonfuls of nostalgia. A full English breakfast, a plateful of Manx bangers and mash or a hearty bowl of homemade soup is the perfect ballast when the weather turns.

'Using loads of Manx produce is right at the top of our priority list,' says Vicky. 'It is vital to play a role in ensuring food security – we use, quite literally, tonnes of Manx spuds, flour, dairy and meat each year. Laxey Flour (page 81) is absolutely pure, no additives whatsoever. Manx meat and dairy herds are mostly grass-fed and live a happy outdoor life. And, to top it off, the carbon footprint is super low as they all come from our beautiful little island. Many of the farmers have become our friends!'

Vicky and Benn grew up in the Isle of Man but lived in Bristol for a decade. During their visits home, they would pass the old radar station while driving along the mountain road and were heartbroken to see it falling into a state of tired disrepair. 'When we moved back to the island, I made it my mission to get the keys to the padlock that held it shut,' Vicky adds. 'It was a battle that took a few years, but it was a battle worth winning.'

The Black Hut car park (/// offered.befit.moonwalk) on the northern side of the mountain is also a handy starting point for hillwalking, with a network of routes starting at the stile directly across the road. The paths stretch up the spine of hills to North Barrule (page 121) and Maughold in the northeast, or down into Laxey Valley – though it is best to have an Ordnance Survey map with you, which has the routes clearly marked, as the paths aren't always easy to make out on the ground.

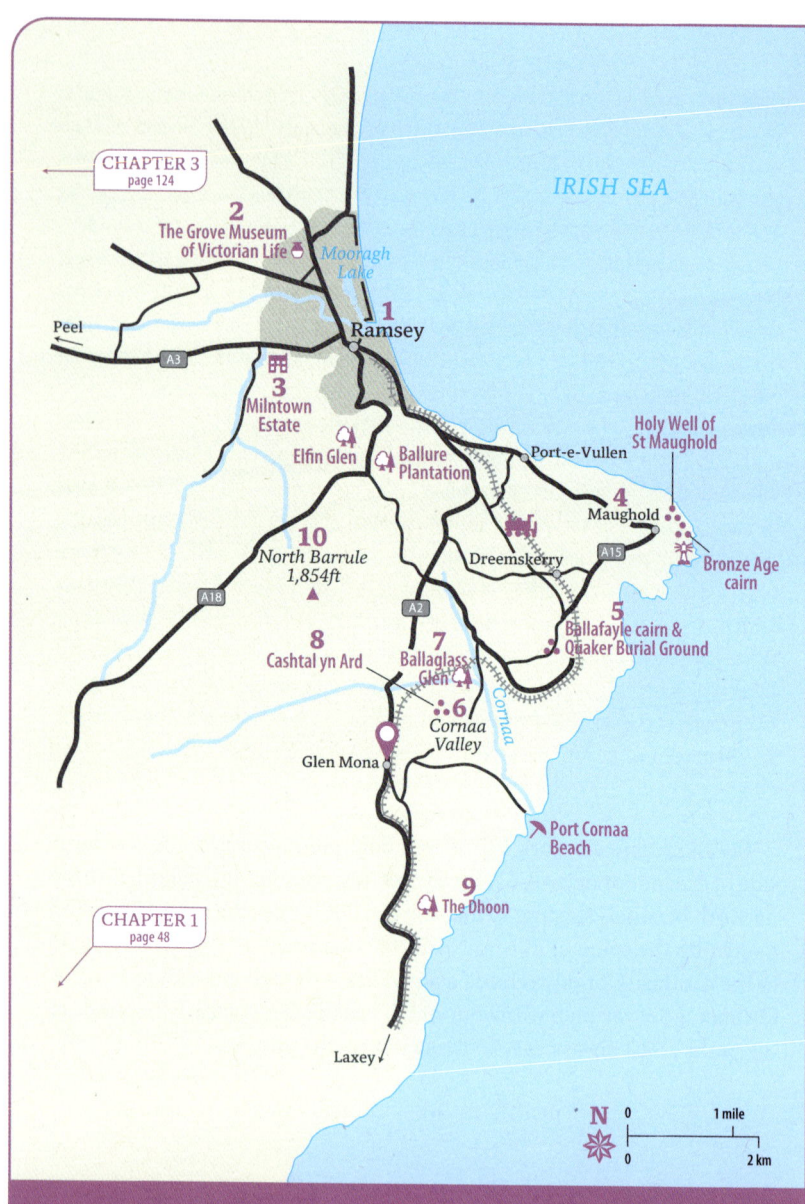

THE NORTHEAST

2
THE NORTHEAST

The northeast of the Isle of Man has historically been a place of arrival. It is where the island's patron saint, St Maughold, first stepped ashore in the 5th century, and where the invasion forces of the Viking king Godred Crovan secured victory over the Manx in 1079. The main town, **Ramsey**, went on to become a hub of fishing and trade, and with the emergence of the tourism boom in the 19th century it became the docking point for thousands of holidaymakers arriving by ferry.

Today, the hordes arrive in the town overland from the west and south. From the west, roaring along the Lezayre Road, come the modern warriors of the TT races each June (page 23) – man (and sometimes woman) battling machine as they tear round the 90-degree bend at Parliament Square. This spot is one of the more famous spectator points around the course, and is well served by cafés for fans who don't fancy spending a day sitting on an isolated hedge in the hills.

From the south come the more sedate visitors travelling from the capital. Cars winding down from the Mountain Road are treated to a spectacular aerial view of the town – the island's largest outside Douglas and Onchan, with a population of about 8,000 – while those arriving by bus or tram come via the scenic clifftops that stretch up from Maughold. The welcome is rather warmer than it was for the 11th-century Vikings, too.

Outside Ramsey, the area is sparsely populated – the craggy coastline around **Maughold Head** is dominated by farmland and is mostly used for livestock. The steep, dark hill of **North Barrule** to the west has a looming presence, but also catches much of the rain as it travels over from the direction of Ireland – Ramsey is known as the island's sunniest area.

A walk along the country roads around the headlands of Maughold and Cornaa makes for a lovely, quiet day out, with points of interest including Neolithic tombs, Viking runestones and the tumbling waterfalls of Ballaglass Glen and the Dhoon.

GETTING THERE & AROUND

Ramsey is well served by public transport, with the 3 and 3a **buses** running along the main A2 coast road from Douglas twice an hour Monday to Saturday and once an hour on Sunday. The 5 and 5c run along the A3 from Peel and the northwest of the island roughly once an hour Monday to Saturday and once every two hours on Sunday.

The only regular bus services to Maughold village are the numbers 16 and 16b, which run twice a day on school days only. Otherwise, buses can be booked 'on demand' to Maughold using the ConnectVillages service from Bus Vannin, which operates during the day Monday to Saturday. Bookings can be made using the MannGO app or by calling 01624 697440 between 08.30 and 16.30, Monday to Friday.

The **Manx Electric Railway** also runs up the coast between Douglas and Ramsey several times a day from March to early November (exact dates vary each year, check iombusandrail.im). There are halts at Dhoon Glen, Glen Mona, Ballaglass, Cornaa and Ballajora (for Maughold village).

RAMSEY & AROUND

The only town in the north, the old fishing and trading port of Ramsey has become known for its independent shops and popular gin distillery. It sits at the end of the MER line, making for a fun day out on the tram from Laxey or Douglas, and has some curious historic sights and stories to tell – not least the use of the promenade as an internment camp during World War II. There are some lovely walks to be done in the woodland on the southern edge of town, and the Raad ny Foillan footpath can be followed north out of town for 5½ miles to the Point of Ayre (page 143).

> ### *i* TOURIST INFORMATION
> **Ramsey Town Hall** Parliament Sq, IM8 1RT 01624 810100 08.45–16.30 Mon–Thu, 08.45–16.00 Fri

1 RAMSEY
🏠 Seabank Cottage

The town of Ramsey, with a population of about 8,000, is dominated by its wide harbour, which can seem like more of a lake in the centre of the community. It splits the seafront into distinct halves, with Queen's Promenade to the south and Mooragh Promenade to the north, joined by the arched, steel swing bridge that crosses the harbour – a small feat of engineering from the 1890s that brings to mind a miniature Forth Bridge. The scattering of pubs and old storehouses along the water's edge hark back to the town's heyday as a fishing and trading port, while the small working shipyard on the northern side is a glinting steel reminder that the sea is still a source of income for many.

Both sides of town have the sort of wide, flat, sandy beach that proved handy for Viking marauders looking for somewhere to park their longships – today, the northern part of the beach is popular with dog walkers (dogs are banned from the southern part) and those out for a stroll, but are a bit exposed to the elements to attract many sunbathers. The broad panoramas and expansive sky are very much a feature of the town – its position on the edge of the northern plain means it avoids feeling overshadowed or hemmed in.

"Both sides of town have the sort of wide, flat, sandy beach that proved handy for Viking marauders."

Most of the action can be found towards the centre of town on the high street, which runs behind the old warehouse buildings that line the harbour; turning down one of the narrow, stone-walled passageways that cut between them is a glimpse of what life was like for the traders and smugglers who once had the run of the port. Emerging from the cool shadows on to **Parliament Street** is to discover an eclectic mix of grand Victorian architecture housing a range of independent boutiques, cafés and gift shops, for which Ramsey has become well known. Perhaps the most eye-catching is Felton's – an old-fashioned ironmongers with a funfair-like red-and-yellow façade.

Other stores specialise in crafts and artwork created locally, Manx produce, or unusual clothes and homewares. Leanne Higgins, an artist who founded the Pink Seaweed Gallery in 2023 (page 105), says the town is fast becoming a creative hub. 'Our high street is full of indie businesses, has the best shops, beautiful street art, plus loads of lovely places to eat,' she says, her vibrant pink hair tying in neatly with the name of her business. 'It's colourful, quirky and friendly.' Keep an eye out for Thomas, the town cat – this ginger regular can often be spotted popping into his favourite shops for a nap.

At the northern end of town sits **Mooragh Park** (⊙ year round), a 19th-century amusement park built on a former salt marsh that today includes a children's play area, skate park, tennis courts and a 12-acre boating lake where pedalos and kayaks can be hired (✆ 01624 814240 ⌂ venturecentre.im ⊙ Easter until end of summer 11.00–16.30 w/ends & bank holidays, plus daily during school holidays; closed during poor weather so call ahead to check). Between the northern edge of the park and the far end of the promenade, where there is little apart from a couple of white houses and a long expanse of beach, one of the island's many moddey dhoos (page 19) is said to stalk the seafront after dark – a

MOORAGH INTERNMENT CAMP

The rows of former boarding houses along Mooragh Promenade tell a familiar tale of the decline of British seaside resorts in the second half of the 20th century. Once bustling with happy holidaymakers, many have now been turned into private flats and look as battered by time and shifting economics as they do by the weather.

However, these buildings also have a less familiar tale to tell. It was here, on 27 May 1940, that the island's first internment camp for 'enemy aliens' since the Great War opened, taking hundreds of male internees who were originally from Germany or Austria but had found themselves in Britain at the start of World War II – many of them Jewish refugees who had fled the Nazis.

The boarding-house keepers had found out only two weeks earlier that their homes and businesses were to be requisitioned by the government. Barbed-wire fencing was placed around the hotels, sectioning off this portion of the promenade, and soldiers were shipped over from the UK to patrol the perimeter. The number of internees ebbed and flowed over the course of the war as rules changed; some were released and others, including Finns, Japanese and Italians, were moved from other camps on the island. It was the last men's camp to close, on 2 August 1945.

Paintings and poetry produced inside the camp highlight the sadness and frustration of those trapped behind the wire. Hugo 'Puck' Dachinger, an Austrian artist who spent seven months in Mooragh Camp in 1940, captured oppressive scenes of Ramsey Bay with dark skies and ominous storm clouds. Others wrote of their 'despair' and 'stubborn hope'.

Examples of work created in the camps, and a glimpse into what life was like for World War II internees, can be seen at the National Art Gallery and the Mann at War Gallery in the Manx Museum in Douglas (page 63).

story that has potentially proved useful to parents wishing to stop their children straying too far from the swings.

On the west side of the park, on the corner of Windsor Mount and Windsor Road, there is a grand white Victorian house with a palm tree in the garden. The property was the final home of the Manx national poet TE Brown (page 22), who lived there from 1894 until his death during a trip to Bristol in 1897. A small metal plaque, placed in 1914 and now green with age, on the outside of the garden wall signifies the importance of the site. Brown's final collection, *Old John and Other Poems*, was published by Macmillan in 1893, shortly before he moved in. The house is said to once have been haunted by a playful spirit that enjoyed stealing teaspoons.

> "Seating shelters dotted along the walkway have been overhauled by local artists and provide some bright splashes of colour."

East of the park is Mooragh Promenade – perhaps because the seafront is spread so wide, the town's promenades are fairly quiet places, dotted with slightly tired blocks of flats dating from the 19th and mid-20th centuries. Efforts have been made to brighten up the northern end: the five seating shelters dotted along the walkway have been overhauled by local artists and provide some bright splashes of colour, taking inspiration from the sea and local history.

Heading south down to the far southern end of Queen's Promenade, the narrow, delicate-looking structure of the **Queen's Pier** (ramseypier.im queenspiertrust summer 14.00–17.00 Sun) reaches nearly 700yds out towards the Lake District, which can be seen on the horizon on a clear day. Unlike the glitzy piers of Blackpool or Brighton, where visitors can expect arcade games and candy floss, this pier is remarkably bare save for a gently Modernist concrete entrance from the 1950s.

The pier originally opened in 1886 as a landing stage for the ferries of the Steam Packet Company and, prior to World War I, some 36,000 passengers a year were arriving here to start their Manx holiday – a tiny train transported them along the pier to land and was undoubtedly all part of the fun. However, by 1969 the number of arrivals had fallen to only 3,000, and in the early 1990s the pier was closed entirely. Saviour came in the form of local volunteers, who are now working to restore the structure. A crowd of hundreds attended the reopening of the first

VISIT ISLE OF MAN

VISIT ISLE OF MAN

ANGELA PICKARD, BRIDGE BOOKSHOP

VISIT ISLE OF MAN

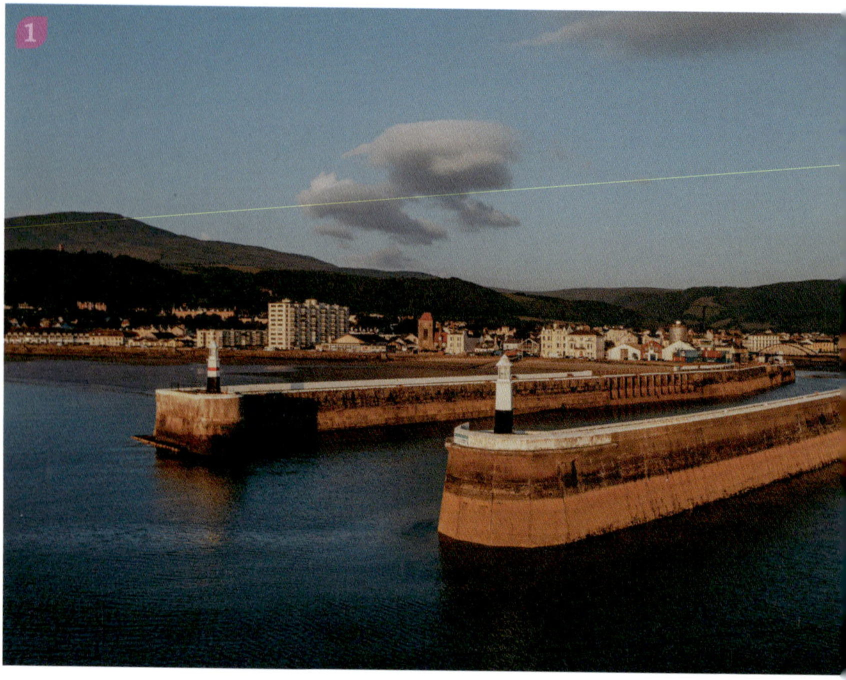

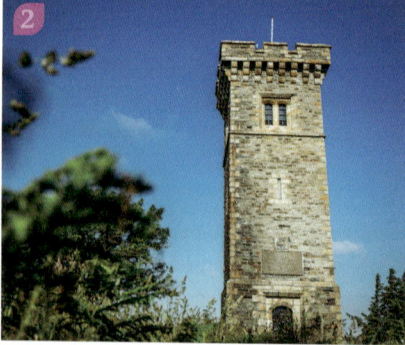

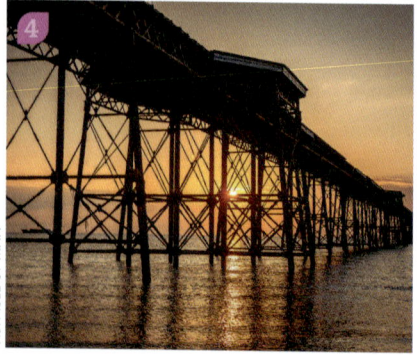

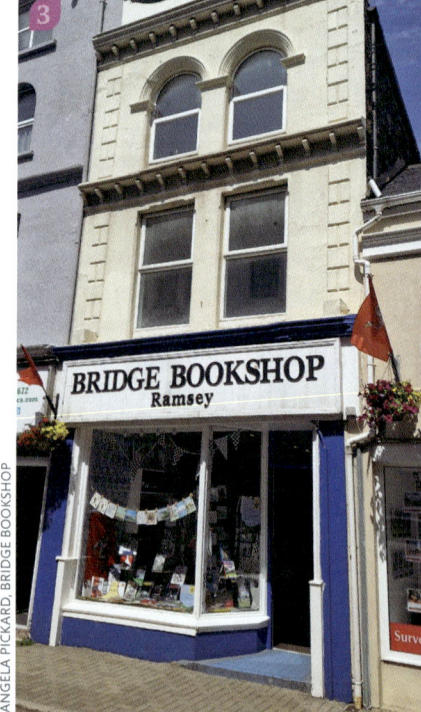

section in 2021, and in 2024 permission was granted for a little red train to take passengers along the first 70yds of track – visitors can now enjoy rides during the open afternoons in summer. *Grandad and the Pier*, an award-winning documentary released in 2023 and directed by Reuben Armstrong (⌂ reubenand.co/grandadandthepier), highlighted the efforts of the restoration group – it was screened around Britain, as well as on the island.

Fynoderee Distillery
Parsonage Rd, IM8 2EE ✆ 01624 812756, ⌂ fynoderee.com ⊖ bar & shop 10.45–18.00 Tue–Thu, 10.45–22.00 Fri & Sat

The fynoderee, a strange creature half-man and half-goat, has been popping up everywhere in the Isle of Man in recent years. He's been spotted at the local bars, lingers in the departure lounge at the airport… and has even been found sitting on the shelves of the big chain supermarkets.

That's because the fynoderee, an established figure of Manx folklore, has become the face of the award-winning premium craft gin brand that has taken the island by storm. Launched in 2017, the small, family-run distillery began by creating flavoured editions for each season with the help of locally foraged ingredients such as gorse and has since expanded its offering to include unusual flavours such as chai, as well as branching out to rum and vodka. The squat glass bottles, decorated with elaborate, fantastical scenes by Ramsey artist Julia Ashby Smyth, are as delicious to look at as they are to drink.

"The fynoderee, a strange creature half-man and half-goat, has been popping up everywhere in the Isle of Man in recent years."

The distillery itself is tucked away behind Ramsey tram station, 150yds south of the harbour, and offers a warm welcome to those joining one of their tasting tours, taking a cocktail class or simply popping into the Fyn Bar for a coffee and one of their signature Manx mezze plates. There are fairy lights, copper vats and a cheerful barman with a moustache

◀ RAMSEY: **1** The harbour dominates the town. **2** The Albert Tower overlooks the town from a nearby hillside. **3** The Bridge Bookshop stocks a plethora of publications on Manx language, culture, folklore and the great outdoors. **4** The Queen's Pier stretches almost 700yds out across the Irish Sea.

THE BUZZ ABOUT MANX BEES

The Fynoderee Distillery (page 101) has its own beehives, the honey from which goes into its Bumbee Vodka, and is keen to stress the global importance of the Manx bee population.

In 2015, the island was recognised by the European Council as being free of Varroa, a mite that attacks honey bees and eventually causes the colonies to collapse. There have been disastrous infestations across Europe, and the parasite has also been confirmed in North and South America, Asia and areas of Africa.

As a result of the 2015 ruling, the island was allowed to ban the importation of bees, while healthy Manx specimens are exported to help boost other populations. According to the Isle of Man Beekeepers Federation, it also means that pure Manx honey is free of the chemicals found in produce from elsewhere as Manx bees do not have to be treated for the disease.

Manx honey can be found in many local shops, but it is also possible to buy honey and beeswax products directly from the producers. A list can be found at ⌀ iombeekeepers.com/honey-for-sale.

worthy of Dick Dastardly. A well-stocked shop carries the full range of drinks plus a selection of merchandise, while toe-tapping trad music keeps everything humming along nicely.

The 90-minute tasting tour, which should be booked in advance via the website, is well worth the time, and is a chance to find out about some of the distillery's more unusual ventures. As well as hearing about seasonal supplies of local flavourings ('if it's not there, it doesn't go in the gin'), there are tales of derring-do on the high seas – including relating to the 200th anniversary of the RNLI in 2024. As the event's official spirits partner, Fynoderee produced a limited edition rum that was left to age for a year inside the wave-lashed Tower of Refuge in Douglas Bay. 'It was a bit scary getting them off again,' says the guide, about the day they had to retrieve the 11 barrels and bring them ashore amid blustery autumn weather. 'I was a bit worried someone might drown.'

Southern Ramsey

On the south side of Ramsey, half a mile from the town centre and tucked away among the bungalows of a modern housing estate, is **Killeaba Mound** (⌗ dance.drummer.nips) – a Neolithic and Bronze Age burial site. It is on the residential street Killeaba Mount, reached by turning onto Lheaney Road from the A18. Today, the mound is just a large grassy knoll, but excavations in the 1960s revealed evidence of burials and cremations – including of both adults and children – along with pottery from the late Neolithic and early Bronze Age. Timber-lined pits at the site were radiocarbon dated to around 3000BC. A recreation of one of the burials, that of a middle-aged man from about 2000BC who was found with a decorated food bowl near his head, can be seen at the Manx Museum (page 63).

From here, continuing south on the A18 brings you to **Claughbane**, the **Elfin Glen** and **Lhergy Frissell** – a trio of adjoining woodlands covering about 60 acres in total. Footpaths, which can be accessed from the Ramsey Hairpin on the A18 (⫽ reform.combo.fudgy), link the three areas and there are some lovely, if steep, woodland walks. Claughbane was established as a commercial plantation and is largely coniferous, though efforts are being made to boost biodiversity. The neighbouring woodlands of Elfin Glen and Lhergy Frissell are home to ash, birch, elm, sycamore and willow. The network of footpaths can be used to reach the **Albert Tower** – a stone folly on the hillside overlooking the town, which was erected to mark the spot Prince Albert paused to enjoy the view during a brief visit in 1847 (Queen Victoria, overcome with seasickness, remained on the royal yacht in Ramsey Bay).

SPECIAL STAYS

Seabank Cottage Church Rd, Port-e-Vullen IM7 1AP ✆ 01624 830200 ⌁ islandescapes. im. This newly built, pint-sized cottage in the coastal hamlet of Port-e-Vullen, just over a mile southeast of Ramsey, has all the cosiness of a modern home with all the character of something that's been there for generations. With one double bedroom and 'his and hers' dressing gowns – plus its own private sauna cabin on the decking – it's the perfect spot for a couple's getaway two miles south of Ramsey.

The blue-clapboard cottage is just 50ft from the quiet beach, and makes the most of its location – the wall of the dining area is entirely glass, giving sensational views out over the Irish Sea. It has a distinct nautical theme, with hurricane lamps in the bedroom and a porthole window above the king-size bed. There is a fully equipped kitchen, including a washing machine, and a welcome pack includes bread, milk, tea and coffee. It sits right on the Raad ny Foillan coastal walking route, and is half a mile away from bus and electric tram stops.

FOOD & DRINK

Good Stuff 6 Peel St, IM8 1JH ✆ 01624 610225 ⌁ goodstuffiom.com ⊙ 11.30–22.30 Mon–Thu, 11.30–23.45 Fri & Sat, noon–16.00 Sun. A funky little restaurant that caters to almost all tastes. From Italian meatball ciabattas to pork-belly ramen and local catch of the

THE NORTHEAST

THE BOAT THAT ROCKED RAMSEY

'We have now stopped and we're about to drop anchor, right here, just in sight of your lovely island...' With these words, uttered after the closing bars of Lulu's *Shout*, the pirate station Radio Caroline announced it had reached its new home off Ramsey on 5 July 1964.

Unlicensed broadcasts of pop music programmes from the MV *Caroline* had begun in the North Sea off Felixstowe, Suffolk, in March that year. By early July, the station had merged with Radio Atlanta – a rival pirate broadcaster that operated on a ship anchored off Essex. Atlanta's ship, the MV *Mi Amigo*, stayed in the area and became Radio Caroline South, while the MV *Caroline* set course for the Irish Sea, where it became Radio Caroline North. Now able to broadcast across most of Britain, the station was able to reach an audience of millions.

'Anchoring in Ramsey Bay made marine sense as the island provided protection from storms in the Irish Sea,' says Peter Moore, Radio Caroline's modern station manager. 'Down south, Caroline soon had other rivals – especially Radio London, which was very polished and professional. But the North ship had no serious rivals and probably subsidised the South ship financially.'

The station set up an office in Ramsey town, occupying the first floor at 9 East Street, directly above where the Penny Farthing vintage furniture shop is today, and its DJs used to stay at the nearby Mitre hotel on

day, the focus is on favourite dishes made with sustainable, locally sourced ingredients. Known for its friendly service and great cocktails.

Studio Umami 2 Bourne Pl, IM8 1JW StudioUmamiRamsey 10.00–17.00 Wed–Sat. A deli, café and artistic hub offering gorgeous coffee and sweet treats. On Saturdays (noon–15.00), it also offers flavoursome, Indian-inspired meals to take away or eat in the bohemian, shabby-chic dining space – the signature roti wraps are worth a trip up north in themselves. The deli side of the business sells products from around the world, and remember to check out the atelier to see if there's an artist in residence – previous artists have included a baritone singer, who serenaded customers over lunch.

SHOPPING

Bridge Bookshop 62 Parliament St, IM8 1AJ 01624 813374 bridge-bookshop.com. One half of a Manx chain (the other branch is in Port Erin), it offers the latest bestsellers as well as an extensive range of publications about the island and books by local writers.

Isle of Man Farmers' Market The Courthouse, 2 Water St, IM8 1JJ 01624 822992 iomfm.co.uk 10.00–16.00 Sat. Held every Saturday in the square outside the old courthouse, with stalls selling a range of crafts and seasonal produce from local artisans and growers.

Parliament Street. Such was the volume of fan mail, the island's postal service had to employ extra staff.

'The arrival of Caroline North was a great boon to the sleepy Isle of Man and the station curried favour by advertising Isle of Man tourism at no charge,' Peter adds. 'Tynwald very much liked Caroline and did not want to ratify the UK law that was supposed to outlaw pirate radio.' That law was the Marine Broadcasting Offences Act of 1967. 'The UK forced the law on them, creating resentment against Britain that may still exist today. So there is mutual affection, and Caroline acknowledges that the Isle of Man tried to fight our corner.'

Radio Caroline North ran until 1968, when the Dutch company contracted to tender the ship – angry over not being paid – cut the anchor and towed it to the Netherlands. Amid legislative and meteorological challenges, Caroline continued broadcasting from the North Sea until 1990, when a lack of fuel forced it to stop transmissions and ended its offshore era. The brand has popped up in various guises since, and the Caroline North name can now be found on air in the form of a monthly link-up with Manx Radio on its AM 1368 frequency, and online at ⌀ radiocaroline.co.uk.

But its stint in Ramsey has not been forgotten. 'Between 1964 and early 1968 Ramsey was a far more happening place than it had been before – and maybe since,' says Peter.

Kermelly's 3 Bourne Pl, IM8 1JW ⌀ 07624 457617 🅕 kermelly. A family-run fishmongers supplied by its own commercial fishing vessel, the *Ramsey Jak*. Stock is seasonal and can include scallops, lobster and crab. Also sells eggs, honey, cheese and a selection of other deli products from Manx producers.

OMA Sustainable Living 31A Parliament St, IM8 1AJ 🅕 omaconsciousliving. An eclectic, fairy-lit jewel box of a store, showcasing products sourced from around the world in an ethical, sustainable and environmentally conscious way. There are clothes made from sumptuous printed fabrics, handcrafted jewellery and accessories, and unique, colourful homewares.

Pink Seaweed Gallery The Flower Building, 73 Parliament St, IM8 1AQ 🅕. A small gallery space that punches above its weight by stocking quirky work from more than 100 local artists and crafters, including paintings, jewellery, ceramics, cards and accessories. 'I wanted to create a vibrant and welcoming space for artists and art lovers,' says owner Leanne Higgins. 'We believe in breaking down barriers, regardless of whether we're supporting a budding artist or an established one.'

Penny Farthing 9 East St, IM8 1DN ⌀ 01624 816150 🅕 pennyfarthingisleofman. Antiques and vintage furniture store. The place to go for a nosey around old china tea sets, carved wooden desks and mid-century armchairs.

THE NORTHEAST

Teare's Butchers 50 Parliament St, IM8 1AN ✆ 01624 812460. An established feature of the high street, this family-run business specialises in Manx beef, lamb and pork. They also make their own sausages, burgers, bacon and cooked meats, as well as dripping.

2 THE GROVE MUSEUM OF VICTORIAN LIFE
Andreas Rd, IM8 2UA ✆ 01624 812686 ⌂ manxnationalheritage.im ⊙ Apr–Oct noon–16.00 Sat–Wed

Set back from the main road that heads north out of Ramsey, the Grove – a grand Victorian house surrounded by tranquil gardens, a duck pond and fields containing native Loaghtan sheep – captures the glamour that was once enjoyed by the town's upper middle classes. It is a treasure trove of knick-knacks harking back to an age when luxury goods were shipped in from every corner of the empire. A tiger-skin rug, complete with glass eyes, takes pride of place among the chinoiserie and rare Broadwood piano in the living room. Portraits of sombre-looking Victorian relatives line the walls of the dining room and bells for calling the servants still hang on the wall in the kitchen.

"It is a treasure trove of knick-knacks harking back to an age when luxury goods were shipped in from every corner of the empire."

But this quirky museum, which takes its name from the house itself, is as much a tribute to its final owners as it is a tableau of Victorian wealth. The house is the former home of Alice and Janet Gibb, the granddaughters of Duncan Gibb – a shipping merchant from Liverpool who bought a cottage on the site in 1838 and extended it to create a summer retreat befitting a wealthy family of the era. The Gibbs eventually moved there permanently.

The sisters never married (some painful correspondence with a suitor, drawn out over many years, can be read on the upstairs landing), instead spending most of their lives at the Grove and seeing out their final years in genteel poverty. They kept their quiet life ticking over in their childhood home by growing flowers and vegetables, keeping bees and managing as best they could as the 20th century forged ahead without them. In their later years, they gave extensive interviews to Manx

---

1 Enjoy a gin tasting at Fynoderee Distillery. **2** Step back in time at the Grove Museum of Victorian Life. **3** Sample unique Manx honey, which is free of chemicals found in honey from elsewhere. **4** Milntown Estate may be haunted, but its 15 acres of grounds are peaceful to walk around. ▶

VISIT ISLE OF MAN

ZAIRON/WC

JOHN WARD

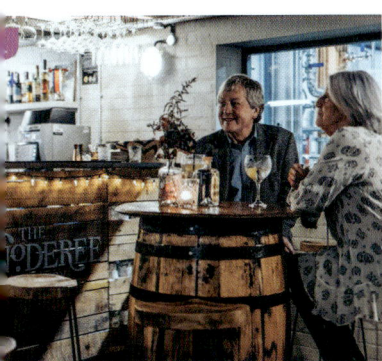

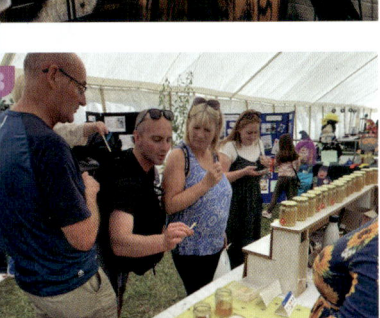

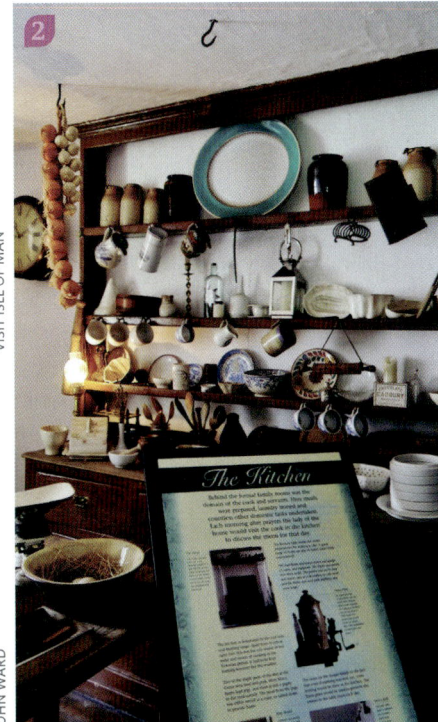

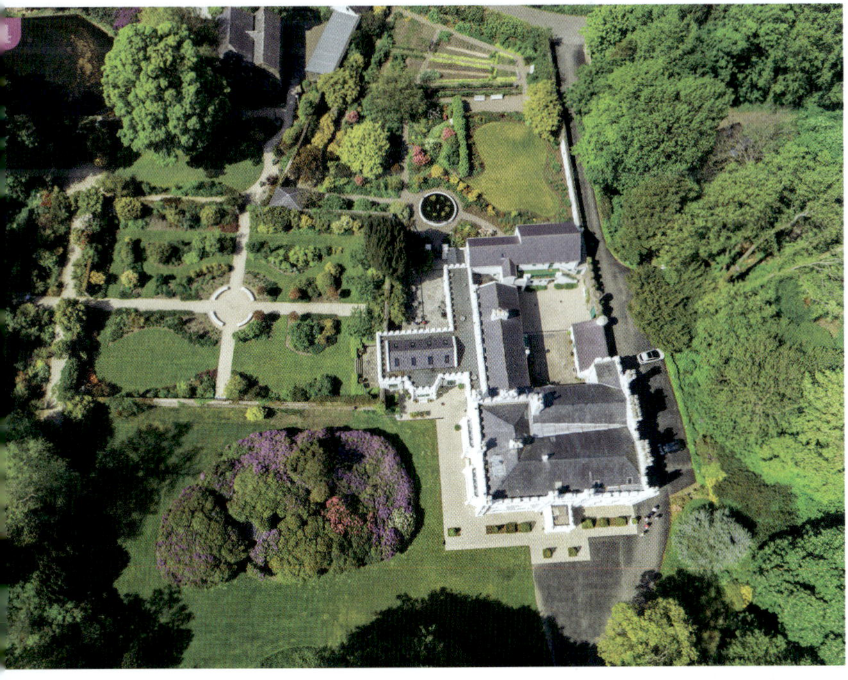

VISIT ISLE OF MAN

National Heritage, allowing them to tell their own story through audio recordings now dotted around the house and grounds, with the estate passing to the organisation after the sisters died in the 1970s.

Highlights of the museum include the clever Victorian shower system (from an age before running water), the glass-fronted beehive that still produces honey (which can be bought in the small gift shop), and the shipping-inspired features Duncan insisted on including in the rebuild – including the hallway with flooring laid like the deck of a ship.

A friendly guide is on hand to greet you at the front door and answer any questions not covered by the excellent information boards. It is a house frozen in time, filled with nostalgia and the sense of a glorious heyday that slipped out of grasp.

3 MILNTOWN ESTATE

Lezayre Rd, IM7 2AB ⌕ 01624 812321 ⌕ milntown.org ⌕ café & gardens 09.30–17.00 Wed–Sun

Set far back off the road behind a shield of mature trees to the west of Ramsey, about a mile from the town centre, Milntown is the former seat of the once-powerful Christian family and some would undoubtedly say that its slightly shady spot is rather fitting.

The dynasty lived at the site for 500 years from the 15th century, with some original parts of the house still surviving. The building was extended over the years and took the form it has today in the early 19th century – an imposing, castellated, almost fortress-like white manor that has more than a whiff of self-importance. The Christians played integral roles in Manx law and politics, and for many generations the senior member of the family was a deemster – one of the island's judges.

The family's most famous son was William Christian, known on the island as Illiam Dhone, who was executed for treason at Hango Hill near Castletown (page 191) in 1663 for his role in the Manx Rebellion during the English Civil War. As commander of the island's militia, Dhone had gone behind the back of the ruling Earl and Countess of Derby to co-operate with the Parliamentarians – debate still rages as to whether he was a traitor or a great Manx hero. A portrait of Illiam Dhone and an embroidered cap believed to have been his are on display in the Manx Museum (page 63).

A later branch of the family produced Fletcher Christian, who led the infamous mutiny on the *Bounty* in 1789. Though born in Cumberland,

A CHILLING NIGHT AT MILNTOWN

'I didn't know what to expect when we started filming,' says Dario Leonetti, 'but strange things started to happen almost straight away.'

Dario is a Manx cinematographer and photographer who, in 2017, went to Milntown with a colleague after dark, where they were joined by a medium and a tour guide to film a piece for a local news website. In true *Most Haunted* style, they were equipped with night-vision cameras – and were careful to keep an open mind. 'I was very aware that I didn't want to put any ideas into my head while we were wandering around,' Dario says. 'I think you can almost start to trick yourself into seeing or hearing things.'

But the first inkling that they were in for a busy night came when Dario's colleague, Ben, was attempting to interview the medium on camera. Laughing, she broke off mid-sentence and, looking at the empty room behind him, said, 'Someone's just been standing behind you, sorry!' From that point on, things never really settled.

'I felt extreme changes in temperature – temperatures changing as soon as we walked into a room,' Dario recalls. 'One room in particular was like walking in through a wall of cold.' He says this room, one of the bedrooms, made him feel decidedly unwelcome. 'I was filming Ben with the night-vision camera and a little orb flew across the room and went past him – Ben almost instantly felt a cold pain in his shoulder.' In the film, a shocked Ben can be seen grabbing his shoulder just as the dot of light whizzes past. The team also heard tappings on the wardrobe, all picked up on camera.

'The strangest experience happened towards the end of the tour, while on the very top floor in the maids' quarters,' Dario adds. 'We all felt the floor shake as if a person was walking very heavy-footed down the corridor. There was only the four of us in the building and we were all standing still in a circle, so it clearly wasn't any of us. The floor shook so much it moved a tripod I had leant against the wall.'

Dario's short film about the visit, *Gef gets spooky at Milntown*, can be found on YouTube. 'I'd love to go back and spend the whole night there,' he says, insisting that his chilling encounters didn't put him off. 'It's a beautiful building with such an interesting history.'

Fletcher later moved to the island because of his family connections; several key players in the rebellion had deep Manx connections (page 78).

Today Milntown is reputedly the most haunted house in the Isle of Man. Staff at the house have reported feeling something (or someone) rush past them on the stairs, while Lady Edwards – one of the last residents – has been seen sitting in her old apartment and a film team has had recording equipment go haywire. A guest who was sleeping in the old maids' rooms in the 1960s claimed to have been thrown out of bed by a ghost, while a moddey dhoo (page 19) has been known to prowl the main road that runs past the house, and uncanny beings allegedly lurk by the mill in the grounds.

If that doesn't unnerve you too much, its 15 acres of grounds and gardens are open to the public with a variety of sections to explore – there are manicured borders, the old corn mill with working waterwheel, a patch of woodland and areas of bountiful, cottage garden-style planting. The café in the conservatory of the main house is a popular spot with locals looking for an afternoon out and a slice of cake – as evidenced by the fact that it serves more than 5,000 cups of tea a year. For transport buffs, the estate also has a collection of vintage vehicles permanently on display, including the island's oldest car: a 1900 New Orleans.

Tours of the house take place on Wednesday afternoons during the summer months – booking ahead is essential.

MAUGHOLD & AROUND

In Celtic Christianity, there are locations that are recognised as 'thin places' – where the distance between heaven and earth is reduced and it is easier to connect with the divine. The sparsely populated Maughold village and surrounding headland – three miles southeast of Ramsey – is an example of just such a place. The area is named after St Maughold, the patron saint of the Isle of Man, who was said to have made landfall here after being put to sea in a coracle as penance for trying to make a fool of St Patrick in the 5th century. The area has held deep spiritual significance since, and the headland is known as 'the cradle of Manx Christianity'.

"The peacefulness of the rolling farmland ties well with the history of spirituality."

The area is quite sparsely populated, but the peacefulness of the rolling farmland ties well with the history of spirituality. The old church in Maughold village has a fantastic collection of carved medieval crosses in the churchyard, and there are wonderful walks to be done along the rugged headland – the area is rich in wildlife and the high cliffs provide a fabulous vantage point for looking out to sea. The village celebrates St Maughold's Week each year at the end of July to highlight

MAUGHOLD & AROUND

Manx Christianity and culture, with events including talks, music performances and guided walks – further information can be found on the Kirk Maughold Facebook page (**f**).

4 MAUGHOLD

The village of Maughold – really no more than a hamlet with a handful of old stone and modern brick houses – lies three miles to the southeast of Ramsey, on the furthest point of the headland that spikes out into the Irish Sea to create the southern boundary of Ramsey Bay. It's possible to walk here from Ramsey via the Raad ny Foillan footpath (roughly 4½ miles), which is a contender for the island's most stunning clifftop route (though be aware that the brief stretch along the beach at Port-e-Vullen can be restricted at high tide – if this is the case, follow the road instead, and there are some steep sections so appropriate footwear is essential). The path takes walkers along the Maughold Brooghs headland, an Area of Special Scientific Interest that blooms with bluebells and gorse in the spring.

At the heart of the village is **Kirk Maughold** (Maughold Rd, IM7 1AS ☉ 09.00–16.00 daily). One of the oldest churches on the island, it can be reached through a wooden gate just off the triangular village green. The existing building is a plain,

"Evidence of religious activity on the site can be traced back as early as the 6th century, when a Christian monastery was set up."

low, rectangular structure that was renovated in the late 19th century, but which still contains elements of the 12th-century construction. Two small sandstone windows on the south side of the nave are believed to be from this era, along with the grey stone font. The carved sandstone pillar inside the church, known as the **Pillar Cross**, dates from about 1300 and includes the oldest known stone carving of the island's three-legs symbol.

However, evidence of religious activity on the site can be traced back as early as the 6th century, when a Christian monastery was set up – the stone wall that surrounds the churchyard marks the original monastic enclosure. It is well worth having a wander around the churchyard, which houses numerous quirky treasures. There are the remains of four ancient keeills – two of which, at the north and east of the site, are still clearly visible and can be entered by modern-day pilgrims. A stone trough said to hold the invisible bones of St Maughold sits just inside the path on the eastern side of the churchyard. There is also the **Hall Caine monument**:

THE NORTHEAST

LOOKING AFTER THE LAND FOR 300 YEARS

'Maughold gets the best sunrises on the island,' says Anna Kerruish, early on a cold Monday morning in January. 'It's an incredible place to live.'

Sunrises are something Anna sees a lot of. As a sheep farmer of 20 years, she is an established early riser and often shares photos of her early starts on Instagram (ManxShepherdess). When we speak, she has just spent the weekend ensuring her flock have plenty of food to see them through a biting cold snap, with bitter winds leaving a sprinkling of snow on the hills. 'The Maughold coastline is rocky and windswept so not ideal for cropping,' she adds. 'We get three times more rain here than Kirk Michael on the west coast and a lot of mist. So grass is what grows best.'

The practical considerations mean Ballafayle Farm – which stretches inland from the water's edge near Port Mooar beach – is a meat producer, with 650 breeding ewes giving approximately 1,000 lambs a year. It is also part of the Biosphere Isle of Man scheme, which promotes sustainability and conservation, and in 2023 won the prestigious Bronze Chough Award for conservation within commercial farming. The award is given out by the Isle of Man's Farming and Wildlife Advisory Group in recognition of efforts to protect biodiversity.

'It's important to recognise our biosphere as a working landscape, shaped by generations of farmers,' Anna says. 'The Isle of Man has over 3,000 miles of hedgerows, which are fantastic for wildlife. It has more hedgerows per square mile than any other country in the world.' She is organising a group of

an art-nouveau obelisk designed by Archibald Knox that marks the grave of the eponymous, celebrated British novelist (page 23).

A superb collection of more than 40 Celtic and Viking carved stone crosses is tucked away in a shelter on the southern edge of the churchyard, including some with runic inscriptions. Among them is **Guariat's Cross**, a large, broad slab dating from the 9th century with five distinctive raised domes, one at each point of the cross and one in the centre. The legend attached to the stone says that a woman once broke the sabbath by spinning on a Sunday and trying to take her wool to the weaver. While on her way, she was blown back by the wind – when she cursed the weather, she and her five balls of wool were turned to stone.

Maughold Head

Car park at /// mystery.that.paperweight

Maughold Head is the easternmost point of the Isle of Man, the cliffs plunging into the Irish Sea just a few hundred yards east of Maughold

volunteers the following weekend to help plant even more – bundles of hawthorn, dog rose, alder, rowan and crab apple are laid out in advance ready for her team of helpers (they will be rewarded with a cup of tea and a slow-cooked lamb bap for their efforts). The new hedge would provide shelter for future generations of lambs in the harsh winds, and plenty of berries and rosehips for birds.

Working alongside nature, rather than trying to force it into submission, is an integral part of the farm's ethos. Anna's mountain-born lambs spend their first six months grazing wild grasses, heather and blaeberries. However, they need more nutrition after weaning, so Anna grows turnips for them – the crop and the weeds that grow among them provide a feeding area for birds such as yellowhammer, skylark and linnet. She also sees buzzards and heron in the field.

Biodiversity and conservation may be modern-day buzzwords, but the Kerruish family have been looking after the land in Maughold for generations; in 2025 they marked their 300th anniversary on the farm. It means Anna knows the area better than most. 'The coastal path from Port Mooar to Maughold village is a must-see,' she says, 'as well as Maughold Head and the path along the brooghs towards Ramsey.' She also recommends a hike up North Barrule in late summer: 'It gives fantastic views of the north and the surrounding hills, purple with heather.'

Ballafayle Farm (Maughold, IM7 1ED) holds open days, and private tours can be arranged by contacting Anna (✉ annakerruish@hotmail.com).

---

village. The headland is gorse-strewn and exposed, with the single-track road that leads out towards the early-20th-century lighthouse lined with pretty daffodils in spring. There is also plenty of wildlife to be spotted out to sea. There is a car park, but the area can easily be reached on foot via the short road from Kirk Maughold.

Even if arriving by car, getting out to explore the headland on foot is the way to get up close to some sites of ancient significance. For the **Holy Well of St Maughold** (/// lambs.bonbons.gateway) – a stone-lined spring renowned for cures and as a place to make wishes – head through the gate on the eastern side of the car park and follow the steep path downhill as far as the gate in the stone wall; the path through here leads down to the well. As well as supposedly being particularly good for healing eye problems, the water is also said to work as a charm against fairies and evil spirits.

The presence of a **Bronze Age cairn** on the top of the headland, 300yds south of the well, reveals that Maughold was an important

PANMAULE/DT

HENRYK SADURA/S

HENRYK SADURA/S

OTTER/WC

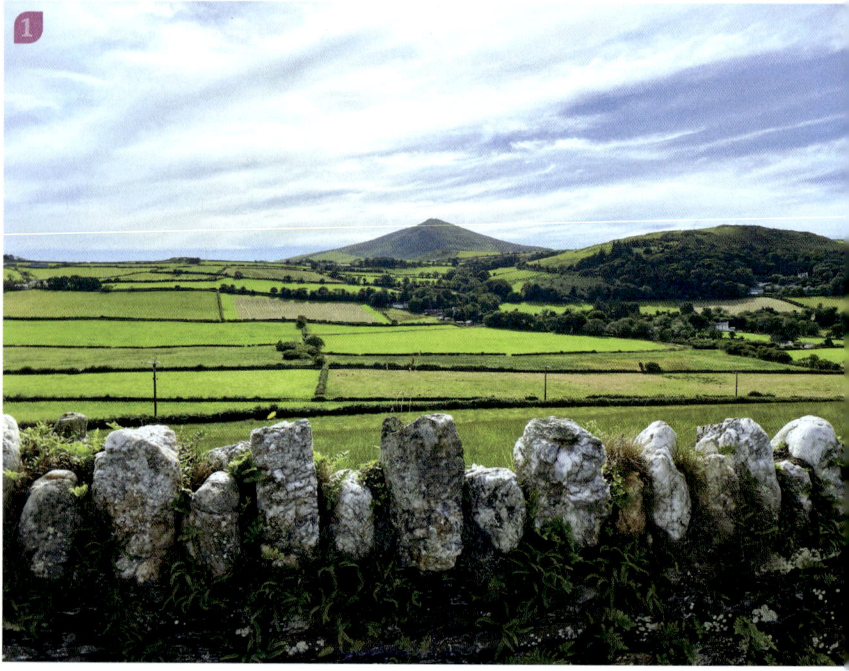

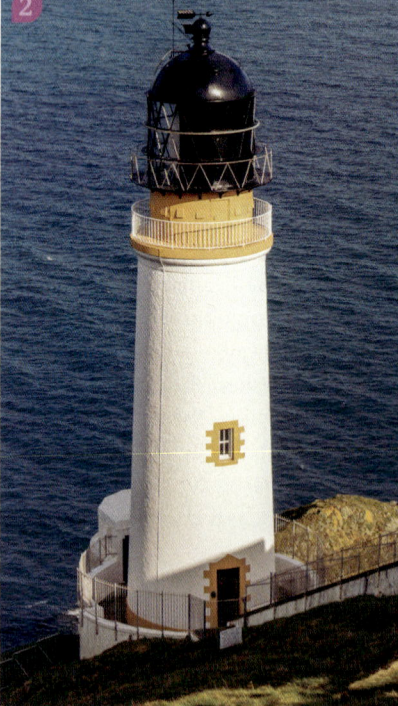

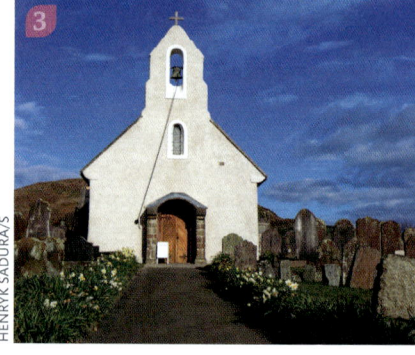

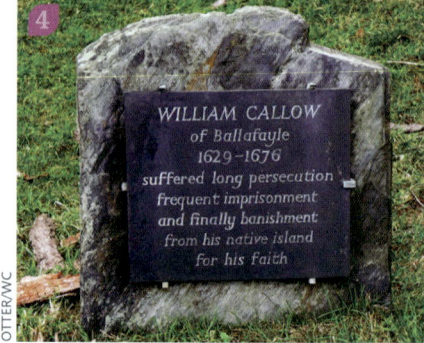

MAUGHOLD & AROUND

defensive position long before the early Christians arrived, with local copper and iron deposits attracting people to the area since prehistoric times. The cairn can be reached by retracing your steps to the car park, then heading 90yds down the single-track road and taking the uneven steps that lead seawards uphill, and is marked by the pile of stones at the summit. A few yards southwards is the right-angled remains of a building that may have been part of a coastal look-out system that existed from the Viking age until the 1600s.

The road leading from the village out towards the headland can be followed east as far as Maughold **lighthouse** – which, as it sits halfway down the cliff face, can be looked down on from the headland despite being 25yds tall. Peregrines can be seen overhead, while razorbills, fulmars and cormorants, which breed on the cliffs in the spring and summer months, can be spotted closer to sea level. The headland is an excellent vantage point for those hoping to spot any of the dolphins that visit Manx waters in the spring and summer months, or the minke whales that move round to the east of the island from September to November as they follow the herring to their spawning grounds.

5 BALLAFAYLE CAIRN & QUAKER BURIAL GROUND
/// magnetic.insolent.vine

There is more evidence of Maughold's longstanding importance as a centre of spirituality to the south of Maughold village. The remains of a **Neolithic burial cairn** at Ballafayle stand beside the road in the corner of a field – the enclosure is accessible to the public. A scattering of standing stones 1–2ft high mark the site, along with the remains of a stone wall running along a narrow trench on the northern and eastern side (it is thought this wall once formed a kerb around the wedge-shaped cairn). The site was discovered accidentally during improvement works in the 1920s, and ash uncovered during the excavation has led to the theory that it may have been used for cremations. Its position on a ridge gives the spot extensive sea views

◀ **1** The area of the northeast around Maughold is dominated by farmland. **2** The headland behind Maughold's lighthouse provides an excellent vantage point for spotting marine wildlife and seabirds. **3** Kirk Maughold is one of the oldest churches on the island. **4** William Callow's grave in the Quaker Burial Ground.

across to the Cumbrian coast, as well as being able to see another Neolithic tomb, Cashtal yn Ard (page 120), across the valley to the southwest.

Directly across the road is the **Quaker Burial Ground** – the only one for Quakers on the island. Sheltered by half a dozen tall trees (an unusual feature in this exposed, windswept landscape) a small, solitary headstone stands at the centre of this tiny graveyard, which can be accessed via a stile in the surrounding wall. The modern headstone is in

THE EXORCIST OF LEWAIGUE

For all the myths and legends that swirl around Maughold, there is one figure who looms particularly large. **Ewan Christian**, a 19th-century evangelist and 'fairy doctor' who lived in the area north of the village, known as Lewaigue, seems to have been the focal point of so many local yarns it is hard not to imagine him as the star of a Gothic masterpiece.

Born in 1803 and a bit of a tearaway in his early years, Christian underwent a radical conversion after allegedly meeting a spirit on his way home from Ramsey one night. He became teetotal and a devoted preacher – yet apparently maintained a good working relationship with the spirits of the dead, who would come to him with messages for their living relatives (often revealing the whereabouts of a hidden stash of valuables). He was also called upon to perform exorcisms of ghosts that refused to move on – one particularly tricky encounter left him bald – and was said to be able to stop someone bleeding simply by saying a charm.

Another report had him called in to tackle a terrifying moddey dhoo (page 19) in the south of Maughold parish, which had been lurking by the side of the road and frightening horses. The first time he addressed it, it told him to come again alone on another night. That he did – and, while the beast was never seen again, Christian returned a changed man and refused to speak about what had transpired between them.

He is also connected to the tale of a talking brass head that could reveal the future. He was said to have built it using materials given to him by the devil, but when the big night came for it to start working, the project was hampered by a meddling servant and the head exploded before it could say anything useful. Another tale claims that he died after meeting the devil on his way home from preaching one night – they had an argument so ferocious that Christian was overcome and never recovered.

Perhaps unsurprisingly, he was allegedly still spotted around the parish long after his death in 1874 – though it has been suggested that all the tales attributed to him are actually an amalgamation of stories linked to various members and branches of his family.

memory of William Callow – a local farmer and Quaker who was born in 1629 and severely persecuted for his beliefs. He and other Quakers were banished from the island in 1665, amid fears they could influence the rest of the population. Callow eventually returned in 1672 and was buried on this spot in 1676, having given part of his land as a grave site for members of the movement – without markers, it is not known how many could be buried alongside him.

> *"Its position on a ridge gives the spot extensive sea views across to the Cumbrian coast."*

Both sites can be reached by continuing south along the A15 out of Maughold village for roughly 1½ miles – cyclists and walkers should bear in mind that the route is uphill for most of the way. Turn right up the single-track road next to the former Methodist chapel, and the sites are on either side of the road at the top of the hill.

SOUTH OF MAUGHOLD & INLAND

To really get away from it all, head three miles south of Maughold village to Cornaa Valley and its surrounds. The area is gloriously quiet, with the stunningly pretty Ballaglass Glen to explore and a brilliant example of a Neolithic tomb at Cashtal yn Ard – which you are quite likely to have all to yourself. It's possible to explore a lot of this area on foot, with easy walks along the country roads that criss-cross between the fields, and so little background noise that it is possible to hear the bees buzzing and gorse flowers popping open in late spring.

6 CORNAA VALLEY

The Cornaa Valley, scraped out by an Ice Age glacier, stretches from the muscular, looming hill of North Barrule (page 121) eastwards to the rocky cove of Port Cornaa Beach. Public transport skirts around the upper edge of the valley through the hamlet of Glen Mona, with the tram line (Glen Mona, Ballaglass or Cornaa halts) largely hugging the main road. East of the tram line, you are on your own. There are only narrow, single-track roads for the two miles from here to the beach, with no cafés or public facilities, and nowhere to fill a water bottle.

But it's the seclusion that makes this section of the northeast coast so appealing. Stepping across the tram line is to find somewhere truly peaceful. The hawthorn-lined roads and footpaths form a basic triangle around the valley from Glen Mona to Ballaglass Glen to the beach and back, allowing for the whole area to be explored on foot (though, it being a valley, it is worth noting that the return trip to the main road will inevitably involve a fair bit of strenuous uphill walking).

Wild swimmers in particular will find **Port Cornaa Beach** has a lot to offer. While the shoreline itself is stony, it is also the spot where the meandering Cornaa River meets the sea – the curve of the foreshore creates a large, inland pool perfect for a dip. Follow the footpath upstream to reach a small waterfall with a wide plunge pool that's a favourite among those in the know. It could well be no coincidence that this is the area associated with a Manx mermaid: a young man who once lived near the beach was said to have met one of the creatures while out at sea one day. The next time he set out he took some apples, much to the delight of his new friend who granted him and his family good luck. Eventually the young man decided it was time to leave for foreign shores, but before he went he was said to have planted an apple tree overhanging the rocks at Bulgham, a short way down the coast, so the mermaid could still have her favourite treat.

7 BALLAGLASS GLEN

Car park at /// dreaming.convergence.shunning

Ballaglass is one of the Manx national glens and covers 16 acres of woodland on the north side of Cornaa Valley. It is renowned as one of the island's prettiest, with a mix of oak, beech and chestnut forming a canopy over the carpet of bluebells that blooms in the spring. There is a surprise around every corner – dotted among the trees are the derelict remains of buildings linked to former corn and flax mills, as well as the stone workings of a short-lived mining venture from the mid-19th century. The most breathtaking spots can be found on the footpaths leading from the car park along either side of the river: the water has carved a series of deep ravines, resulting in a mixture of crashing waterfalls, bubbling plunge pools and still, sun-dappled ponds.

---

1 Cashtal yn Ard is a Neolithic chambered tomb from around 3000 BC. **2** Ballaglass Glen is carpeted with bluebells in the spring. **3** A three-mile footpath leads to the peak of North Barrule, which dominates the landscape of the island's northeast. ▶

THE NORTHEAST

8 CASHTAL YN ARD
/// transparency.sitting.fussed

In the corner of a field near Ballaglass Glen is one of the island's most recognisable archaeological sites. Cashtal yn Ard, which translates as Castle of the Heights, is a superb example of a **Neolithic chambered tomb** from around 3000BC, revealed in its full glory by excavations in the 1930s.

Fallen stones were re-erected as part of the works in the early 20th century, with new, clearly dated stones put in place where others were obviously missing. Today the site is one of deep stillness and reflection, far from any traffic or other distractions. A semicircle of standing stones is pierced by the low, cramped entrance to what was once a series of covered chambers, now open to the air, which the excavation suggested held burials and pottery. Unrestricted access means the chambers and forecourt can be explored up close. The dark presence of North Barrule to the west and the expanse of sea and sky to the east make it a powerful place.

"The dark presence of North Barrule to the west and the expanse of sea and sky to the east make it a powerful place."

The site is completely open to the public and accessed via an overgrown path leading up from the nearby road (the road is reached by turning east off the A2 opposite the Glen Mona Hotel). The footpath is marked with a small green sign; after 200yds, clamber over a stone stile to get into a field. The tomb is immediately on your right, and there is a gate for entering the enclosure at the far end of the railings.

9 THE DHOON

A steep, rugged glen five miles south of Ramsey, the Dhoon is not for the faint-hearted (or weak-ankled). However, there are rewards for those brave enough to take on the challenge of the mile-long descent through the mossy, mature woodland to the cove at the base of the valley.

The entrance to the glen is on the main A2 road between Douglas and Ramsey and has its own stop on the Manx Electric Railway; there is also a dedicated car park directly across the road.

The path through the narrow glen follows the river through the trees and leads past the base of the beautiful, tumbling Inneen Vooar – or Big Girl – waterfall, one of the highest on the island with a drop of about 40yds (it is one of those idyllic spots that makes a belief in fairies seem perfectly reasonable). It eventually reaches the secluded stony beach at the bottom of the glen, which is enclosed by steep headland on either side, making it a quiet spot for a picnic; the distinct vertical lines in the cliffs also provide a good example of Manx Group geology and the sedimentary layers from which it was formed. Look out for choughs and peregrines, and see if you can spot any of the feral goats that roam the headland to the south.

FOOD & DRINK

Zen at the Glen Dhoon Glen entrance and tram stop, IM7 1HL zenatdhoonglen ⊙ 10.00–15.00 Wed–Fri, 10.00–16.00 Sat & Sun. A small but perfectly formed kiosk with outdoor seating beside the entrance to the glen, serving organic coffee, light bites and cakes. It also runs a 'nature spa', with hot tubs and ice baths among the trees.

10 NORTH BARRULE

North Barrule, which sits just to the south of Ramsey, is the dominant feature of the landscape wherever you stand in the northeast of the island. At 1,850ft above sea level it falls just short of being a mountain, but what it lacks in height it makes up for in steepness.

The peak can be reached via a three-mile footpath over very uneven, sometimes boggy ground from the Black Hut car park on the Mountain Road (decoy.rehearsing.buffoon) – a moderate walk along a ridgeline. A much steeper, craggier route up the northeast side can be taken from

THE WORST AVIATION DISASTER IN MANX HISTORY

The sudden, looming presence of North Barrule led directly to the worst aviation disaster in Manx history. On 23 April 1945, a B-17 Flying Fortress carrying American servicemen from southeast England to Northern Ireland slammed into the side of the hill, which was swathed in mist. Thirty-one people lost their lives.

A farmer working on the slopes below saw the plane seconds before the collision and believed it to be flying at only 500ft. The impact and resulting fireball were so great that the only recognisable part of the aircraft was a small section of the tail.

The men were flown back to England so they could be buried at the American Military Cemetery near Cambridge, but they are still remembered on the island. An American flag is raised at the site each year on the anniversary of their deaths, and a memorial plaque marks the spot on the eastern hillside.

Ramsey – a digital map is available for 'Manx Summit Route 2' on the ⌀ visitisleofman.com website.

As the highest summit in the north, North Barrule has played a central role in Manx folk practice. A bonfire used to be lit at the peak on Oie Voaldyn (the evening before 1 May) and at Hop tu Naa (page 29) to ward off bad luck and evil spirits. Meanwhile, a helpful glashan, a large, hairy, fairy-like creature, is said to assist farmers on the hillside by rounding up straggling sheep.

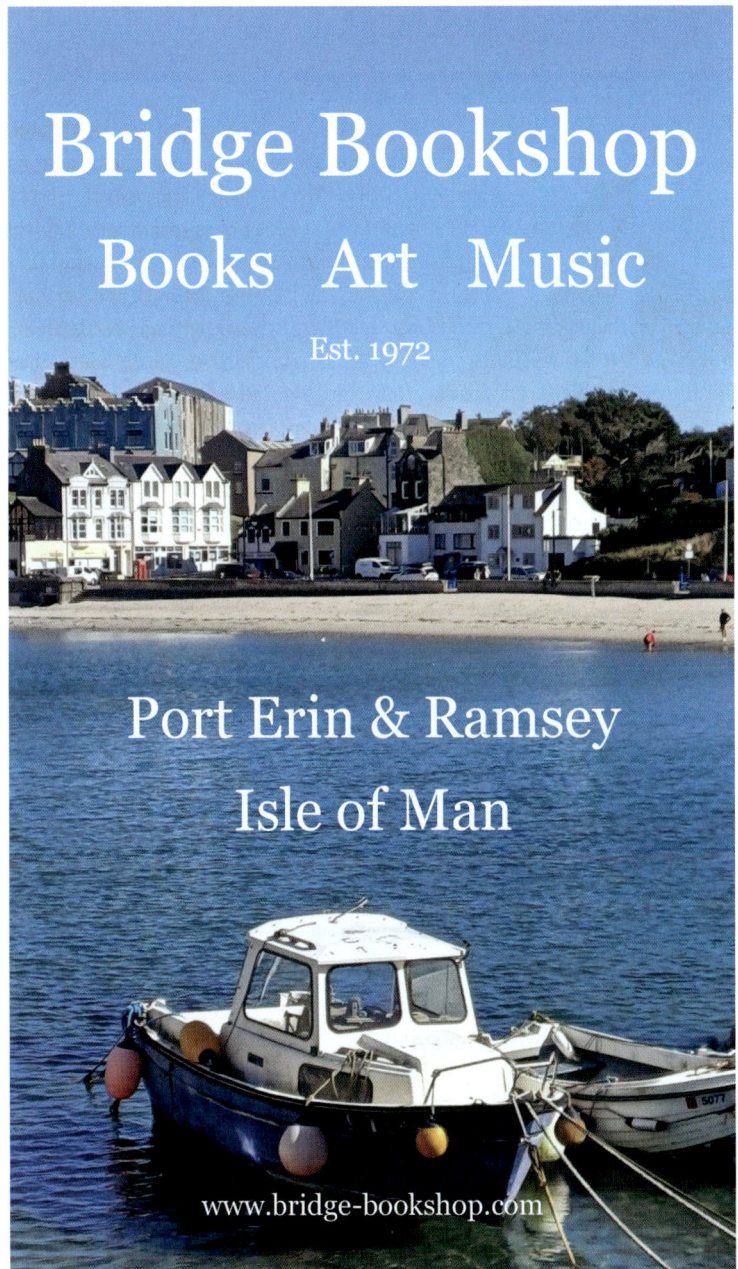

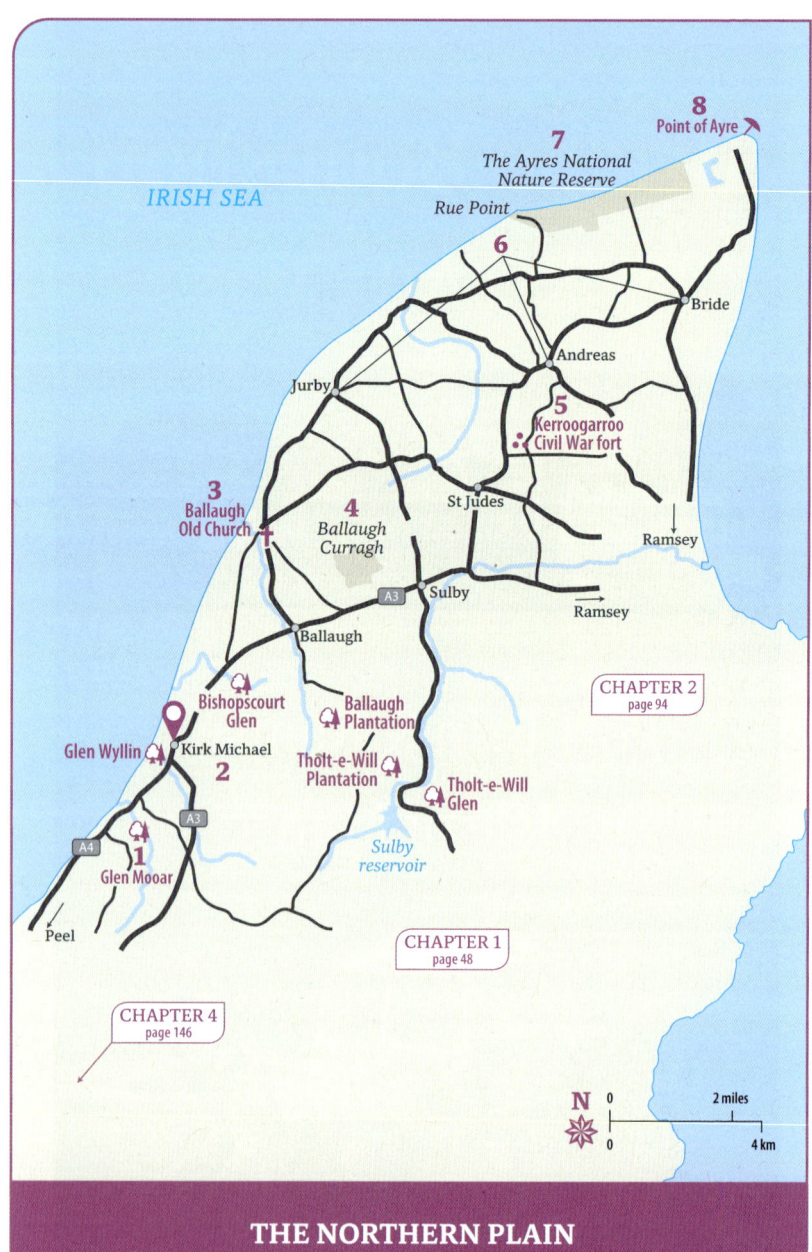

THE NORTHERN PLAIN

3
THE NORTHERN PLAIN

The northern plain represents something of a gear change for those travelling up from the south. Whereas the rest of the island is hilly, rugged and dotted with the remains of the mining industry that make it more akin to Cornwall, the northern plain is low-lying, largely flat and has the kind of broad skies that bring Norfolk to mind. The shift happens suddenly: at a line drawn roughly from **Kirk Michael** village in the west across to Ramsey in the east, the hills suddenly drop away and the tip of the island rolls out before you like a map.

The reason for this marked difference in appearance is geology. Most of the island is made up of sedimentary rocks laid down over hundreds of millions of years; the northern plain, however, is the result of glacial deposits that are just thousands of years old. Between 70,000 and 10,000 years ago, ice sheets are thought to have advanced and retreated over the island several times. When the glacier melted for the final time, it dropped the sediment it was carrying to form the northern plain – including rocks from the mountains of Scotland, which can now be found as pebbles on the northern coast.

The knock-on effect of this unusual geology is that the plain has historically been the most sparsely populated area of the island. There are no natural harbours, so no ports have sprung up and consequently no large towns. There is a scattering of small villages and hamlets across the landscape – the largest being Kirk Michael – but otherwise the land is largely given over to farming, areas protected for wildlife, and a little sand and gravel quarrying. The area is so flat, the military made use of it by setting up airfields during World War II (page 137) – and the Manx even refer to heading that way as going 'down north'.

This very much has its benefits for visitors. The area is ideal for a day of unchallenging walking or cycling in the countryside, with the **Raad ny Foillan** footpath tracing along the coast and taking in the **Ayres**

Nature Reserve (page 139) and the most northerly tip of the island at the **Point of Ayre** (page 143). Inland, picturesque country lanes criss-cross the landscape, and the boggy wetlands of **Ballaugh Curragh** (page 134) provide a habitat that is unique on the island.

The thin population and lack of marine traffic has made the northwest coast a haven for sea birds such as gannets and curlew, while the flat sands at **Glen Wyllin and Glen Mooar beaches** are ideal for a stroll. Some of the island's most famous furry residents also make the area their home – a large population of **wild wallabies**, descended from escapees from the local wildlife park, roam in the northwest of the island and sightings are common, particularly in the curragh.

GETTING THERE & AROUND

Buses 5, 5a and 6a travel between Douglas and Ramsey via Peel, following the coastal route along the A4 and A3 via Kirk Michael, Ballaugh and Sulby. The villages of Andreas, Bride and Jurby are covered by the ConnectVILLAGES bus service, which operates on demand (⊙ 08.40–19.00 Mon–Fri, 06.30–19.00 Sat) and can be booked using the MANNgo app or by calling ✆ 01624 697440 (⊙ 08.30–16.30 Mon–Fri).

THE NORTHWEST COAST FROM GLEN MOOAR TO SULBY

Dotted along the A3 are the small villages of Kirk Michael, Ballaugh and Sulby, which will be familiar to anyone who has ever taken an interest in the TT (page 23). Each just a small cluster of houses with the occasional church, shop or pub, during race fortnight they become a showcase for the skill of the riders, who must weave their 1000cc machines at 160mph between the painted stone cottages that line the narrow roads.

Outside race season, the area is a lot more peaceful, with precious little in the way of commercialism. There is a long flat beach, nature reserve and glen to explore, with natural curiosities, such as the thriving local wallaby population, and manmade attractions, such as an ancient chapel and carved rune stones, tucked away in hidden corners.

Options for **walks** in the area include the beach at Glen Wyllin to the west of Kirk Michael, which is part of the broad shoreline that curves all the way along the northwest coast to the Point of Ayre (page 143),

12 miles to the northeast. On this section of coast, to the west of Kirk Michael and Ballaugh, the shingle and sand beach is overlooked by tall sand cliffs that give a sense of seclusion – with no promenade, shops or ice-cream vans on hand, it's the perfect spot for anyone who wants to play at being a castaway for a day. There are marked walking routes around the area and a coastal footpath – signposts can be found at the beach car park. Further up the coast at Ballaugh beach, the wreck of a fishing trawler that ran aground in bad weather in 1931 can be found at low tide (all 13 men on board survived). The tide can turn quickly on the flat beaches, so beware being cut off. Byways also run from the villages of Kirk Michael and Ballaugh up into the hills to the east, with bracing hikes up to the Ballaugh and Tholt-e-Will plantations.

1 GLEN MOOAR

/// hallmarks.dudes.cigar for the entrance gate to the glen, teacup.relatives.stainless for the car park 200yds west at the beach

As well as being a beautiful stroll that is filled with bluebells in spring, this magical little woodland hides mystical sites dating back over 1,000 years along its half-mile length. Sitting a mile south of Kirk Michael (page 129), the glen covers ten acres and follows a trickling stream through the valley, with gorse-lined fields surrounding it on either side. The path through the trees is a 'there and back again' walk tracing the length of the narrow, corridor-like glen.

Just a few steps beyond the little wooden gate that leads directly off the A4 main road are the vast stone pillars that once carried a railway viaduct across the valley. Following the path deeper into the trees reveals the ruins of Cabbal Pheric, or **St Patrick's Chapel** – a tiny keeill within a small enclosure, accompanied by the remnants of a priest's cell. The site is thought to date from between the 8th and 10th centuries, and is completely open to visitors who wish to explore. The walls, now just a couple of feet high, are a yard thick; excavations in the early 20th century revealed that it once had a flagstone floor and an altar against the eastern wall. It is a deeply peaceful and reflective place, a little haven of spirituality among the trees.

> *"It is a deeply peaceful and reflective place, a little haven of spirituality among the trees."*

A potential reason for its existence, and why the site may have been considered sacred long before the arrival of Christianity, lies at the

THE NORTHERN PLAIN

A walk from Kirk Michael to Bishopscourt & Glen Mooar

❋ OS Landranger map 95; start: the car park in the centre of Kirk Michael, on the corner of the A3 and Station Rd ⚲ SC316907; 5 miles; easy

This walk can be completed in its entirety, or split into the northern loop via Bishopscourt and the southern loop via Glen Mooar. Both loops are fairly flat, but include uneven, unpaved surfaces – the second loop involves walking on a sandy beach.

LOOP 1: BISHOPSCOURT (2½ MILES)

1 From the car park, turn right and walk 100yds down Station Road to the old level crossing, where there is a small section of railway tracks and a white and red gate. Turn right into the grounds of the fire station and follow the route of the old railway line directly ahead, keeping the old station building and the garage housing the fire engine on your right.

2 After about a mile, you'll reach a metal gate on the left with a wooden signpost pointing out the Raad ny Foillan and other public rights of way, and a dog bin on your right. Turn right

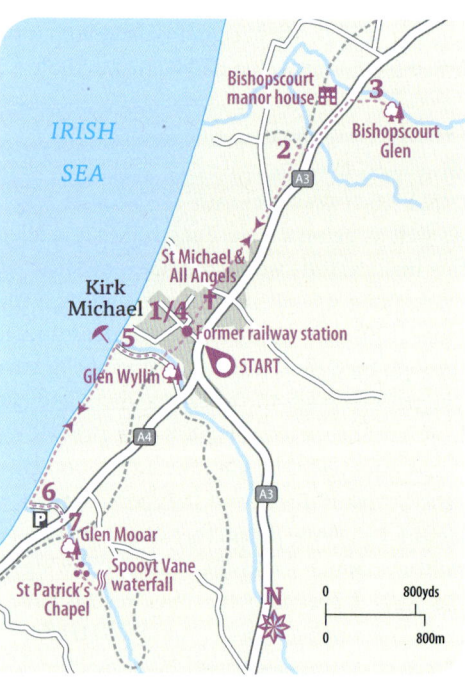

southern end of the glen: **Spooyt Vane waterfall**. One of the highest waterfalls on the island (the name means 'white spout' in Manx), the cascade tumbles down three tiers of rock face into a deep, dark, atmospheric hollow. While it technically sits just outside the boundary of the glen, the landowner welcomes visitors, who can view the falls from the rocks at the base via a steep flight of steps.

past the dog bin and walk the few yards down on to the road. Follow the narrow road the few yards up to join the main road, and turn left onto the boardwalk. Follow the main road for about 500yds until Bishopscourt manor house – identifiable by the distinctive stone chapel attached to its northern side – is on your left.

3 Directly opposite, on the eastern side of the road, is a pair of white gate posts with bishops' hats painted on them. Go through this gate into Bishopscourt Glen, where there is a looped path taking visitors past a miniature Tynwald Hill, a former mill pond and a hermit's cave – the loop can be completed in either direction. Afterwards, return to the main road to retrace the walk back to Kirk Michael village, from where you can return to the car park, with the option to continue on the Glen Mooar loop.

LOOP 2: GLEN MOOAR (2½ MILES)

4 From the car park, turn right and walk 100yds down Station Road to the old level crossing. At the old level crossing, turn left and follow the former railway line south about 250yds until you reach Glen Wyllin campsite. Cross the footbridge over the stream and turn right on to the road that runs through the campsite. Follow the road 700yds down to the beach.

5 Turn left on the beach and head south, keeping the sandy cliffs on your left. Walk for about a mile until you reach the river that runs across the beach. Turn left and head up the gravelly path into Glen Mooar beach car park.

6 Cross to the eastern end of the car park and follow the narrow road for 250yds up to the main road – there will be a small gate into Glen Mooar directly opposite. Cross the main road and go through the gate.

7 Follow the path through the glen (page 127), passing the remains of St Patrick's Chapel and going as far as Spooyt Vane waterfall. After visiting the waterfall, retrace your steps back through the glen and down onto the beach to return back to Kirk Michael.

2 KIRK MICHAEL

The most southerly, and the largest, of the three villages in this area is Kirk Michael, which has a main road lined with little cottages, a traditional butcher and a pretty tea room, as well as an imposing church at its centre housing some impressive medieval crosses. The arrival of the steam railway connection from St John's (page 169) in the 1870s

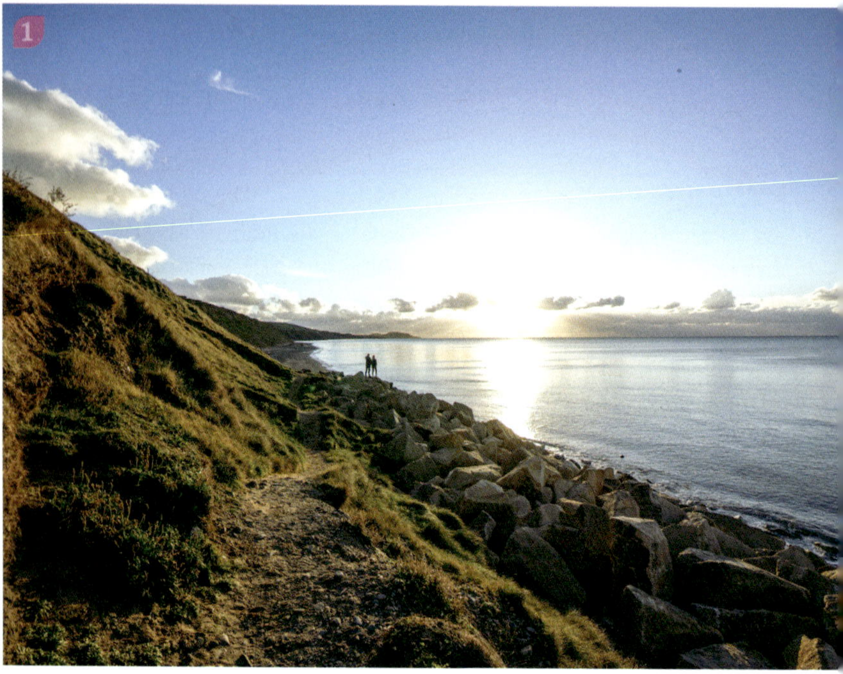

VISIT ISLE OF MAN

TIMOTHY CRAIG

STEPHEN RICHARD MCADAM/S

VISIT ISLE OF MAN

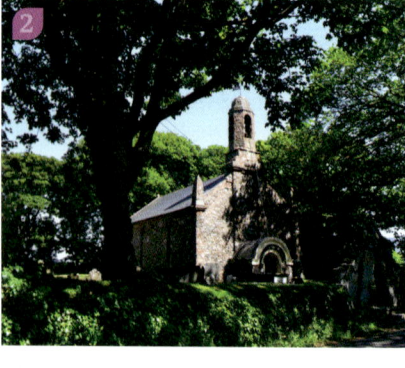

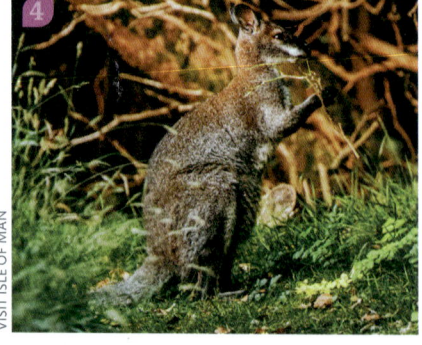

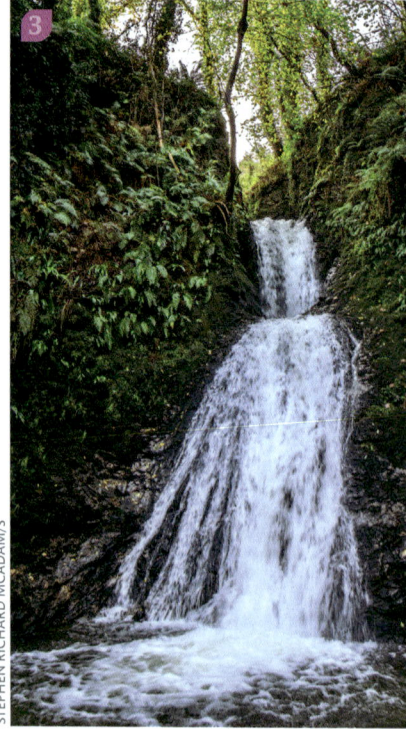

brought the gloss of tourism to the village and a few rows of grand Victorian houses, and the 20th century saw the addition of a scattering of bungalows.

The big draw in Kirk Michael is **St Michael and All Angels Church** (☉ 10.00–16.00 daily), after which the village is named. The Gothic-style building that exists today, along with its domineering clock tower, was built in the 19th century, but the site is believed to have been sacred since the middle of the first millennium. The church has a collection of 12 Manx crosses from as early as the 6th century on display inside, including the beautifully carved slab known as Grim's Cross: only about 18in from the top of this carving remain, but it carries stunning knotwork, runes down the side and what could be a very early depiction of Christ flanked by a cockerel and an angel on one of the faces (it isn't known for definite who the figure is, as it is clothed and has no stigmata, leaving it open to interpretation). The opposite face of the slab reflects the older Viking beliefs with what appears to be a carving of an eagle, thought to be linked to Norse mythology.

"The church has a collection of 12 Manx crosses from as early as the 6th century on display inside."

Thanks to its proximity to Bishopscourt – the sprawling the 17th-century manor just up the road that was once the official residence of the island's bishop (now in private ownership) – there are five bishops buried in the old graveyard, which sits immediately to the right after entering the church grounds through the black arched gateway off the main road. A less celebrated but rather more moving grave marker is that of an unknown woman whose body washed ashore on the nearby beach in December 1880. The body was never claimed; however, newspaper reports at the time said she had been wearing a black cashmere dress, silk stockings and a wedding ring – leading to speculation that she was someone well-heeled who had fallen overboard from a ship. A small posy of flowers is still frequently placed on her modest headstone, which stands on the westerly edge of the graveyard near the church door.

◀ **1** The Raad ny Foillan coastal path includes the beach near Kirk Michael. **2** Nature seems to be trying to reclaim the bewitching Ballaugh Old Church. **3** Spooyt Vane ('white spout') is one of the highest waterfalls on the island. **4** There are thought to be around 1,000 wallabies roaming wild in Ballaugh Curragh.

THE NORTHERN PLAIN

The railway line through the village closed in the 1960s, leaving what has become a fantastic, level **walking route** along the old trackway that is perfect for an easy stroll. Part of the original track still survives in the village, down the aptly named Station Road: a small memorial plaque marks the few yards of remaining ironwork, directly opposite the gingerbread house-style old station building, which has now been amalgamated into the modern fire station.

Kirk Michael's village pub, **The Mitre**, is the oldest on the island and dates from at least the 1780s – Fletcher Christian (page 78) was reputedly one of its customers before he set off to commit mutiny. Its low-rise stable building still stands next door and is now the home of the local rifle club, while the small Victorian courthouse complete with castellations and tall, arched windows – where a case was last heard in 1950 – adjoins the pub car park. The pub itself boasts a roaring fire, locally brewed ale and, during the steam-railway era, was a popular destination for honeymooning Manx couples who sought a bit of privacy.

FOOD & DRINK

The Dovecote Tearooms Main Rd, Kirk Michael IM6 1ET ⌕ 01624 878534 thedovecoteiom ⊙ 09.00–16.00 Thu–Sat. A sweet, cottagey tea room in the heart of the village doing homemade cakes, lunches including soup and pies, and – of course – afternoon teas. A cute and cosy place with floral tablecloths, pastel-coloured furniture and vintage crockery.

SHOPPING

Lee Mayers Traditional Butchers Main Rd, Kirk Michael IM6 1ER ⊙ 09.00–17.00 Tue, 09.00–13.00 Wed, 09.00–17.00 Thu & Fri, 09.00–15.00 Sat. Bills itself as 'the ultimate candy shop for meat lovers' and it's not hard to see why. The pick 'n' mix of sausages in all manner of interesting flavours – such as beef, sweet onion and Guinness – is hard to resist, and there are crates of vegetables to help you make up a meal.

3 BALLAUGH OLD CHURCH

/// ambushed.buzzword.destination

Two and a half miles northeast of Kirk Michael is the smaller village of **Ballaugh**, which is essentially a cluster of houses with a corner shop and a good pub. The unmissable humped road bridge in the centre of the village is a notorious TT black spot, with its jump-and-corner combination ending many riders' races – and sometimes even their lives.

A mile north, along the A10, is the bewitching Ballaugh Old Church (☉ 10.00–15.00 Sat & Sun). It was the locals' main place of worship for 600 years until the early 19th century, when a new church was built to accommodate the growing population of the village. Gnarly old trees now breathe down on the squat, rectangular building with its rough-hewn stonework – giving the impression that nature would be only too keen to reclaim the site given half a chance. Rooks make a racket in the branches, and the two imposing gateposts lean drunkenly towards each other (it is said that when they finally touch, the world will end). It has all the air of a place where rural superstition sat equally alongside religious faith; indeed, the church was once used as a place of reprimand for one Alice Cowley, a local woman who was convicted of sorcery in the

THE SULBY GIANT WHO RAN AWAY TO THE CIRCUS

Fairies were said to live under Ballaugh Bridge and were known for capturing passing farmers and using them as decoys so the 'little people' could get served at the pub. Two and a half miles up the road at Sulby, however, a very big – and much more real – person was achieving an almost mythic status too.

Arthur Caley, also known as the Manx Giant, was born to a farming family in a cottage just outside the village in 1824. He continued growing until well into his twenties, eventually reaching a height of 7ft 11in and weighing 28 stone. With these proportions, a life in showbusiness beckoned and in 1851 he left for the bright lights of Manchester and London, eventually ending up in the salons of Paris, where he apparently died a year later – shortly after a life-insurance policy was taken out for him. His mother received a letter informing her of the death, and yet…

A few years later PT Barnum, the famous circus entrepreneur behind The Greatest Show on Earth, presented an incredible 'Arabian Giant' to audiences in New York. The giant was seen by thousands of people a day, and went on to appear in numerous exhibitions and circuses. It was only on his deathbed in 1889 that it was revealed that the Arabian Giant was in fact the Manxman Arthur Caley, who hadn't died in Paris at all.

Caley is still remembered at Rose Cottage, two miles to the north of Sulby on Regaby West Road (50yds to the east of the crossroads with Kerroogarroo /// lift. disused.town), where an iron cast of his huge hand is affixed to the top of the gatepost at a height of 7ft 11in. The cottage is thought to have been owned by a former employer of Caley. Another cast of his hand and one of his boots are held by the Manx Museum in Douglas (page 63), and a book about his life, *The Manx Giant: The Amazing Story of Arthur Caley*, has been written by John Quirk.

early 18th century after selling a love charm to a young man. She spent a month in prison before being ordered to do penance at this church.

The old building no longer hosts services but is looked after by volunteers, who use it for events and have rewilded part of the grounds. Inside, it is simple, plain and white – a calming spot for a moment of reflection.

🍴 FOOD & DRINK

The Raven Ballaugh Bridge, Ballaugh IM7 5EG, 🖉 01624 896128, TheRavenBallaugh. A solid country pub serving classic, chef-prepared meals such as slow-cooked pork belly and mash. It makes the most of its vantage point on the TT course: the walls are covered in race memorabilia. It also sells an exclusive brew from the local Okell's brewery, Raven's Claw, which is only available at this pub.

4 BALLAUGH CURRAGH

Car park: Windmill Lane, Ballaugh Curragh /// symptom.twinge.raindrops

The Ballaugh Curragh, a designated Area of Special Scientific Interest a mile northeast of Ballaugh, covers 82 hectares and includes areas of willow scrub, mature woodland, marshy grassland and peat bogs. Boardwalks criss-cross through the gnarly, twisted willows and a petrol-like sheen caused by the peat – or 'turf', as it is known locally – sits on top of the dubs that pockmark the lurid green moss. ('They're called "ponds" in English,' explains John 'Dog' Callister, my guide, when asked what a 'dub' is.)

It is an eerie, magical landscape. John points out wild mint, ragwort and bog myrtle among the willow trunks – the purple flowers of spotted and marsh orchids can be seen in summer. It hosts the largest winter roost of hen harriers in western Europe and is a summer breeding site for water rail, curlew, woodcock and grasshopper warblers; a specially built birdwatching hide can be reached along level boardwalks a few hundred yards from the reserve car park.

The curragh – the Manx name for marshland – formed in the basin of what was, 10,000 years ago, a glacial lake. Over the course of millennia, decaying vegetation built up in the basin to form peat up to 12ft deep; it is now the most important wetland on the island and a site of international significance.

John pushes a low-hanging branch aside and strides along the slightly bouncy boardwalk. 'They're about the size of an Alsatian,' he says, 'but the other way up.' The creatures he is describing are wallabies. Because it turns out wallabies love a northern wetland. They particularly love a northern wetland when they have escaped from a local wildlife park and realised there are absolutely no predators.

John, a willow weaver, poet and former countryside warden with Manx National Heritage, has been visiting Ballaugh Curragh for over 50 years, caring for the unique landscape and holding great affection for the unusual fauna.

'If one needed attention, sometimes I'd catch it and take it into the school,' he says, referring to the primary in nearby Ballaugh village. On one occasion he took in a wallaby and after a while the children suddenly erupted with excitement. 'I couldn't work out why,' he said, 'then I realised a little face had poked out of its pouch.' He's confident that those pupils are probably still talking about that day decades later.

The wallabies hopping about today are the descendants of the escapees from nearby Curraghs Wildlife Park. They have been happily breeding in the area since the 1960s – there are now thought to be about 1,000 roaming wild, according to a survey in 2024. Keep a sharp eye on the middle distance as you walk through the trees and there is every chance you will spot a grey furry face peering back through the branches, or hopping away for cover. It is gloriously absurd. 'I've never actually

BUMBEE CAGES

John 'Dog' Callister (see opposite) hands me what looks like a tiny woven rattle, with a handle and cage on top containing a shell. This, he explains, is a bumbee cage.

Bumbees – how older generations of Manx referred to bumblebees – were said to be naughty fairies who had been transformed into insects as punishment. Traditionally, children would weave a bumbee cage from rushes and trap one of the creatures inside by placing it over a flower.

Once the child had gone to sleep, their parents would free the beleaguered bee and replace it in the cage with a stone or shell. The child would be told in the morning that the fairies had decided the bee had suffered enough punishment and allowed it to escape, but had left the stone or shell to ensure the child still had their toy.

Luckily for the bees, the practice has now died out (there are suggestions that the appeal of such outdoor pursuits waned with the arrival of television) – though the skill of making the intricate cages is kept alive by weavers such as John.

A video of John weaving a bumbee cage can be found on his website ⌔ willowmann. im/bumbee-cage-videos-willow-mann.

seen one sitting like that before,' says John, when we spot a particularly relaxed wallaby sitting on its haunches like a lemur.

There are mixed feelings towards the wallabies among locals. Some think they should, as a non-native species, be eradicated entirely – there are concerns about their impact on native fauna, and worries about the long-term health of the animals with such a large population coming from a tiny gene pool. However, many residents have taken the wallabies to their hearts, and the Manx Wildlife Trust says they are 'arguably now a part of Manx culture'.

Bus routes 5, 5a and 6a out of Ramsey stop outside the Curraghs Wildlife Park, and it is then a flat two-mile walk to the curragh car park down single-track roads. John – who is a former Manx Bard (the island's equivalent of the poet laureate) – takes visitors round the curragh on request (he can be emailed at ✉ dog@iom.com). He doesn't charge but is more than happy to be taken for lunch in return.

THE FAR NORTH

The Isle of Man's most northerly point can accurately be described as flat, sparsely populated and rather windswept. The wide-open skies and long flat beaches make the coast in the area a glorious place to watch seabirds, but bear in mind there really is nothing between you and the weather, which can be fierce.

Inland, medieval stone crosses and a civil-war fort speak to the centuries of human history that have played out in the area – and the two 20th-century airfields reflect its slightly unexpected role in more recent conflicts. Today, it has very much returned to the state of relative isolation that attracted by far its most famous resident: the comic actor Sir Norman Wisdom.

5 KERROOGARROO CIVIL WAR FORT
/// discounts.pudding.frill

Set far back from the nearest road, surrounded by fields on all sides and enclosed by a wide ditch, are the remains of a fort built during the English Civil War. These impressive earthworks – now just a massive grass bank, large enough for a footpath to run around the perimeter – still clearly show the star-like shape of the site as it would have been when it was built in the 17th century by James Stanley, the 7th Earl of

THE FAR NORTH

Derby and the Lord of Man, who was ultimately betrayed in 1651 by his Manx receiver-general, Illiam Dhone.

Stanley left the island in August that year to fight for the Royalist cause – however, in his absence, Illiam Dhone eventually decided to surrender to Oliver Cromwell's troops. Kerroogarroo initially resisted the order, though it would be wrong to suggest that there was any major bloodshed – the dispute over the fort ultimately came down to a heated exchange between the two sides and some rude remarks about the countess, who had remained on the island. Nonetheless, its fall signalled Illiam Dhone's seizure of control of the island, which surrendered to the Parliamentarians a few days later. It was also the moment that sealed Dhone's fate after the English monarchy was restored (page 191).

A footpath marked with a green signpost leads to the site off the A17 road, about two thirds of a mile northeast of St Judes village, taking you across farmland for 250yds, through gates and over a stile. A QR code on a sign at the entrance to the fort provides an audio guide.

6 ANDREAS, JURBY, BRIDE & AROUND
Yn Thie Thooit

These three villages – which could arguably be said to be barely bigger than hamlets – are the most northerly on the island and, with a sparse population of about 2,500 spread across an area four miles wide, feel a long way from the hustle and bustle of Ramsey or Douglas. During World War II, however, the area erupted into a hive of activity as the RAF made use of the flat landscape to establish airfields at Andreas and Jurby. Both airfields were used as training grounds, though fighter squadrons were sometimes also sent up to take on German bombers menacing the

"If the tower of the church looks unusually squat, that is because it was shortened during World War II."

likes of Belfast and Glasgow. The airmen who lost their lives in accidents while training are buried at St Andrew's Church in Andreas, which has 25 military graves, and St Patrick's Church in Jurby, which has 43.

Today, the village of **Andreas** has returned to being just a quiet cluster of houses – a mix of modernised stone cottages and more modern homes – with a corner shop and a pub, The Grosvenor, doing standard pub grub. As well as the military graves, **St Andrew's Church** (which stands 200yds south of the village, on the A9 road ⊙ daylight hours daily)

137

also houses a collection of 11 medieval carved stone crosses, including one known as Thorwald's Cross, which dates from roughly AD1000 and depicts the Viking god Odin alongside the Christian imagery. The modern church building was constructed in the 19th century but stands on the site of a much older place of worship dedicated to St Columba (though no visible structure remains). If the tower of the church looks unusually squat, that is because it was shortened during World War II to make it easier for planes to land at the airfield.

The RAF stopped using Andreas in 1946, and the airfield is now in private hands. The airfield at **Jurby**, four miles to the west, continued to be used by the military until the 1960s – it is now partly an industrial estate, the location of the island's prison and the home of two motor museums, which are very much the village's biggest draw.

The smaller of the two is **Jurby Transport Museum** (◯ Apr–Sep 11.00– 16.00 Sun) in an old wartime hangar. The museum has a collection of vintage buses dating from as early as 1927, plus an assortment of old cars, motorbikes and memorabilia. The larger of the two, **Isle of Man Motor Museum** (⊘ isleofmanmotormuseum.com ◯ Apr–Sep 10.00–17.00 daily), is a paradise for petrolheads, containing more than 500 vehicles parked up in a hangar-size building to wander round at your leisure. Highlights of the collection include a 1953 Humber Super Snipe used by Queen Elizabeth II on her coronation tour of the Commonwealth, an original P50 from Peel Engineering (page 151) and a former White House limousine. The collection includes more than 300 motorbikes, including TT race-winning machines from the likes of Joey Dunlop and John McGuinness.

St Patrick's Church (◯ Mar–Nov 10.00–16.00 daily; Dec–Feb 10.00– 15.30 daily), a mile southwest of the transport museums, is a local landmark thanks to its pristine white façade and imposing location on the northwestern headland, making it easy for sailors to spot and use for navigation while out at sea. The existing building is from the early 19th century, though it stands a few hundred yards from an 8th-century keeill and there are some 10th-century cross slabs in the porch. The stained- glass windows include three panels commissioned by the RAF, showing images of 1940s aircraft, to commemorate its connection to the area.

The tiny village of **Bride** sits seven miles northeast of Jurby, and amounts to a scant handful of stone cottages, a small primary school and a church right at the centre. At Bride Church (IM7 4AT ◯ daylight hours daily) lies the unassuming black headstone marking the grave of **Sir Norman Wisdom** (page 64), which sits in the modern extension to the graveyard. Immediately adjacent to the central walkway, towards the eastern end of the graveyard, the short stone is easy to miss – all of the graves in this section look much the same. Yet look closer and the distinctive feature jumps out: Sir Norman's iconic peaked cloth cap, carved into the stone with the words 'Remembered With a Laugh'. His former home, four miles west, near the village of Andreas, is called 'Ballalaugh' – a mixture of Manx and English meaning 'the home of laughter'. A ghostly figure has been reported approaching people around the church; however, as sightings began in the early 20th century, it seems unlikely to be Sir Norman seeking out a new audience.

SPECIAL STAYS

Yn Thie Thooit Lhen Bridge, The Lhen, Andreas IM7 3EP ⌀ 01624 830200 ⌀ islandescapes.im. Manx holidays don't come much more traditional than this: a single-storey, two-room thatched cottage in the countryside. Inside this tiny, whitewashed gem – which is a registered historic building owned by Manx National Heritage – the space is split into a cosy living room/kitchen with a log-effect stove and a double bedroom, all in a setting tranquil enough to hear the distinctive call of curlews outside. It is a retreat in every sense: the nearest shop is over two miles away in the village of Jurby to the south, and there is just a small handful of houses nearby. The beach and small Cronk-Y-Bing Nature Reserve are 200yds to the west. Just off the A10, the cottage is easy to reach by car or determined cyclists; it is also covered by the ConnectVILLAGES on-demand bus service.

FOOD & DRINK

The Old Guardhouse Jurby Industrial Estate, IM7 3BZ ⌀ Apr–Sep 10.00–16.00 daily; Oct–Mar 10.00–16.00 Thu–Sun. Located in a former World War II guardhouse on the edge of the old airfield, this functional and friendly little café is also right next door to the Isle of Man Motor Museum. It has a simple but tasty menu of sandwiches, chips, soup and jacket potatoes, plus fry-ups and bacon baps for a late breakfast. Finish off with one of the homemade cakes.

7 THE AYRES NATIONAL NATURE RESERVE

Car park and visitors' centre at /// carnivore.daytime.eternally

A haven for seabirds, rare plants and unusual fungi, this narrow corridor of protected land runs for three miles along the far northwestern coast – and feels very different to anywhere else on the island. While the beaches further south are enclosed by rugged cliffs and bracken-strewn headlands, the Ayres is a flat, scoured landscape created by deposits of sand and shingle that have been swept up the west coast since the retreat of the Ice Age glaciers some 10,000 years ago. The sand deposits continue to this day, making the Ayres the 'newest' part of the island; Rue Point, at the southwestern tip of the reserve, has extended 30yds towards the sea in the past 50 years. The word 'Ayres' itself comes from the Norse for 'gravel bank' and refers to the undulating waves of sand dunes that lead from the scrubby flatlands out towards the shingle beach.

"Exposure to the elements has buffed the wooden viewing platform to the colour of driftwood."

It is a stunning place, the low-lying marram grass whispering in the breeze and appearing to have been almost bleached of colour by the salt that whips off the sea in a gale. Exposure to the elements has buffed the wooden viewing platform beside the sole car park to the colour of driftwood. Flocks of gannets plunge into the water offshore (they hit the surface at about 60mph) while jittery oystercatchers and curlew scuttle about at the water's edge. The air is so clean that the grey-green lichen *Usnea articulata* – which is highly sensitive to pollution – is found here in large quantities.

Some 780 species of flora and fauna have been counted in total at the reserve, and a great place to start finding out about them is at the small **Discovery Centre** (*m* carnivore.daytime.eternally ⊙ May–Sep 13.00–16.00 daily) beside the car park. It runs a short film about the wildlife, and has hands-on displays covering the geology and birds, plants and habitats.

But the best way to experience the reserve is to get out among the dunes. Three colour-coded, marked trails of varying length – from 500yds to three miles – and terrain trace across the reserve. In spring, the pink and purple flowers of early and northern marsh orchids can

---

1 Holiday stays don't come much more traditional than the two-room thatched Yn Thie Thooit cottage. **2 & 3** An oystercatcher flies over the Ayres National Nature Reserve, where the dunes and flatlands are markedly different from the rugged cliffs of the coast further south. **4** The 'Winkie' light, with the Point of Ayre lighthouse behind it. **5** St Patrick's Church in Jurby stands out from the landscape, a useful beacon for sailors. **6** The Isle of Man Motor Museum includes a collection of more than 300 motorbikes. ▶

THE NORTHERN PLAIN

> ## A PRICKLY SUBJECT
> When, exactly, the non-native hedgehog arrived in the Isle of Man is unlikely to ever be proved. However, one theory is that they first made landfall at Rue Point following a shipwreck in 1800. The *Isle of Man Daily Times* reported in 1958 that the schooner *Hooton* had got into trouble off the north coast after leaving Whitehaven in Cumbria; someone on board had a box of hedgehogs, which were brought ashore and promptly escaped. The common hedgehog is now found throughout the island.

be found in the hollows between the dunes, while orange-tip butterflies look for a place to lay their eggs and the occasional osprey can be seen overhead. In the summer months the top of the beach becomes a nesting ground for little terns, oystercatchers and ringed plovers, which have amber, amber and red ratings respectively on the Britain-wide list of Birds of Conservation Concern; warning signs at the reserve during nesting season ask visitors to walk close to the waterline to avoid crunching any of the well-camouflaged eggs underfoot.

The extensive area of lichen heath that spans the raised part of the beach is of particular importance – it is a globally rare habitat, and this is the sole example in the Isle of Man. The lichens grow among the low-lying heather and gorse, creating what appears to be a greyish, prickly carpet. Skylarks and meadow pipits make their nests among the protective plants, and common lizards can be spotted darting for cover.

The area that now makes up the 673-acre reserve, which was officially created in 2000, hasn't always been so closely protected: until the 1980s, sand was taken from the dunes to be mixed into concrete. Stones from the beach have also historically been used for building, the marram grass was used for thatch and sheep were grazed on the heathland. Due to its remoteness, it was also used as a training ground for the military during World War II – bullet casings still turn up occasionally (though any munitions should be left in place and reported to the police).

The 20a bus runs twice a day, on schooldays only, to the village of Bride, from where the Ayres car park and visitors' centre is a flat, two-mile walk (the first mile is along the A10 without pavements, the last mile along a quiet, single-track road). The ConnectVillages bus service can also be booked in advance to reach Bride. Alternatively, the reserve is a fairly flat, seven-mile cycle along the A10 out of Ramsey.

THE FAR NORTH

8 THE POINT OF AYRE
Car park at ///tinting.peculiarly.drip

It is said that a powerful witch who lived on the island many centuries ago foretold that one day the Isle of Man and Scotland would grow so close that a Manx woman and a Scottish woman would be able to fold their washing across the gap.

It's not quite there yet – but the northerly tip of the island is most definitely on the move. Just 14 miles from the Isle of Whithorn in Dumfries and Galloway, anyone on the beach at the Point of Ayre is closer to Scotland than they are to Douglas, and is standing on a piece of land that did not exist 150 years ago. The windswept foreshore is made up of banks of stone and shingle that were left behind after the retreat of Ice Age glaciers, and it is gradually being swept round to the east by the strong currents that run up the island's western coast. Buoys mark the undersea sandbanks created by the tides, while powerful eddies at the surface reveal where the flows that come up each side of the island slam against each other. It is a place that demands respect for the sheer brute force of nature.

With no bus services and just a single narrow road leading the three miles up from Bride, it can feel a little like visiting the end of the Earth (it can also be reached on foot via the Raad ny Foillan from Ramsey, a route of roughly 5½ miles). The landscape is etched with signs of industry – the sand and gravel have long been extracted from pits for building materials – and there is little else to interrupt the views over the flat, scrubby expanse, apart from the candy-cane **red-and-white lighthouse** that sits just back from the beach.

On arrival at the car park it becomes evident that there are in fact two lighthouses: the traditional tall pillar surrounded by a gaggle of keepers' houses, and a short, squat light out on the shingle. The taller building, with a height of 98ft, is the original and is still in use: it was completed in 1818 and was the first to be built on the island by the Northern Lighthouse Board. However, the shapeshifting coast soon meant that a second light was needed to mark the new banks of shingle, and the smaller tower – affectionately known as Winkie – was built in 1890 about 250yds closer to the sea. Winkie then had to be moved a further 250yds in 1951 as the beach morphed again; it was ultimately

"It is a place that demands respect for the sheer brute force of nature."

LUNDY, FASTNET, IRISH SEA...

'All you can hear is the sound of the birds and the waves and the pebbles,' says Amanda Litherland. 'You can stand at the edge and feel like you are completely surrounded by the sea.'

Amanda is a continuity announcer for BBC Radio 4, so spends most of her time in London. But she also grew up on the island, and when the *Shipping Forecast* marked its centenary in early 2025, she chose the Point of Ayre as the location for a special commemorative broadcast.

'The Point of Ayre is one of my favourite birdwatching spots,' she says, explaining her choice, 'especially for oystercatchers, cormorants and gannets, which I love to watch diving into the sea. You'll often meet seals sunbathing on the rocks, or popping out of the shallows to get a good look at you. It can be a very peaceful place, but also a very windy one!'

Amanda's dispatch for *The Shipping Postcards* can be listened to on BBC Sounds.

---

decommissioned in 2010. The old diesel-powered foghorn trumpets also still stand nearby, though they fell silent in the 1980s.

Four hundred yards to the east of the original tower lighthouse are the remains of an **old saltworks**, which were once connected to the herring industry: a brine lake was discovered underground in the 19th century, and the concentrated salt was pure enough to extract and use as a preservative for the fish. Seabirds flock to the area, and arctic terns nest on the beach from late spring into the summer.

JOURNEY BOOKS
CONTRACT PUBLISHING FROM BRADT GUIDES

DO YOU HAVE A STORY TO TELL?

- Publish your book with a leading trade publisher
- Expert management of your book by our experienced editors
- Professional layout, cover design and printing
- <u>Unique</u> access to trade distribution for print books and ebooks
- Competitive pricing and a range of tailor-made packages
- Aimed at both first-timers and previously published authors

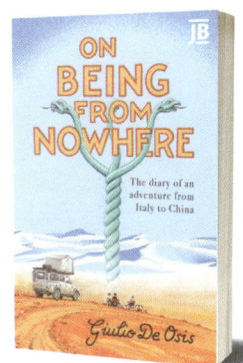

"Unfailingly pleasant"… "Undoubtedly one of the best publishers I have worked with"… "Excellent and incredibly prompt communication"… "Unfailingly courteous"… "Superb"…

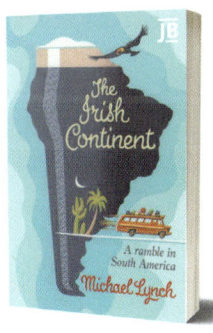
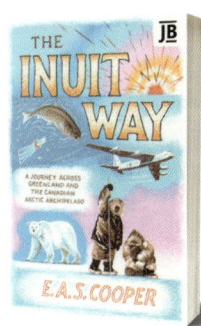

For more information – and many more endorsements from our delighted authors – please visit: **bradtguides.com/journeybooks.**

Journey Books is the contract publishing imprint of award-winning travel publisher, Bradt Guides. All subjects are considered for Journey Books, not just travel. Our contract publishing is a complement to our traditional publishing, not a replacement, and we welcome traditional submissions from new and established travel writers. Please visit bradtguides.com/write-for-us to find out more.

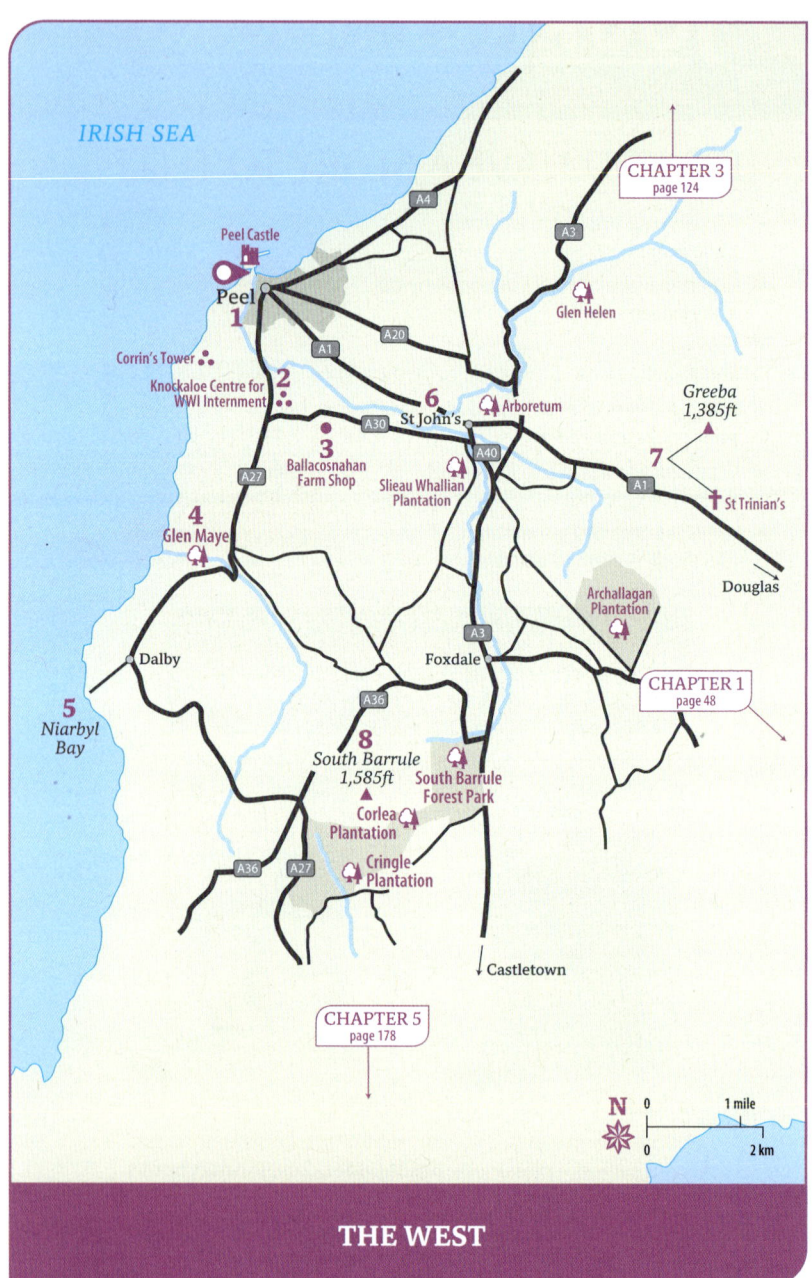

THE WEST

4
THE WEST

The overwhelming feeling in the west of the island is one of protection. The great Viking fortress of **Peel Castle** dominates the coastline of the area's main town, daring anyone to attempt to invade and providing shelter for the fishing boats that snuggle in behind it in the safety of Peel harbour. The RNLI lifeboat station is also nestled in its shadow, the crews ready to leap into action to help those at sea. Even sunbathers on the butter-yellow sands of Peel beach are shielded from the worst of the prevailing winds by the steep headland to the south.

And the protection doesn't stop at the mere physical, either. The area has become a focal point for those wishing to preserve the more intangible elements of Manx culture – ensuring that it doesn't simply grow dusty in glass cases in museums but lives and breathes. While the Manx National Heritage sites in Peel are a brilliant entry point to learn about the history of the island's culture (especially the medieval clash of Celtic and Viking ways), there is plenty of opportunity to see how it manifests in the 21st century, too.

The village of **St John's**, inland to the east of Peel, is home to Culture Vannin – the body that protects Manx cultural heritage – and hosts the annual Tynwald Day ceremony in recognition of the island's parliament and political independence. It is also the home of the only Manx language primary school and is the scene of the annual cammag match (page 171) between the north and south of the island (the game, played with sticks and a ball, has been dubbed 'killer hockey'). Meanwhile the farmers at **Ballacosnahan** to the south of Peel are leading the charge to save the highly endangered Manx Loaghtan sheep.

For those craving a frisson of danger, the stories of the ghostly moddey dhoo of Peel Castle (page 154) and the fearsome buggane of St Trinian's (page 172) should send a shiver down your spine. If you're in search of an adrenaline kick that won't keep you awake at night, the great

> **TOURIST INFORMATION**
>
> **Peel Visitor Information Point** Manx Wildlife Trust gift shop, Market Place, Peel IM5 1AB
> ⊙ 10.30–17.00 Mon–Sat, 13.00–16.30 Sun

rolling headland that spans south from Peel is recognised as the most strenuous coastal walking on the island. This stretch of the **Raad ny Foillan footpath** climbs up to steep vantage points before descending into secluded coves – it's a tough route, but the views out to sea are invariably sensational, stretching across the Irish Sea to the Mourne Mountains in Northern Ireland and offering plenty of opportunities to spot the telltale fins of basking sharks as they glide through the water.

So head out west for an ice cream and to top up your tan – but be prepared to leave with a head full of ghost stories, Manx Gaelic and thoughts of Viking longboats emerging from the mist.

GETTING THERE & AROUND

The A1 main road from Douglas to Peel is well served by buses, with the routes 5 and 6 running frequently throughout the day. The 4n covers the area south of Peel, taking in the village of Patrick and Niarbyl, twice daily on weekdays.

The Raad ny Foillan footpath traces along the entire western coastline – the six-mile section from Niarbyl to Peel provides wonderful views of the rolling clifftops to the south as far as the Calf of Man (page 229), while much of the route north out of Peel follows the old railway line. There is a charming bunkhouse in the hamlet of Dalby, four miles south of Peel, that provides low-cost overnight stays perfect for long-distance walkers or those exploring the island by bicycle – it is part of the hamlet's old schoolrooms; for more information, see ⌀ stjamesdalby.org.

1 PEEL

Peel is known as the Sunset City for good reason. Located halfway down the island's west coast, it benefits from uninterrupted views of spectacular sunsets over the Irish Sea, particularly in the summer months. It is the perfect place to spend an evening lingering over a crab bap after a lazy day at the beach, watching the sky light up pink and orange as seals pop their curious heads out of the surf below. Once twilight descends, the sprawling castle that dominates the bay transforms into something out of a fairytale, illuminated by spotlights.

In the centre of town is **Cathedral Isle of Man** (Derby Rd, IM5 1HH ⊙ 09.00–18.00 daily), the seat of the Bishop of Sodor and Man – and the reason Peel sometimes calls itself a city, despite only having a population of 5,700. Dedicated to St German, the 5th-century missionary who was the island's first bishop, the church is a Victorian Gothic construction of sandstone that glows orange in the late afternoon sun. It is deeply peaceful and welcoming – and the grand sandstone arches inside give more than a nod to the architecture of the castle across town. The cathedral is also an enthusiastic host of exhibitions and music events, both religious and non-religious, so there is always something fascinating to look at. The gardens tell the story of Manx Christianity and include a replica keeill, which it is possible to enter, and a 'sky gazing' outdoor room.

Peel was once a busy fishing port and the area around the harbour, half a mile west of the cathedral, and close to the seafront still has streets of fishermen's cottages and old warehouse buildings, often built from the distinctive red sandstone that was also used to construct the castle. A particularly pretty example is **Charles Street** – set just back from the promenade, the traditional red stone cottages along this narrow little lane have brightly painted doors and are usually adorned with blooming hanging baskets and pots in summer.

The warren of narrow streets and alleyways was also ideal for the smugglers who used to operate around the port. The **Old Bonded Warehouse** near the harbour (29 Castle St, IM5 1AL ⊙ 11.00–16.30 Tue, Fri & Sat) is today an Aladdin's cave of antique furniture and collectibles spread across three floors – but the basement of the building, which appears on maps as early as 1764, still includes the old smuggling tunnels. Castle Street is lined with former merchants' houses and is believed to be the oldest street on the island, and is said to be haunted by icy hands that feel their way up to pedestrians' necks (the culprits are thought to be the spirits of naughty schoolboys).

Immediately to the west, on East Quay, the independent little **Leece Museum** (⊙ 10.00–16.30 Tue–Sat) holds a collection of classic motorcycles in what was once a basement prison cell used to hold those accused of being drunk and disorderly or prostitution. Upstairs is a treasure trove of knick-knacks from the island's past, including memorabilia from the internment camps of World War II and the last birching stool to be used in Peel.

On Station Place, a few hundred yards south of the museum, is the immersive and interactive **House of Manannan** (manxnationalheritage.im 09.30–16.30 daily), where the story of the Isle of Man's human inhabitants and their relationship to the sea is seen through the eyes of the eponymous Manannan – the Celtic sea god and the island's protector.

The journey begins in a wooded grove, where a bearded Manannan invites visitors to follow him through over 1,000 years of history. From there you are invited to sit round the fire at a Celtic roundhouse for story time on a wild winter's night, where tales of the ancestors mix with the crackling sparks. Then experience the upheaval of the arrival of the Vikings, including listening in on a conversation between a Viking settler and his Manx wife and walking on the beach as raiders pull their longship up on to the sand.

Later, you'll experience the chaos of the 19th-century quayside and see what it would have been like to be a herring girl (one of the women employed to gut the herring being made into kippers), before arriving at the present day when you can try your hand at steering the ferry into Douglas Harbour. The whole experience is spooky, surprising and great fun, and takes about two hours to get round. A temporary exhibition space next to the foyer also includes a different exhibition on aspects of Manx life each year (these temporary displays are free admission).

Another 150yds to the south is **Manx Transport Heritage Museum** (The Old Brickworks Office, Mill Rd, IM5 1TA Easter–Sep 13.00–17.00 Sat & Sun; free admission), housed, as its address suggests, in the office of a former brickworks. The island's smallest museum, it contains film clips, photographs and memorabilia covering all forms of Manx transport, including scale models of railway stock and maps of the island's rail network over the past 150 years.

The star exhibit is an original P50 microcar, which was created in Peel in the 1960s and has become a collectors' item (page 151). The museum also holds a replica of the TT racing bike ridden by George Formby in the 1935 film *No Limit*. The museum sits directly across the road from a small surviving stretch of the Peel railway line, complete with level-crossing barrier and signal, plus the original water tower and a lovingly looked-after, three-compartment passenger coach.

THE SMALLEST CAR IN THE WORLD

Peel is famous for being the home of a little car. And it's not just 'city runaround' little – at 54in long and 39in wide, it is the smallest production car ever made.

The three-wheeled P50 was created by Cyril Cannell and Henry Kissack of Peel Engineering Company, at their factory a few yards from where the House of Manannan (see opposite) stands today. It was designed to carry 'one adult and a shopping bag' and was launched at the Earl's Court Motor Show in London in 1962. It has held the Guinness World Record for the world's smallest production car ever since.

Much of the car's appeal lay in its simple design. It had no reverse gear – instead, a handle on the back allowed the 130lb vehicle to be manoeuvred into position. The windscreen wash was kept in a bottle that was simply squeezed when needed, and the petrol tank gauge was just a transparent panel. It had a single windscreen wiper and one headlight.

Marketed as being almost cheaper than walking, the P50 – which was equipped with the 49cc engine from a moped – could do 100 miles to the gallon with a top speed of 38mph. Despite its diminutive size, it has always been road legal in Britain, and was intended to be used by urban shoppers. The original model cost £199, the equivalent of around £4,500 today.

Peel Engineering Company ceased trading in 1974 after making only 50 of its flagship cars. Just 27 are thought to still exist, meaning they have become collectors' items – one sold for $176,000 at a Sotheby's auction in the US in 2016. At the time, Sotheby's said only four of the cars had appeared at auction in the previous 30 years.

However, in recent years the brand has been revived. In 2008 the company Peel Engineering Ltd was established in Kent, southeast England, by the businessmen Gary Hillman and Faizal Khan, who subsequently received investment to revive the car on the BBC programme *Dragons' Den*. The company offers petrol and electric models, which are hand built to order in Nottinghamshire. In 2018 it was reported that Peel Engineering sells around 15 P50s annually, for about £15,000 each.

In 2007 the P50 made a star appearance on an episode of the BBC's *Top Gear*, with Jeremy Clarkson proving the usefulness of such a genuinely tiny car by driving it to work and carrying it single-handedly through the doors of Television Centre – before the newsreader John Humphrys was shown steering it around the office corridors.

The chance to get up close to some of the island's **marine life** is a big attraction in Peel. The seals are the stars, and seem just as keen to watch the humans on land as humans are to watch them. Keep an eye out for them in the outer harbour along the breakwater, where they hang around the unloading fishing boats in the hope of being thrown a treat by one of the softer fishermen. Another good place to see them is from

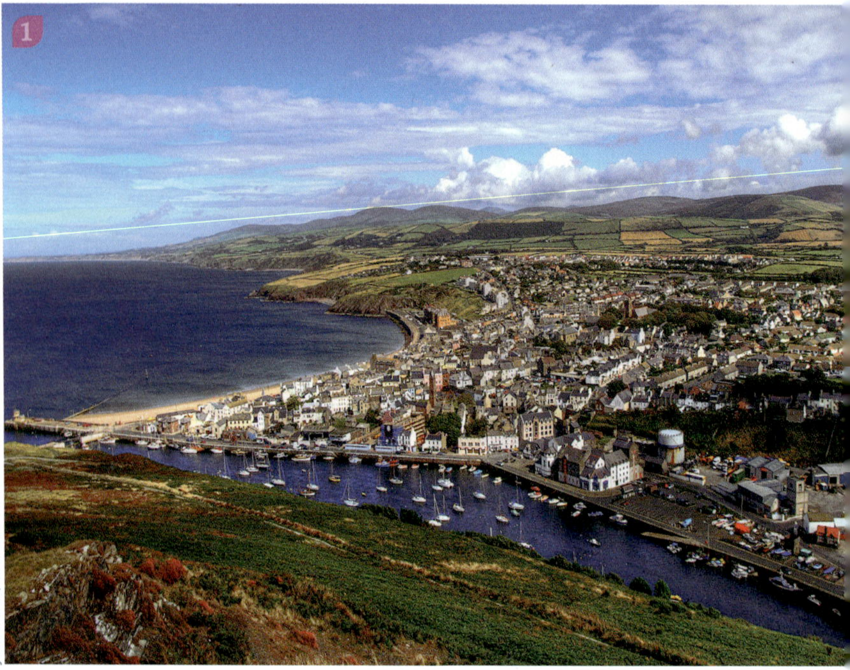

JOHN HALL/CULTURE VANNIN

VISIT ISLE OF MAN

GRAHAM TAYLOR/DT

VISIT ISLE OF MAN

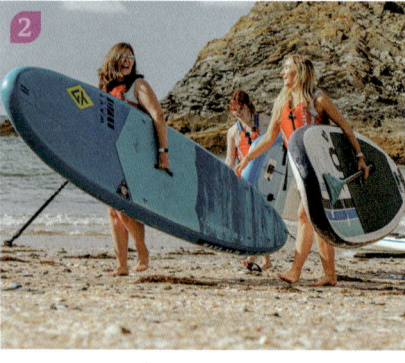

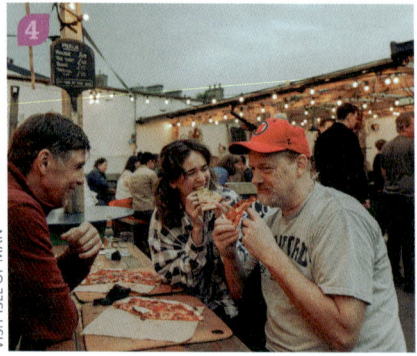

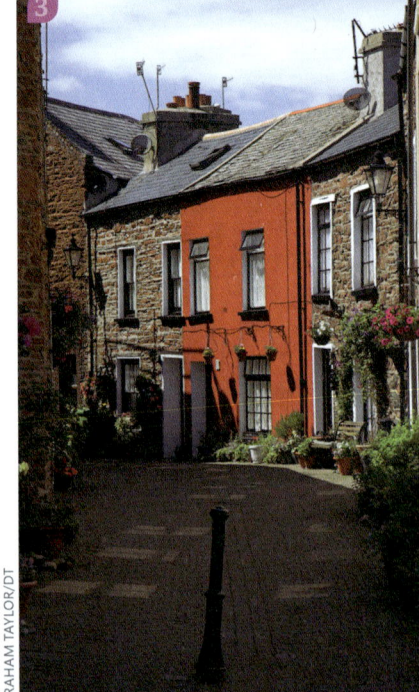

the public footpath that runs around the back of the castle (page 154) – they often surface opposite the low concrete viewing platform behind the breakwater. Cormorants can be spotted diving for fish, or standing on the rocks with their wings out to dry. The path behind the castle is also a great place to spot the island's famous basking sharks (usually in the form of a fin cutting through the surface of the deeper waters) and Risso's dolphins – a pair of binoculars will come in handy in case anything pops up further out to sea.

Peel has two beaches, thanks to the causeway that connects the mainland to St Patrick's Isle (page 154), on which the 11th-century castle stands. The **main beach** along the promenade is a fine sandy stretch that is hugely popular on a bright day in the summer holidays – arrive early if you want to find a spot to put down your towel. **Fenella Beach**, the cove created on the western side of the causeway, is much more secluded and is often used as a launch spot for kayakers and paddleboarders. The water in the inlet can be crystal clear after a few calm days, and the beach itself

"The water in the inlet can be crystal clear after a few calm days, and the beach itself is covered with scallop shells."

is covered with scallop shells. (The beach is named after the character Fenella in Sir Walter Scott's 1823 novel *Peveril of the Peak*, which is set partly around Peel Castle.) The headland on the south side of Fenella is a great spot to watch the ferocious waves that break over the causeway when conditions are stormy. No day at the beach is complete without a trip to **Davison's Ice Cream Parlour** in the middle of the promenade (page 158).

There are lovely walks up over the headlands at both ends of the bay. The stone tower of **Corrin's Tower** can be reached by following the footpaths that cross Peel Hill (page 154) to the south. The four-storey tower was built in 1806 by the landowner, Thomas Corrin, as he loved the view – its high vantage point commands a stunning vista out across the Irish Sea towards Ireland. Corrin used to sit reading by the fire on the third floor (the windows on the seaward side were blocked up after complaints from shipping that the light was confusing) and is buried

---

◀ PEEL: **1** Peel is protected by headlands on both sides. **2** Fenella Beach is a popular spot for paddleboarders. **3** The warren of narrow streets includes pretty fishermen's cottages. **4** Black Dog Oven, in a former working yard on the quay, is a popular place for a bite to eat.

THE WEST

A walk from Peel up the headland to Corrin's Tower

❋ OS Landranger map 95; start: Fenella Beach car park ♀ SC242844; 2½ miles moderate (the route is steep up to Corrin's Tower, with the first half of the walk on uneven, unpaved surfaces)

This walk takes you up over Peel Hill to Corrin's Tower (page 153), with spectacular views towards the Mourne Mountains in Northern Ireland before heading back into Peel along the tranquil River Neb. The climb up to the tower is very steep and uneven under foot, but it levels out once down at the river. Expect the walk to take about two hours.

1 Go up the steps just inside the entrance to the car park, next to the carved wooden statue of Fenella. Follow the concrete footpath until the concrete runs out, the continue along the grass path. You will cross over a narrow gravel roadway, then a narrower dirt track – keep following the footpath directly upwards towards the top of the hill.

2 Once you crest the top of Peel Hill, you will see the tower of Corrin's Towe due south, ⅔ mile away. Follow the path along the spine of the hill, passing through the metal kissing gate in the wall, and continue to the tower.

3 At the 19th-century tower, you will see the footpath continues directly south down the hill. After taking in the sweeping views out to sea, follow this path to the bottom, about 350yds down a moderately steep incline, where it meets a dry-stone wall; turn a sharp left and follow the wall for 300yds until you reach a stile with a green footpath arrow signpost.

4 Climb over the stile and follow the track down through a farm for 200yds. Where the route forks just after the house, take the track on the left.

5 Follow the path as it zigzags between the fields – the narrow footpath is always between two hedgerows (beware accidentally wandering into a field if you come across an open gate).

alongside his wife and two children in a small graveyard next to the tower. Alternatively, if you're heading for the paths along the clifftops at the northeastern end of the bay, be sure to touch the cliff face at the end of the promenade as you pass – it is supposed to bring good luck.

ST PATRICK'S ISLE & PEEL CASTLE
⌖ manxnationalheritage.im ⊙ Apr–Oct 11.00–16.30 daily

The ruins of **Peel Castle**, which sprawl in an almost organic way over the whole 7½ acres of **St Patrick's Isle**, look as though they might have been there forever. They are a motley collection of red sandstone walls,

After 600yds, the path enters woodland, and after another 150yds it emerges from behind a white cottage on to a main road.

6 Cross the road, turn left and after 50yds cross over the stone bridge. Descend the flight of steps on the right-hand side of the bridge down to river level, then make a sharp left and pass back underneath the bridge. You will be walking in the same direction the river is flowing. Move left off the cycleway and on to the footpath as soon as you can. Follow the footpath for $2/3$ of a mile until it brings you to the top of the harbour. Cross the road bridge and head back down the harbour to return to Fenella Beach car park.

imposing towers and what remains of various religious sites and garrison buildings. Yet the fortification of the island, which began towards the end of the 11th century, is only a fraction of its history – artefacts found on the site show it has been in use for thousands of years, spanning the entire human occupation of the Isle of Man.

The islet's strategic position at the mouth of the harbour meant it caught the eye of Viking rulers and the castle today is the result of 800 years of adjustments and expansions to the original fort. The remnants of early Christian habitation still stand at the centre, the old cathedral within the grounds is from the 13th century, the gatehouse (and public entrance) is from the late 14th century and the walls encompassing the whole area are from the 15th century. The Isle of Man was jointly controlled from Peel Castle and Castle Rushen (page 183) until the middle of the 17th century, and the last gun battery was decommissioned by 1870.

What stands today is a deeply atmospheric, open-air castle where it is possible to explore a millennium of history within a couple of hours. The audio guide is highly recommended as you follow in the footsteps of early monks, Civil War soldiers and the prisoners who were led

THE MODDEY DHOO OF PEEL CASTLE

There are reports of ghostly black dogs dotted around the Isle of Man, but the terrifying beast said to stalk Peel Castle is by far the most notorious moddey dhoo (the name means 'black dog' in Manx). The usual telling of the tale begins during the late 17th century, after the monarchy had been restored in England. It was a time when Peel Castle was still manned by soldiers, and the guards were responsible for ensuring the castle was locked and secure each night.

A passageway was said to run from the guardroom to the captain's office, by way of one of the old churches within the castle grounds. Each night after locking up, the soldiers would take it in turns to go along the passage to take the keys to the captain.

One night, as the soldiers were settling down in the guardroom for the evening, an enormous black dog appeared from the passage and made itself comfortable in front of the fire. Terrified, the soldiers refused to disturb it – and at dawn it got up and disappeared back from where it had come. This became a nightly occurrence and, fearful of what they might encounter, the men insisted they would only go in pairs through the passageway to deliver the keys.

As time went on, the soldiers became slightly more at ease with the creature that appeared each night to sit in front of the fire. One evening they took to drinking and, emboldened, one of the men bragged that he wasn't afraid and would take the keys to the captain alone. He disappeared down the passageway – and the beast silently rose from the guardroom and followed him. After a tense silence, there followed a series of unearthly screams. The soldier eventually staggered back to the guardroom, as white as a sheet and unable to speak from fright.

The other soldiers never did find out what had transpired between him and the beast. He died of terror three days later, having not uttered a single word.

That was the last the men saw of the moddey dhoo, but it can still be heard howling on a windy night. Some might say the noise is simply the sound made by the gales whipping round the old castle buildings, but the children of Peel who dive under their duvets when they hear it might disagree.

down into the crypt after falling foul of the ecclesiastical court (be sure to count the 13 pillars while down in the crypt, to avoid bad luck).

One of the great discoveries on the site, made during excavations in the 1980s, was the grave of the 'Pagan Lady'. Found in a medieval cemetery close to the old cathedral, it is one of the richest burials of a female from the Viking era uncovered outside Scandinavia. Among the items buried alongside her were a necklace of glass and amber beads from across the Viking world, and a long iron rod – initially thought to be a cooking implement, more recent research suggests the staff could have been a symbol of power for a respected 'wise woman'. Her possessions are now on display at the Manx Museum in Douglas (page 63).

Elsewhere in the grounds, flints have been found dating from 6000BC, a stone axe from 2000BC and the foundations of dwellings from between 650BC and 600AD. A Celtic monastery was founded on the site as early as the 8th century, probably by Irish followers of St Patrick – who myth says landed on the island after outwitting the defences of Manannan. The walls of the stone church that replaced the earlier monastic buildings in the 10th or 11th century still stand, as does the round tower (these narrow, cylindrical towers were common monastery features in Ireland and were used as refuges in case of attack).

> "Among the items buried alongside her were a necklace of glass and amber beads from across the Viking world."

One evening each summer a visiting acting troupe makes the most of the stunning surroundings of the castle by putting on a Shakespeare performance in the grounds – keep an eye on the Manx National Heritage Facebook page () for upcoming performances. Curling up on a blanket with a flask of tea as the sun sets and Romeo cries out for his beloved Juliet is truly one of life's great pleasures.

FOOD & DRINK

The Black Dog Oven East Quay, IM5 1AR IOMBlackDog 16.00–23.00 Thu & Fri, noon–23.00 Sat, noon–22.00 Sun. This former working yard on the quay has been transformed into a family-run bar and grill, centred on its wood-fired pizza oven. With a focus on local produce for its pizza toppings, it has some indoor seating but is mostly al fresco – and is very Instagram-friendly with wooden tables, exposed beams and strings of bare lightbulbs. It often has live music and is a favourite with locals.

THE WEST

The Boatyard East Quay, IM5 1AR ⌘ theboatyardpeel.com ⊙ noon–13.45 & 17.30–20.45 Wed–Sat, noon–16.00 Sun. A proper sit-down restaurant with a cosy nautical theme and classic menu focusing on freshly caught local seafood. If you really want to push the boat out, as it were, go for the Afternoon Sea Platter – a twist on traditional afternoon tea, with lobster, oysters and homemade kipper pâté (the exact combination depends on the season).

The Creek Inn 14 Lake Ln, IM5 1AT ⌘ 01624 842216 [f] ⊙ 10.00–23.00 Sun–Tue, 10.00–midnight Wed–Sat. A beloved red-and-white painted pub next to the House of Manannan, complete with cartwheels hanging on the outside and floor-to-ceiling paintings and memorabilia of Peel on the inside. It is cosy and friendly, with a broad menu offering classic pub dishes done to a delicious and generous standard. The battered fish-finger sandwich with mushy peas will keep you going for days. Booking recommended as it has limited space and fills quickly.

Davison's Ice Cream Parlour 3 Castle Court, Shore Rd, IM5 1AQ [f] PeelIceCreamParlour ⊙ Apr–Aug 10.00–17.30 daily; Sep–Mar 10.00–16.30 daily (winter hours weather dependent, check Facebook). This third-generation family company has been going since the 1980s and its outlet on the seafront has a queue that stretches out onto the street on hot days. Its award-winning ice cream comes in an ever-evolving selection of more than 30 flavours – including all the classics, plus novelty flavours such as 'Iron Brew', Guinness and kipper – and is made exclusively with Manx double cream, milk and butter.

The Fish Bar East Quay, IM5 1AR ⌘ manxfish4u.co.uk ⊙ 11.00–16.00 daily. A deceptively plain-looking take-away van selling exquisite little pots of flash-fried queenie scallops (page 32). Have yours with bacon, chorizo or truffle oil. One for the purists.

Peel Breakwater Kiosk Next to the lifeboat station on the breakwater [f] ⊙ Apr–Oct 09.00–17.00 daily; Nov–Mar 09.00–15.00 daily. This no-frills little kiosk has achieved cult status for its friendly service, generous portions and fabulous location. Try a homemade pie or scone, or treat yourself to one of its legendary kipper baps and a cup of Bovril. Outdoor seating only, but it's the perfect place to linger as you watch the fishing boats unload or the seals frolicking in the harbour. It closes in poor weather, so check the Facebook page if you're unsure. And beware the seagulls.

Roots by the Sea 26 Shore Rd, IM5 1NH [f] ⊙ 10.00–16.00 Fri–Sun. Coffee shop known for its fruity porridge bowls and hot bagels including Manx crab and BLT, with bacon from the butcher's up the road. It also does a gorgeous selection of brownies (try

---

PEEL: **1** It's a steep walk up the headland to Corrin's Tower. **2** The atmospheric ruins of the 13th-century cathedral at Peel Castle. **3** The House of Manannan explores the island's relationship with the sea. **4** An original P50 microcar, the smallest car in the world, which now lives at the Manx Transport Heritage Museum. **5** St Patrick's Isle sits in a strategic position at the mouth of the harbour. ▶

SAMANTHA FLETCHER

SAMANTHA FLETCHER

VISIT ISLE OF MAN

MRSBAIN/S

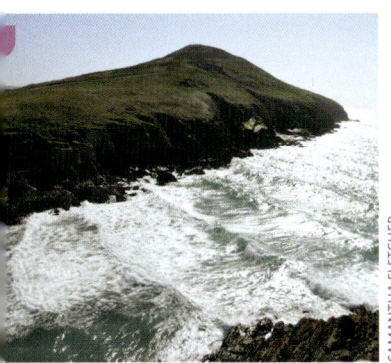

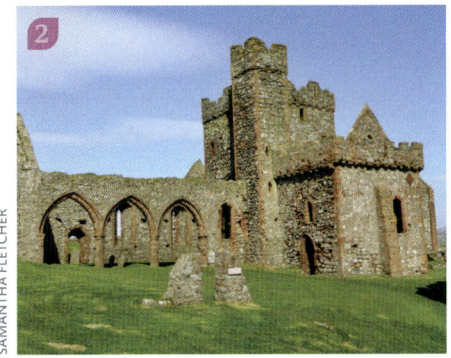

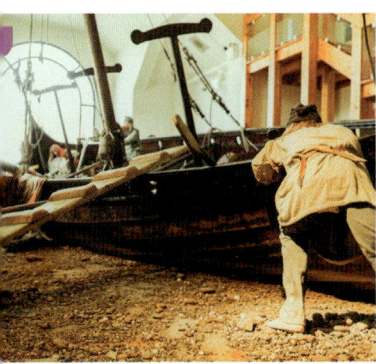

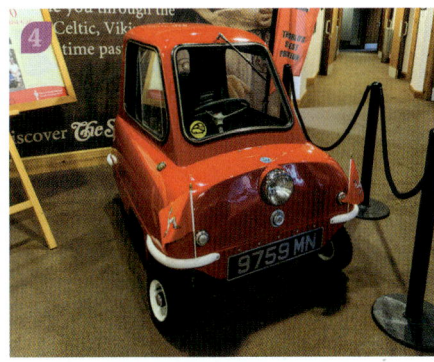

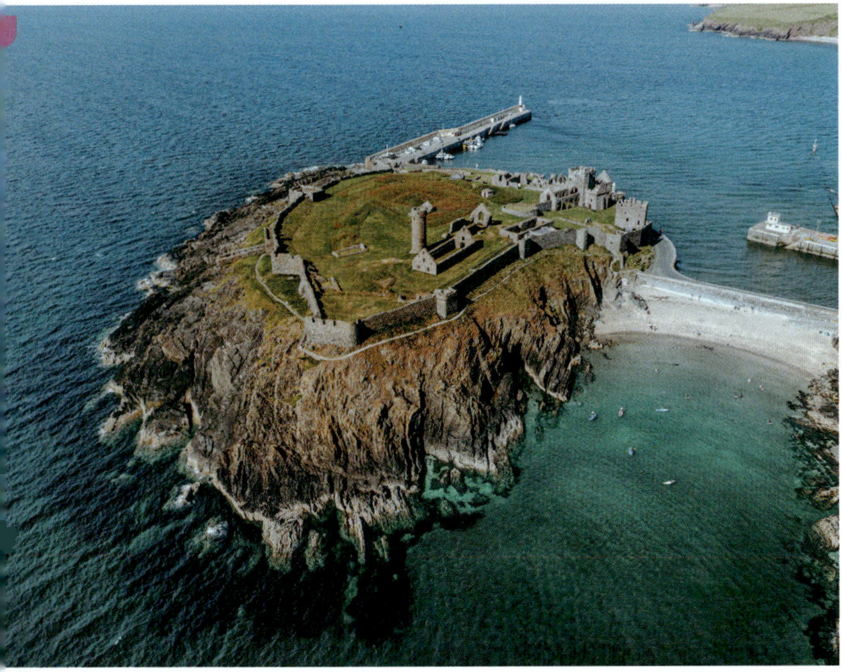

VISIT ISLE OF MAN

the Mars Bar or Curly Wurly varieties for some real decadence) and has its own unique coffee blend, roasted by Noa Bakehouse in Douglas.

SHOPPING

Devereau's Factory Shop Mill Rd, IM5 1TA ⌀ isleofmankippers.com ⊙ 09.00–16.30 Tue–Fri; 09.00–13.00 Sat. The place to buy locally produced kippers, which are cured in the Devereau's factory near the harbour. The 140-year-old company also has a fishmonger's at 33 Castle Street, Douglas.

Manx Wildlife Trust 7–8 Market Pl, IM5 1AB ⌀ mwt.im ⊙ 10.30–17.00 Mon–Sat. The gift shop for the local wildlife charity has all the usual themed toys, books and binocular sets

THE WRECK OF THE SAINT GEORGE

Anyone walking past Peel lifeboat station, in the shadow of the castle at the landward end of the breakwater, is likely to spot some yellow-clad RNLI volunteers tying things up after their last shout or getting ready for a training session. Peer closer through the open doors, however, and you will spot a strapping, larger-than-life man dressed all in royal blue with a dark cape draped around his neck.

This is Saint George – the muscular wooden figurehead from the ship of the same name that was wrecked off Peel on 7 October 1889. The 200ft cargo vessel from Norway, laden with coal and pipes, became distressed in a fierce northwesterly and signalled for help, triggering the launch of the Peel lifeboat. A crowd of thousands gathered on land to watch as the drama unfolded.

The embattled lifeboat crew rowed for three hours through the towering sea, and were swamped more than once. Eventually they were able to secure a line to the *Saint George*, which was by this point already disintegrating, and begin the rescue of all 23 on board. Each person had to jump into the raging water in a lifebuoy then be hauled into the lifeboat – the one exception being nine-month-old Sigrid Thoresen, the captain's daughter, who was carried in a canvas backpack by the ship's carpenter. The *Isle of Man Times* reported that, when they arrived back to harbour and word got round the assembled onlookers that all had been saved, 'a ringing cheer went up… the like of which has never been heard in Peel before'.

The ship itself was fit only for salvage. The following month, the RNLI's in-house *Lifeboat Journal* reported that a rainbow had appeared in the western sky just as the rescued sailors made landfall. 'There was not a soul of us on board our vessel… that expected to be saved,' the ship's master is quoted as saying.

The lifeboat crew were awarded medals by the Norwegian government for their bravery. The poet TE Brown later immortalised 'the fury, and the din, and the horror, and the roar' of the rescue in his poem *The Peel Lifeboat*, and the salvaged figurehead was kept as the lifeboat station mascot.

that you would expect, but also sells art and handcrafted goods from respected local artists and artisans, as well as work from its in-house artist. Products include Fair Trade jewellery, handmade candles and carved homewares.

Tate's Traditional Butchers 12 Michael St, IM5 1HB ⌀ tatesbutchers.com ⊙ 08.00–17.00 Tue–Sat. This family-run butcher's shop stocks the usual Manx beef, lamb and pork, but the knock-out products are its homemade sausages, cured bacon and cooked hams. With all the production done in-house, it also branches out into unusual flavours such as scallop sausages and bacon cured in Jack Daniels.

SOUTH OF PEEL

The area to the south of Peel is one of peaceful rolling farmland, rugged coastlines and tiny hamlets with some fascinating stories to tell. Life here was turned upside down during World War I with the arrival of thousands of internees at Knockaloe – a visitors' centre now explains this history in detail – while two decades later a farmhouse a couple of miles south became a focus of the London press thanks to tales of a spooky talking mongoose.

There are renowned beauty spots at Glen Maye and Niarbyl, and the chance to pick up some rare Loaghtan sheep wool at Ballacosnahan Farm Shop. The area is covered by the 4n bus route, which runs out of Douglas twice a day (Monday–Friday).

2 KNOCKALOE CENTRE FOR WWI INTERNMENT
Old School Rooms, Patrick Corner, Patrick IM5 3AL ⌀ knockaloe.im ⊙ visitors' centre: May–Sep 10.00–15.00 Tue–Thu; walk-through camp area: open-access year-round

The Centre for WWI Internment, in the hamlet of Patrick two miles south of Peel, addresses one of the biggest upheavals on the island during World War I: the establishment of an internment camp for 'enemy aliens' at a farm called Knockaloe. The world's largest internment camp during the Great War, it eventually came to house 23,000 men in 23 compounds within a three-mile perimeter. Some 695 miles of barbed wire were used to keep them in.

The internees were nationals of countries that were wartime enemies of Britain, who had found themselves in the UK when war broke out and did not qualify for exemption from internment. Considered a threat to national security, they came from Germany, Austria and Hungary, among others, and were shipped over to the island from November 1914 to be housed in barracks-style huts of 30 men each. Conditions were cramped and some internees developed a psychological condition that became known as 'barbed wire disease' – a sort of cabin fever borne out of the stress of their situation coupled with the lack of privacy – with some taking their own lives.

Today the site has long since been returned to rolling farmland. A large sign by the road, directly across the road from the visitors' centre, marks the entrance to Knockaloe Farm, with the fields now given over to grass. Far from the hustle and bustle of Peel, it is a quiet, rather beautiful spot with big skies and hills rising to the south. The difference to how it must have been when crowded with men from across Europe is stark.

"It is a quiet, rather beautiful spot with big skies and hills rising to the south."

The small visitors' centre is based in the old village school, and tells the personal stories of those held in a moving and engaging way. Artefacts and photographs from inside the camp show some of the efforts that were made to make life inside more tolerable: sport and amateur dramatics were encouraged, and there was a tailors' workshop and library. The centre also holds a scale model of how the camp would have looked, and descendants of internees who wish to find out more about their relatives can email the centre ahead of their visit to request an 'internee review', which will be gone through in detail on the day.

There is plenty to explore outside the centre too. A short guided walk can be taken around the area using the Knockaloe app – a QR code on the sign on the outside wall of the old schoolroom directs you to where it can be downloaded – which can be done regardless of whether the centre is open or not.

The graveyard of **Patrick Church**, immediately next door to the centre, is also well worth a visit – both for the graves connected with the camp, and those dating much further back in history (some of the early markers are from the mid-18th century). The graves of most of the internees who died during the war were later moved to Cannock Chase in Staffordshire, but the headstones of seven Turkish men still stand together in their own small corner of the churchyard. Close by are the headstones of two Jewish internees, which stand beside a small oak tree grown from an acorn brought from Auschwitz Concentration Camp in

THE ORIGINS OF PILATES

One of those interned at Knockaloe during World War I was **Joseph Pilates**, a German circus performer in his early 30s whose troupe was in Blackpool when the conflict broke out.

While in the camp, Pilates – who had grown up around gymnastics and boxing, and took a keen interest in anatomy – developed his ideas for his own exercise methodology that also took spiritual wellbeing into account. One story goes that he was inspired by the stray cats he saw running around the camp, and the way they kept stretching out their muscles even while resting. Another version of events is that he worked in the camp hospital, where he devised a set of exercises to help the invalids regain their strength by adapting the springs on their metal beds.

Pilates returned to Germany after his release in 1919, where he continued to build on his techniques, eventually moving to the US and patenting his iconic 'Universal Reformer' bed in 1925. He was a shrewd marketer, and succeeded in promoting his techniques to the point where they are now practised by millions around the world.

In an essay entitled 'Your Health' in 1934, Pilates said his goal was 'to offer a real service to humanity from an altruistic and philanthropic point of view', adding that the ultimate aim for anyone undertaking his regime was 'health and happiness'.

Poland. The tree, clearly marked with a plaque, was planted in 2018 in recognition of those interned on the island during both world wars.

3 BALLACOSNAHAN FARM SHOP

Patrick IM5 3AW ✆ 07624 333756 ⌖ manxloaghtanproduce.com ⏰ 09.00–18.00 daily (call the phone number on the board outside the shop on arrival and someone will come and open up), except during the Southern and Royal Agricultural Shows

Half a mile east of the Knockaloe Centre for WWI Internment, along the only road leading east out of Patrick, is Ballacosnahan Farm. Turning up the tree-shrouded single track, either in the car or on foot, feels rather like heading on a treasure hunt. Photos of brown-fleeced faces, attached to small boards beside the track, lead like a trail of breadcrumbs between the hedgerows – until, after 350yds, you emerge into a sunlit farmyard that is a tribute to all things Loaghtan.

The Loaghtan is the Isle of Man's only native sheep, descended from animals brought to the island by the Vikings. With only about 1,500 registered breeding ewes across Britain, it was added to the 'urgent priority' list by the Rare Breeds Survival Trust, a conservation charity, in 2025. It has a brown fleece, a distinctive set of four horns (though

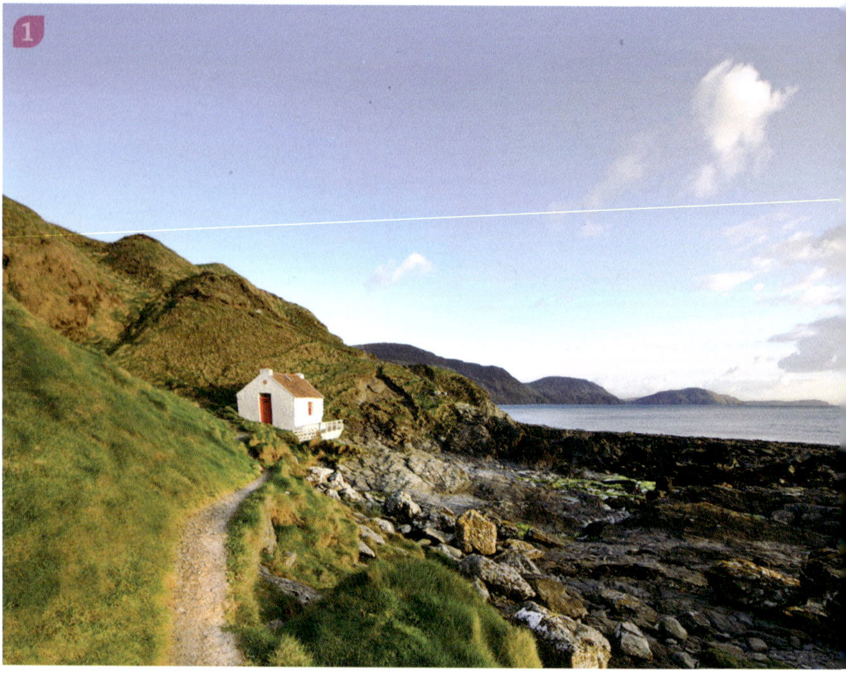

TR3GI/DT

SAMANTHA FLETCHER

BALLACOSNAHAN FARM

VISIT ISLE OF MAN

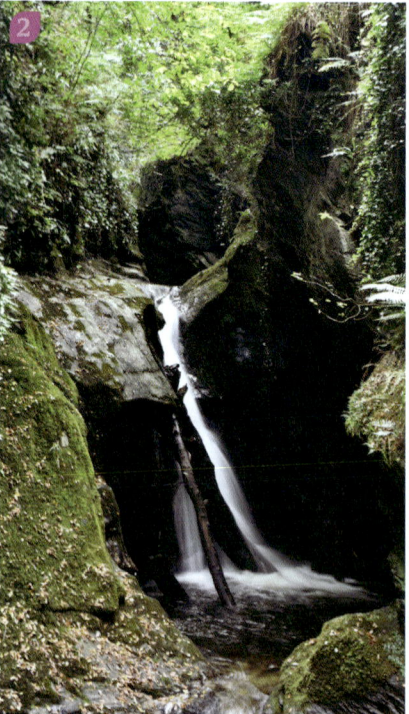

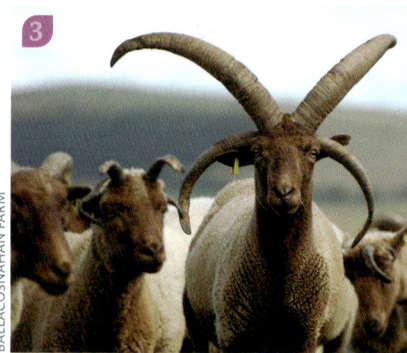

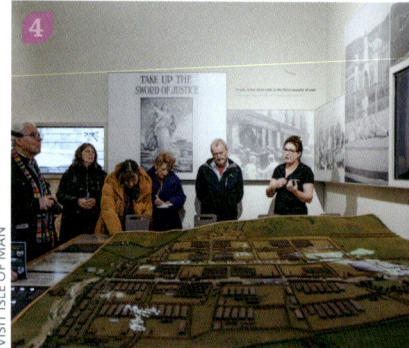

sometimes they even manage six) and is a hardy animal perfectly adapted to surviving on the harsh Manx uplands.

Today a flock of 600 of the creatures is managed by Jenny Shepherd and Rawdon Hayne on their 200-acre farm – and they care deeply about the survival of the breed. 'We felt the only way to protect these uniquely Manx sheep was to try and create a viable commercial future for them,' says Jenny.

The way they have done that is through their farm shop, which is well worth making the effort to visit and has gone from strength to strength since Ballacosnahan produced its first balls of wool over a decade ago. 'We had 1,800 balls of wool. That all sold in about a year and we haven't looked back,' says Jenny. The enterprise initially began on their kitchen table, but now visitors are welcomed to a perky blue cabin in the farmyard where they can peruse all manner of Loaghtan produce. Balls of wool in varying shades of brown are stacked neatly on the tables, luscious chocolate-coloured sheepskin rugs hang on the walls, and a fridge in the corner stocks packets of their award-winning charcuterie. A pen has been built immediately outside to show off some of the sheep themselves.

> *"Behind the scenes, Jenny and Rawdon use their animals as part of broader conservation efforts to increase biodiversity."*

'We have been breeding for good wool for over 15 years,' says Jenny. 'When spun it is naturally a beautiful dark brown colour – while being light, it is hard-wearing but still soft and very versatile.' The volume of rosettes proudly displayed in the shop are testament to the effort they have put in to breeding high-quality fleece, and their wool is prized by knitters and spinners. Visitors to the shop are welcomed warmly – Rawdon delights in telling visitors about the importance of the Loaghtan, and their own story of how they came to be custodians of such a unique piece of Manx heritage (the farm has been in Jenny's family for over 60 years).

Behind the scenes, Jenny and Rawdon use their animals as part of broader conservation efforts to increase biodiversity. Loaghtans can

---

◀ **1** The curving bay of Niarbyl is one of the island's great beauty spots. **2** Glen Maye's strikingly pretty woodland surrounds a bridged gorge and waterfall. **3** Manx Loaghtans at Ballacosnahan Farm. **4** A scale model reveals what life would have been like for internees at the Centre for WWI Internment in Knockaloe.

WHAT DOES MANX LOAGHTAN TASTE LIKE?

As well as producing gorgeous, squidgy balls of wool, in 2023 Ballacosnahan Farm (page 163) branched out into charcuterie. Within months their Manx Loaghtan chorizo had scooped three stars at the Great Taste awards, while their Manx Loaghtan salami won two stars. Rawdon and Jenny employ a full-time chef to work solely on the charcuterie, and a visit to the curing shed in the farmyard is a real treat (it smells like a rustic Italian deli).

'Manx Loaghtans are slow maturing, taking about 24 months before they can be eaten,' says Jenny. 'The meat is a dark colour, finely grained, low in fat and cholesterol, and has a unique, intense flavour that is delicious and more like venison than conventional lamb.

'We used to sell some meat but not enough to contribute a significant amount to the farm income. In 2023, we decided to try a different tack and go into charcuterie as we all love it and it would add extra value to the meat. We started selling a charcuterie in December that year and were surprised how popular it was. In early 2024 we entered the Great Taste Awards – and were completely stunned. Out of about 16,000 entries only about 1.5% win three stars, so not bad for a very new producer!'

---

graze where other animals can't, in doing so creating new habitats for ground-nesting birds, hares and wild orchids. 'Manx Loaghtan are ideal for conservation work and thrive on rough grasslands and flower meadows,' says Jenny. 'We stopped the use of all fertilisers, weedkillers and chemicals nine years ago and already see the benefit. Bird species are increasing, as well as increases of hares, hedgehogs, insects and bats.'

In 2024, Ballacosnahan Farm won the prestigious Bronze Chough award, given out by the Isle of Man Farming and Wildlife Advisory Group in recognition of commercial farmers who work alongside nature.

4 GLEN MAYE

Car park at eaters.kittens.class

The glen and secluded beach of Glen Maye sit on the west coast three miles south of Peel, offering a picturesque stroll.

The strikingly pretty woodland – once known as the Luxuriant Glen – is one of the Manx National Glens, and has 11 acres of trees and ferns including relics of some of the ancient forests that once covered the island. The majority of the trees are ash, sycamore and elm, but the glen also supports plants that are not found anywhere else on the island, such as the dainty purple wood vetch flower, the tufted 'hairy brome' grass and the 'Glen Maye bramble' – a micro-species variant of the common blackberry. The abundance of luscious ferns can be attributed to the glen's mild, sheltered climate.

There is a footpath leading through the glen down to the beach, which can be a bit of a clamber with a few steep steps. There is also a good-sized car park at the top beside the glen entrance, on the edge of the fairly nondescript hamlet of Glen Maye.

The biggest draw is the spectacular bridged **gorge and waterfall**, where lush, Jurassic-looking plants trail down the cliff face and the narrow wooden walkway looks down on the rushing water below. The ghost of a man drowned by a glashtyn (a Manx goblin that often takes the form of a horse and lurks by pools and rivers) is said to haunt below the waterfall.

At the base of the glen stands the large stone casing of the old **Mona Erin waterwheel** – the only evidence now remaining of the mining that took place here during the 18th and 19th centuries. The beach is a small cove surrounded by headland and, as it is only accessible by foot, is almost guaranteed to be quiet. The shoreline is fairly stony, but the river mouth tumbling over the pebbles adds interest, and there are wide views over the Irish Sea towards Ireland. The beach is also held in folklore to have been the site of a great battle between Manx and invading Irish fairies (the Manx fairies were victorious).

5 NIARBYL BAY

One of the island's great beauty spots, **Niarbyl** is a remote promontory curving out into the Irish Sea about four miles south of Peel. The single narrow road that cuts half a mile across the headland from the hamlet of Dalby leads directly down to **Niarbyl Bay**, a secluded cove with breathtaking views stretching down the rolling coastline as far as the Calf of Man. The stony beach – the final descent to which is steep – has a tail of rocks that extends out into the bay, and a pair of idyllic thatched cottages with pretty red doors are nestled into the base of the headland. It's the perfect spot for sensational sunset views, and with virtually no light pollution offers some spectacular stargazing. A coastal footpath leads from the bay to the pebbly cove of White Beach, 500yds to the south.

Niarbyl Bay is also a place of great geological interest, where you can stand with each foot on rocks that once belonged to different

GEF THE TALKING MONGOOSE (AKA THE DALBY SPOOK)

The tale of Gef the talking mongoose began with the apparent sound of scratchings at a farmhouse in the 1930s. The story was still going strong by 2023, when it was the subject of the film *Nandor Fodor and the Talking Mongoose*, starring Simon Pegg and Minnie Driver. In between, it caused a sensation in the British tabloid press, was the focus of psychic investigations, and as the subject of numerous books, radio programmes and podcasts.

The isolated farmhouse, just over half a mile to the east of the hamlet of Dalby, was home to the Irving family: James, Margaret and their 13-year-old daughter, Voirrey. In September 1931, they claimed to have heard rustlings and scratchings coming from within the walls of their home. The cause of the noises allegedly introduced itself as a creature named Gef that had been born in India in 1852 and claimed that it was 'an extra, extra clever mongoose' and an 'Earthbound spirit'. Voirrey said Gef was small and yellow with a large bushy tail.

Gef was said to speak many languages using a high-pitched voice; he was often conversational but could sometimes be threatening, and found a particular friend in Voirrey. The story soon spread among locals, and before long had reached newspaper desks in London, who dispatched reporters to the island. Eventually even the BBC got involved, sending the renowned psychic investigator Harry Price to inspect the claims.

Unfortunately, Gef proved shy around visitors. Attempts by the Irvings to prove his existence also quickly crumbled: hair said to be Gef's was found to belong to the family dog, as was a footprint. Sceptics suspected that Gef was an invention of Voirrey's and that her parents were in on the hoax – it was noted that the walls of their house had gaps behind the wooden panelling that meant sound would travel well between rooms. Voirrey was also accused of using ventriloquism to create Gef's voice. Believers said the mongoose was some form of poltergeist.

In an interview in 1970, Voirrey – who died in 2005 – told a magazine reporter that she last remembered Gef being around the farm in 1938 or 1939. The girl and her mother sold the house in 1945 after the death of James, and the subsequent owner claimed to have shot and killed the creature.

Today, Gef is widely understood to have been an invention. However, even if he failed to prove the power of the spirit world, he did prove the power of a good story.

---

continents. The distinctive white line marking the Niarbyl Fault is visible in the rocks on the shoreline just north of the beach car park. To the north lies the sandstone that once formed part of the continent of Laurentia, of which North America and Scotland were part. The dark grey rocks to the south are 480 million years old and come from Gondwana, of which southern England and Africa were part. The collision of the two some 400 million years ago left a suture that runs across northern England, through Ireland, and reaches as far as the US and Canada.

The quaint beachside cottages may also be familiar to anyone who has seen the 1998 film *Waking Ned*. Though set in Ireland, the comedy was filmed in the Isle of Man – largely at the village of Cregneash (page 223). However, the cottages at Niarbyl were used as the home of the reclusive Ned Devine, whose death sets the capers in motion.

ST JOHN'S & INLAND

St John's has long been a focal point for Manx political identity, thanks to the Tynwald Day ceremony that is held on the distinctive four-tiered grass hill at the centre of the village each summer. But the village is worth a visit year-round, as it also has the headquarters of Culture Vannin (the island's cultural body), a beautiful arboretum and the opportunity for a bracing walk up the darkly looming Slieau Whallian hill to the southwest.

Further east, Greeba Mountain has spectacular views from the summit (despite not really being a mountain) and comes with a frightening tale of an angry ogre, while heading south will take you to South Barrule, offering walks through cool plantations and the site of an Iron Age hill fort.

6 ST JOHN'S

The village of St John's, which sits two miles east of Peel, is where all the pomp and formality of Manx government meets the ferocity, weirdness and humour of the island's folk culture.

It has two visually dominating features: the expansive flat green in the centre on which sits Tynwald Hill – a 12ft-high, turf-covered mound resembling a four-tiered wedding cake, which is the symbolic centre of Manx parliamentary life – and Slieau Whallian, the dark, coniferous hill to the southwest that often has wisps of fog circling its summit. The main road to Peel runs between the two, lined with the headquarters of Culture Vannin, the Manx-language primary school and The Tynwald Inn – a pub with toasty open fire that has also taken on the role of the village corner shop (it's the place to head to enjoy a pint of beer while sitting among shelves of biscuits).

Tynwald Hill comes to life every 5 July, when the Manx executive, legislature and judiciary descend for their annual outdoor sitting. Tynwald Day, as it is known, is a grand celebration of the island's democracy and political uniqueness, and is marked with a national bank holiday. The ceremony – which takes place on the nearest Monday if the date falls on a weekend – begins in the **Royal Chapel of St John's**, a smart little granite church built in the 19th century with a distinctive tall, narrow spire. Those involved file in procession down the gravel path to the hill, taking their place on the tiers according to seniority. New laws for the year are read out in English and Manx, and it is an opportunity for residents to present 'petitions' for new legislation that will then be taken away and discussed. There is a fair for local artisans, Manx dancing and music, and a village of Viking re-enactors on the area surrounding the hill.

The hill itself is thought to have been constructed in the 13th century, using stones held together with soil from all 17 of the island's ancient parishes – though there is speculation that it might have been built on a much older burial mound. The outdoor ceremony is believed to have been established by the Vikings, with the site's proximity to roads that link the north, south, east and west of the island a possible explanation for why this location was chosen. For a deeper history of Tynwald Day, head into the **Culture Vannin** building (⊙ 10.00–16.00 Mon–Wed & Fri, 11.00–16.00 Thu), across the road, which has a small exhibition about the event, short films about Manx culture, and a collection of books about Manx language and music to peruse.

Away from the formalities, **Slieau Whallian** – half a mile to the southwest of Tynwald Hill, on the outskirts of the village – is where the island's witches were said to have been tested. They were allegedly placed in a barrel lined with metal spikes, then rolled down the hill: anyone who survived the ordeal was obviously in league with the devil (however, despite the tenacity of the story, there is no evidence that this actually took place). Today, the plantation that now covers it is a popular destination for fell runners and walkers – there are great views from the 900ft summit down towards South Barrule and across to Peel. There is an entrance gate with a stile at ▦ potatoes.candidate.succeeds, with a clear network of paths through the trees.

> *"There is a fair for local artisans, Manx dancing and music, and a village of Viking re-enactors."*

THE BOXING DAY CAMMAG MATCH

'Not the dog! NOT THE DOG!' the cry went up at my first cammag match, as the ball and ensuing scrum pummelled into the field wall where spectators – and pets – were standing. At my second match, the winded goalie for the South had to be helped off the pitch. 'I don't think I've ever seen someone actually carted off before,' said the gentleman on the wall next to me as one of the other players – who happened to also be a GP – checked the goalie over (he was OK and later returned to the match).

Cammag is the annual battle between North and South islanders that takes place on the green in front of Tynwald Hill at St John's. It begins each year when the Royal Chapel bell strikes 14.00 on Boxing Day, and lasts until 15.00 with two short breaks in between. It has similarities to Scotland's shinty and Ireland's hurling in that all the players are armed with sticks and the aim is to get the ball through the other team's goal posts. However, the game has remained resolutely unreconstructed and is essentially an hour of anarchy. There are no team bibs or colours, the number of players on the pitch can easily reach a couple of hundred, and the sticks for hitting the ball can be anything from beautifully carved wood through to well-shaped gorse branches – or even a golfing umbrella with a slipper taped to the end (the use of hockey sticks is frowned upon).

'The only rule is there are no rules,' says John 'Dog' Callister, a proud northerner who is usually found defending the goal for his side, in a film about the match on the Culture Vannin website. The winning side is the one to have scored the most goals.

There is a scattering of interesting stones to be found around the village, including the so-called **Giant's Grave**, a Bronze-Age burial mound close to Tynwald Hill – what remains of it are the large slabs of a grave that can be clearly seen making up part of the wall on the western side of the minor road that runs alongside the hill. In the porch of the Royal Chapel stands **Asruth's Cross**, a stone slab decorated with interlaced Viking carvings and runes from the late 10th century, while directly across the main road stands the **Pinfold** – the area where any stray animals found wandering the village used to be held, which also contains a collection of stones from the Mesolithic that were excavated nearby.

The **Tynwald National Park and Arboretum**, the main car park and entry gate for which is 55yds east along the main road from the Royal Chapel, offers an expansive area to explore, with 25 acres of ornamental and native tree species on show. An hour or two spent among the whispering trees, watching the moorhens on the pond or seeking out the various sculptures within the park is a lovely, slow way to pass an afternoon, and there are plenty of spots to sit. Scrambling up to the stone shelter on the hill in the northern corner of the park rewards you with a good view back over the village and Slieau Whallian. (Watch out on the concrete paths immediately after the gate when entering the arboretum, as they are steep and slippery when wet.)

FOOD & DRINK

Greens Café Main Rd, opposite Tynwald Hill, IM4 3NA ⌘ greens.im ⊙ 09.00–17.00 daily. A deliciously cosy little café offering home-cooked food from a menu that's barely changed in 35 years, with plenty of vegetarian options. Warming lunches include homity pie and a quiche of the day, but the café is renowned for its filling salad bowls – think herby beetroot pasta, curried lentils and homemade coleslaw. It's also excellent for coffee and a slice of cake, or order 48 hours ahead for afternoon tea.

SHOPPING

Element Isle Tynwald Mills, IM4 3AD ⌘ elementisle.com ⊙ 10.00–16.00 Mon–Fri, 10.00–17.00 Sat. A family-run jeweller that has both its store and workshop in the Tynwald Mills shopping complex to the north of St John's. Contemporary pieces heavily inspired by the island's landscape, nature and shoreline, with an ethos rooted in sustainability and handcrafting. The company was chosen to produce the Isle of Man's gift to Queen Elizabeth II to mark her Platinum Jubilee, creating a gold brooch in the shape of the island inlaid with gemstones (a duplicate is on display in the shop). The store is stylish and welcoming, and windows onto the street allow passersby to see into the workshop.

7 ST TRINIAN'S & GREEBA MOUNTAIN

The small 14th-century chapel of **St Trinian's** sits 100yds back from the roadside in a private field, but is visible from the pavement on the northern side of the A1 between Crosby and Greeba Castle, just under three miles east of St John's. There is no child in the Isle of Man who does not know the terrifying tale of the Buggane of St Trinian's; to children, it is known as 'the church with no roof' – for reasons that are self-evident.

Exactly why the chapel has no roof is unlikely to ever be established: one theory is that the political turmoil of the early 14th century, when

---

1 The village of St John's comes to life every July for Tynwald Day, when celebrations include Manx dancing. **2** The 14th-century church of St Trinian's. **3** With players armed with sticks, and with no rules, the Boxing Day cammag match in St John's is not for the faint-hearted. ▶

control of the island passed repeatedly between the English and Scots, meant it was simply left unfinished.

Folklore has rushed to fill the vacuum of facts, however, and the story begins with the buggane that lived on Greeba Mountain immediately to the west (bugganes are a type of shape-shifting Manx ogre, and Greeba is not a true mountain as it only reaches a height of 1,385ft).

Unhappy at the prospect of having church bells ringing within earshot all day, the buggane set out to ensure that the construction of the church was never finished. Each time the roof was put on, he would come down at night and tear it off, until a local tailor bet that he could spend a night in the church – making a pair of trousers as he did so. He sat up sewing by candlelight well into the night until the furious buggane, with fierce tusks, a thick black mane and blazing eyes, broke up through the floor of the chapel and roared taunts at the tailor. With a flourish, the man added the last couple of stitches to his trousers then fled – tearing down the road to the consecrated ground of nearby Marown churchyard. The buggane flung the roof off St Trinian's and gave chase as far as the edge of the churchyard where, outraged that he couldn't step on the holy ground, he tore off his own head and threw it at the tailor. It was the end of the buggane, but the tailor lived to tell the tale – and, thanks to the finished trousers, collected his bet.

The now buggane-free **Greeba Mountain** can be climbed via a path through the plantation on its slopes, accessed from the main road at its base (the entrance gate is at /// recoil.ramble.naptime). Greeba Castle, a decidedly Gothic Victorian manor house that is privately owned, can also be glimpsed through the trees from the road. It was the home of novelist Hall Caine (page 23) from the 1890s to his death in 1931; he had a writing studio set deep in the woodlands in the castle grounds.

8 SOUTH BARRULE & SURROUNDING PLANTATIONS

At 1,585ft, the hill of South Barrule, roughly equidistant between Peel and Castletown, is the tallest in the south of the island. The name 'barrule', like its sister hill in the north of the island (page 121), comes from the word 'wardfell' – a place where watchmen were stationed to keep a lookout for potential invaders. The summit, rich in archaeology, remains a fabulous spot for views across to Ireland, the Lake District and even as far as Snowdonia on a clear day. The top can be reached via a short, straight footpath rising fairly steeply from the A27 road – it starts on the eastern side of the road (◉ nevertheless.fictional.charged), about 200yds south of the crossroads with the A36 at Round Table. There is a car park 600yds south (◉ niceness.podcasts.flying), on the western edge of the Cringle Plantation.

South Barrule has long been seen as the home of Manannan, the Celtic sea god and protector of the island, and it is tradition for the Manx to carry a bundle of rushes to the top of the hill on Midsummer's Eve or 4 July (the day before Tynwald Day, page 170) as a form of rent. The southern side of the hill is also said to have once been overrun with fairies.

There is rather more concrete evidence, however, for an early Iron Age hill fort at the summit. The entire top of the hill is encircled by the remains of a rampart, with the stones used to construct it still clearly visible (if now toppled over thanks to strong winds and the passing of time). A multitude of round pock marks cover the site, sometimes made more visible by being filled with water. These were the locations of thatched roundhouses, with more than 70 of them in total, thought to date from around 500BC. The doorways of each hut faced east, away from the prevailing wind, and the larger ones were about 18ft across. Pottery found during excavations in the 1960s suggests the community was made up of local people, rather than invaders who had arrived from elsewhere.

The highest point of the hill is marked by an Ordnance Survey triangulation pillar, which stands on a cairn about 30ft wide and 3ft high. Though no artefacts have been found, the construction of the cairn from pieces of local slate is typical of Bronze Age burials.

> *"A multitude of round pock marks cover the site, sometimes made more visible by being filled with water."*

Plantations run around the west and southern base of South Barrule, including **South Barrule Forest Park**. One of the island's most popular woodlands for outdoor adventure and leisure activities, the forest's 128 hectares are perfect for walkers and mountain bikers. First planted in the 1880s, the main types of trees are sitka spruce, lodgepole pine and Japanese larch. The woodland also contains Ape Mann Adventure Park (✆ 07624 494252 ⌘ apemann.info ⊙ 10.00–17.00 Tue–Sun; booking essential) with rope courses and zip wires, and Laser Mayhem (✆ 07624 234555

⌀ laser-mayhem.com ⊙ 09.30–16.00 Sat & Sun, plus school holidays; booking essential), a military-inspired laser tag.

Footpaths lead through the forest park to the neighbouring **Corlea and Cringle plantations** to the west, which offer the same enticement to ramble, without some of the busyness of being near the zip wires or laser warriors. The area is home to some of the island's rarer birdlife, such as short-eared owls and hen harriers, and keep an eye out for jewel-like dragonflies around the glassy Cringle Reservoir on the southern side of the plantation.

The Forest Park is not easily accessible by public transport, but can be reached by car or bicycle via the A3: follow the road to a mile south of Foxdale village, then turn west onto the A36 – the car park is on the left after 200yds.

FOOD & DRINK

The Coffee Cottage Next to Laser Mayhem, South Barrule Forest Park, Foxdale IM9 3FB
thecoffeecottagesouthbarrule ⊙ 09.00–16.00 Mon, Thu & Fri, 08.30–17.00 Sat & Sun. A cosy stone cabin nestled among the trees of the forest park, this is the ideal spot to refresh (and potentially warm up) after a brisk walk around the plantations. With a roaring wood stove and stacks of logs lining the walls, it is an inviting place to linger over a bowl of homemade soup, cake, a reviving coffee or one of its signature hot chocolates.

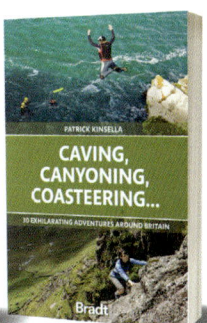

bradtguides.com/shop

ADVENTURES IN BRITAIN

@bradtguides

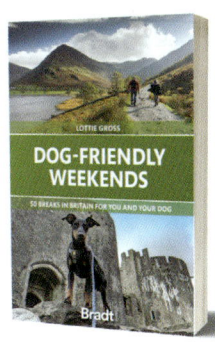
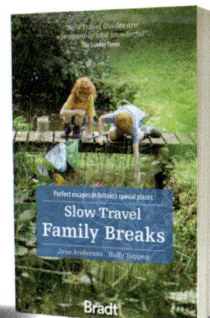
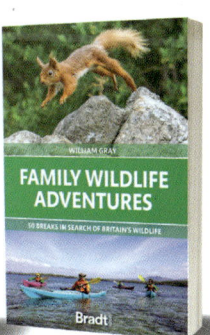

TRAVEL TAKEN SERIOUSLY

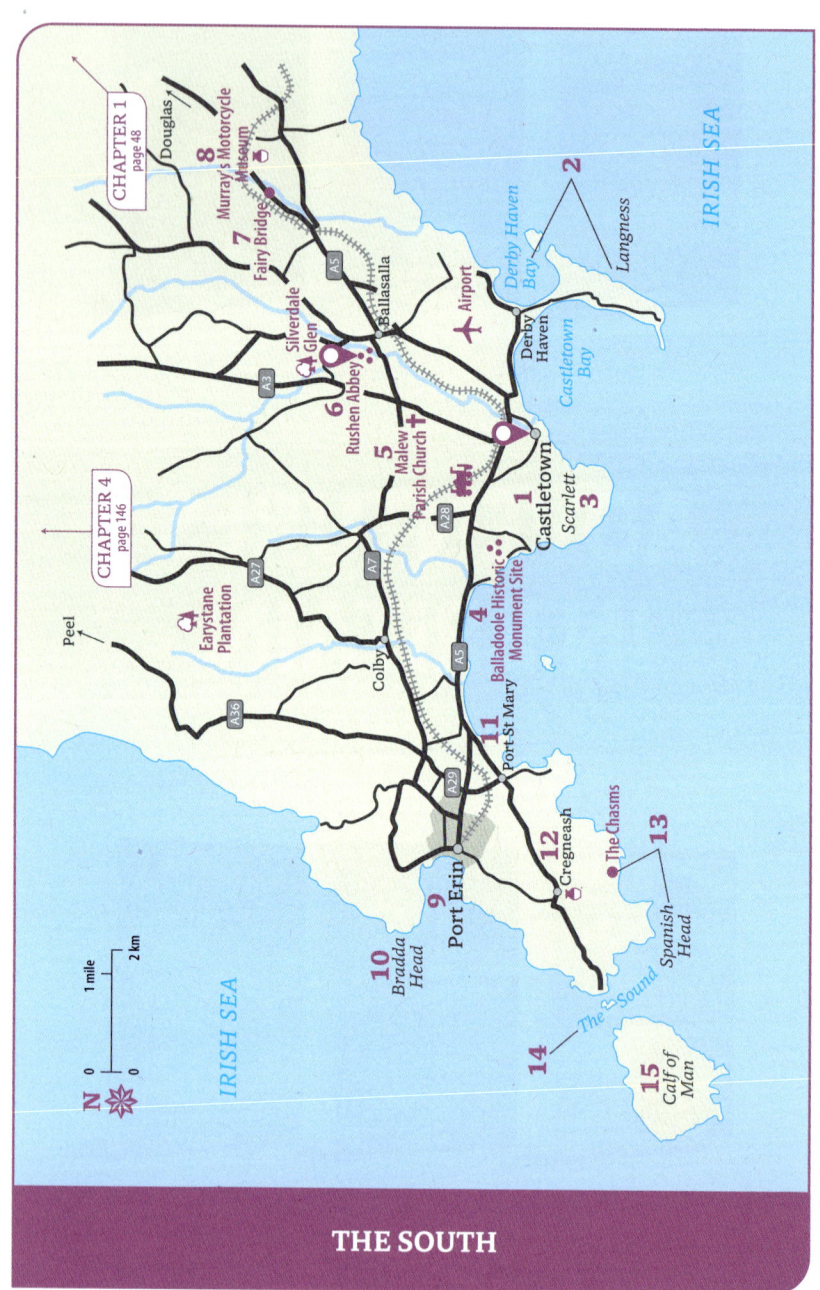

THE SOUTH

5
THE SOUTH

The home of the island's ancient capital, **Castletown**, the south of the Isle of Man has retained an olde-worlde charm that is hard to resist. The coastline resembles a cookie that has had several big bites taken out of it, creating numerous bays and natural harbours that have allowed a dense collection of small towns and villages to thrive. From kings to smugglers via crofters, fishermen and merchants, for centuries this was where all layers of Manx society jostled cheek by jowl.

The 19th-century decision to move the island's capital to Douglas goes a long way to explaining the sense that the south has been frozen in time. When the political circus moved north, it allowed Castletown and the surrounding villages to breathe out, relax and settle into their new status as relative backwaters. Narrow streets of fishermen's cottages survive unscathed in Castletown and **Port St Mary**, while **Port Erin** has embraced its identity as a seaside holiday resort that can be traced back to the Victorians. Toy-coloured leisure boats bob sleepily in the harbours, while happy swimmers emerge from the waters on to the curved, sandy beaches to reunite with their flasks and Dryrobes. The space between villages is green and pastoral, crisscrossed by hedgerows with a soundtrack of bleating sheep.

The area is superb for walking, with the Raad ny Foillan coastal path looping around the entire southern tip. Coastal walks on the southeastern side are fairly level, with a good number of opportunities for a pitstop at one of the cafés along the way; the western coast is more challenging but comes with the rewards of isolation and the beauty of the rolling landscape. The Bayr ny Skeddan footpath cuts inland from Castletown, heading northwest to Peel and crossing areas that are much more sparsely populated, with just a smattering of hamlets leading up into the hills that mark the southern end of the chain that runs the length of the island.

The area is awash with human history, beginning with a Neolithic tomb on Meayll Hill that is unique in Britain, taking in a Viking ship burial near Castletown and the medieval Castle Rushen, and culminating in the wonderful folk village at Cregneash, which showcases what life was like for 19th-century crofters. Evidence of much earlier creatures can be found on the slab-like limestone rocks of Scarlett, which contain the ghostly fossils of sea life that have been hundreds of millions of years in the making.

GETTING THERE & AROUND

The main villages and towns in the area are well served by buses, with the routes 1, 2 and 12 passing through Castletown, Port Erin and Port St Mary; the Steam Railway (page 34) also stops off at these points, terminating at Port Erin.

CASTLETOWN & AROUND

Castletown is the main town in the south of the island, and as the old seat of power has a rich and fascinating history. Much of that history has been preserved, with Castle Rushen (page 183) and the Old House of Keys (page 186) among the heritage sites to be visited, as well as the site of a Viking ship burial (page 203) further round the coast.

Today the town, which was built largely of limestone from the nearby quarries, is rather sleepy – except when the World Tin Bath Championships (page 182) are on. There are fantastic, relatively flat walks to be done along the coast, either north to the wildlife-rich Langness peninsula (page 195) or south round the geologically fascinating Scarlett (page 200).

1 CASTLETOWN
The Witches' Mill

The Isle of Man's ancient capital – perched on the southeastern corner of the island, with a small population of about 3,000 – is nothing if not aptly named. Built at the mouth of the Silverburn River, all the roads and cottages dance around the slab-like 13th-century **Castle Rushen** (page 183) like bees around a queen. Even when it's not directly in view (which is likely if you're exploring down the twisty, narrow streets), the

> **TOURIST INFORMATION**
>
> **Castletown Tourist Information Point** Civic Centre, Farrants Way, Castletown IM9 1NR
> ⊙ 09.00–13.00 & 14.00–15.00 Mon–Fri
> **Port Erin Visitor Information Point** Commissioners Office, 12 Bridson St, Port Erin IM9 6AN ⊙ 10.00–12.30 Mon, 09.00–12.30 Tue–Fri

presence of the castle still feels palpable – after standing guard for 800 years, it still emanates power and strength.

While the Vikings had initially focused on maintaining their base in Peel and the west, which was on the marine superhighway between the Scottish islands and Dublin, by the 13th century attention was shifting to the English court, and Castletown had become the seat of the King of Man and the Isles. It remained the island's capital until 1869, when the Manx parliament moved to Douglas in recognition of the town's growing economic links with Liverpool.

Today, Castletown is a much quieter little town than it once was. But this means that its history is all the better preserved – and it has plenty to offer anyone who enjoys delving centuries into the past. It is also a good base for walks along the coast, with the coast road leading south out of town to the nature reserve at Scarlett (page 200), and the route running north along the beach – a long stretch of sand and pebbles – heading up to Langness and Derby Haven (page 195).

The **Market Square** sits immediately to the southwest of the castle, in the shadow of its curtain wall. Pedestrianised and kitted out with deckchairs in summer, it is an enjoyable place to pause with a take-away drink from a nearby coffee shop, or something from one of the artisanal food vans that regularly park up. The buildings surrounding the square still hold all the Georgian grandeur of the town's heyday, with tall sash windows set into grey stone walls constructed out of limestone taken from the nearby quarry at Scarlett.

On the northeastern edge of the square, beside the castle wall, stands a squat little column commemorating a visit in 1777 by the Methodist preacher John Wesley (he stayed nearby, at 47 Arbory Street). He preached near the castle – one fisherman was said to have been converted on the spot, after realising that Wesley had appeared in his dream the night before as the man who had saved him from drowning. The neoclassical column in the centre of the square marks the site of the old market cross and carries a memorial to a mother and son who were convicted of witchcraft and burnt to death in the square in 1617. For an informal connection to Manx political history, pop in to the **George Hotel** on the edge of the square for a drink or meal – built in 1833, it briefly played host to Tynwald while the parliament was looking for a permanent home.

The shops along Malew Street to the north of Market Square have long since faded and the old high street now offers little in the way of retail therapy, but carry on along its length and follow the neat terraces of stone cottages (Hope Street, Mill Street and the northern end of Malew Street) that branch off towards the harbour for a sense of how the workers of the town – sailors, boatbuilders, quarrymen, and those who did well off the back of these industries – once lived. There is also a good reason for the noticeable winding narrowness of the streets: they were said to have been built like that to break the force of the wind.

The harbour splits the town in two and is now used mostly for leisure craft. On the southern edge of the harbour, directly opposite the entrance to the castle on Castle Street, is the Old Police Station. This almost medieval-looking building, with tall slit windows and a squat

THE WORLD TIN BATH CHAMPIONSHIPS
⊘ worldtinbath.com

The hope for most people sitting in a bath is that it will at least keep the water in. For those entering the World Tin Bath Championships, however, the goal is to keep the water out.

Held on a Saturday each summer (the exact date depends on tide timetables), the riotous event in Castletown Harbour sees more than 100 competitors attempt to paddle round a 350yd course in 5ft-long tin baths. The baths must abide by tight regulations – though they are not always entirely seaworthy, and many are decorated with carnivalesque constructions that rather hinder aerodynamics. The winner is either the first to cross the finish line or the one who covers the furthest distance before sinking.

'I sank twice before the start line last time I entered,' says Boris Kitching, who organises the race on behalf of the Castletown Ale Drinkers Society, which founded the event. His top tip to anyone taking part is to 'relax before and after you sink' (he suggests 'a couple of beers' are likely to help with this).

The races have been going for over 50 years and attract a crowd of thousands, including celebrity guests. In 2007 the adventurer Ben Fogle ended up in an ambulance with mild hypothermia after the bath he was racing in sank.

turret, was actually built in 1901 and designed by the renowned Arts and Crafts architect Mackay Hugh Baillie Scott. A registered building and something of a local landmark, it was used by the constabulary until 2017 – there are now hopes it can be repurposed for the local community, but plans are yet to get off the ground.

The harbour is also the starting point for the Herring Road (Bayr ny Skeddan) footpath, which follows alongside the Silverburn before crossing the island to Peel. The 2½ mile section of the footpath between Castletown and Silverdale Glen to the north is being developed as an art trail, with a giant 26ft steel heron unveiled beside the harbour in 2024 to mark the start. Made by the local artists Darren Jackson and Stephanie Quayle, the heron weighs ten tonnes and took 1,300 hours to construct.

Castle Rushen
⌂ manxnationalheritage.im ⊙ Apr–Oct 09.30–16.30 daily

'Who goes there!' The shout catches you off guard. Standing at the top of the drawbridge, you look around and realise you are standing directly under the portcullis. Didn't you read somewhere that a portcullis was used to trap unwanted visitors so rocks could be tipped over them? To your right, you realise an archer is watching you through a narrow slit in the wall – his bow and arrow raised in your direction. Ah. That would be the source of the shout. Maybe you're not welcome here after all?

Then you spot a friendly guide with a walkie talkie in the courtyard and calm is restored. The chap with the bow and arrow is in fact a lifelike mannequin, and his cry has been delighting children (and the childlike) for decades. The guardroom he stands in not only overlooks the drawbridge but also contains the entrance for the castle's oubliette (from the French word *oublier*, the deep, dark hole is where prisoners could be thrown to be completely forgotten about). This dutiful guard is one of many mannequins to be found throughout the castle, all dressed in appropriate period clothing, engaged in some task or other to keep this great organ of state functioning.

The earliest record of Castle Rushen comes in chronicles written by the island's monks, which state that the Viking king Magnus died there in 1265. Construction work is thought to have begun under the rule of his uncle Reginald, who took power in 1188 and had connections to Anglo-Norman castle builders. Initially on a spit of dry land between the Silverburn River to the east and bogs to the west, the site was easily

CASTLETOWN & AROUND

defendable and by the mid 13th century had taken over from Peel Castle as the island's main seat of power. Building material was also readily available, with the limestone at Scarlett to the south ideal for cutting into blocks.

The castle as it stands now is the result of centuries of remodelling and extension. The original stonework is still visible in the sloped footings at the base of the keep (the main building in the centre of the complex) – the rest of the keep and curtain wall is largely from the later medieval period, while further outer defences were created in the 16th century to deflect cannonballs. Derby House, a grand residence tucked into an inner corner of the wall by the gatehouse, was built in the 1580s to give the Lord of Man somewhere more comfortable to stay than the draughty medieval halls.

"A short patrol around the ramparts makes it easy to see just how hard it would have been to attack the castle."

Today, the whole site is recognised as one of the best-preserved medieval castles in Europe, and it is a brilliant place to experience what life would have been like for the island's rulers throughout the centuries (or, for younger visitors, play at being a prince or princess). Each visit starts with a short film about the history of the kings and lords of Man – do keep an eye on the courtyard as you head into the cinema room, as a ghostly monk has been reported crossing the flagstones just as people look away.

Then it is up to the top of the main tower which, at 80ft high, gives fabulous views out over Castletown and the surrounding countryside. A short patrol around the ramparts makes it easy to see just how hard it would have been to attack the castle; any invader would have been seen coming from miles away. A room at the top of the main tower also contains artefacts from the castle's time as the island's prison and asylum in the 19th century – the gruesome 'hangman's mittens' on display were used to stop those being executed from scrabbling at the rope around their neck.

From here, head down the spiral stairs into the dressed rooms, where you can join a no-expense-spared banquet in the early 1500s (complete with a stuffed peacock centrepiece), have a peek into the king's bedchamber and peer over the shoulders of 17th-century diners.

◀ Castle Rushen has stood guard over the island's former capital, Castletown, for 800 years.

Further on there is a trip to the smoky kitchens to see (mannequin) cooks at work.

Unsurprisingly for an old building that has been a place both of great power and great human distress, the castle is riddled with ghost stories. Along with the monk in the courtyard, a little servant girl is said to haunt the medieval banqueting hall, while a malevolent spirit is said to stalk the stairs that lead up to the walls from the gift shop. Children have also been known to complain about people that the adults around them cannot see.

The Old Grammar School & the Old House of Keys
Both are set back off Castle St ⌂ manxnationalheritage.im ⊙ guided tours covering both sites Apr–Oct noon & 14.00 Wed & Sat; book in advance

A couple of hundred yards south of the castle, down a narrow lane that turns off Castle Street, the **Old Grammar School** is an unassuming stone building on a patch of grass near the town's breakwater. Single-storey, painted white and not much larger than the traditional thatched Manx cottages, it actually began life as a chapel serving the castle and, dating from as early as the 13th century, is the oldest roofed building in the Isle of Man.

"Deep grooves in one of the old sandstone arches show where monks used to sharpen their tools."

It was converted into a grammar school for boys in 1710 amid a push for better education on the island, and continued operating until 1930. Today the building – which has had a small extension since its days as a chapel, to create a classroom – is kitted out to look as it did in its Victorian heyday, with information boards detailing the history of the site and displaying charming black-and-white class photographs.

Markers of its past are still etched into the building: deep grooves in one of the old sandstone arches show where monks used to sharpen their tools, while an exquisite little sailing boat carved into one of the classroom benches suggests a lad in the 1700s was not paying as much attention to the teacher as he should have been.

A copy of one pupil's exercise book makes for fascinating reading (the beautiful handwriting putting most 21st-century visitors to shame), while details of the old school register is well worth a flick through: the number of pupils who are listed as having gone to the US is a reminder of the extent of emigration in the late 19th century, while others are recorded as having gone on to become judges, lawyers and businessmen. It was a good school, despite its small size, and many pupils went on to win scholarships to the nearby King William's College (page 191).

The **Old House of Keys**, which stands on a small square just off Castle Street, beside the lane that leads to the Old Grammar School, dates from 1821 and was the centre of the island's political life for much of the 19th century as the home of the island's parliament, Tynwald. A square little Georgian building, it is not much grander than a good-sized house; those who sat in its chamber were often keen to avoid close scrutiny. Members of the House of Keys – who now sit at the Tynwald buildings in Douglas (page 61) – were at the time essentially part of an oligarchy, selected from the powerful old Manx families and recommending a replacement among themselves whenever a vacancy arose.

Visitors to the renovated building are invited to sit in the Keys' meeting room itself, with a guide explaining the fight for democratic elections that unfolded over the course of the 19th century. One of those who spearheaded the calls for reform was James Brown: the grandson of a freed American slave, he had moved to the island after marrying a Manx woman and became editor of the *Isle of Man Times*. He endured a

VOTES FOR WOMEN!

One of the subjects discussed during a visit to the Old House of Keys (page 186) is the Election Act of 1881: the legislation that made Tynwald the first national parliament in the world to give women the vote – 37 years earlier than similar rights were won in the UK.

The act was part of broader reforms to enfranchise more of the population – and it had initially been aimed at men. However, the simple decision to remove the word 'male' from the legislation meant that spinsters and widows over 21 who owned real estate worth at least £4 were also given the vote.

Unlike in the UK, there had been no mass campaigning of the sort organised by the suffragists and suffragettes. Instead, the change in the law was largely the result of work by individual politicians – though they were undoubtedly supported by women and other allies, whose names are now lost. Universal adult suffrage based on residency was introduced in 1919, along with the right of women to stand for election themselves.

Despite the lack of campaign movement for women's rights on the island itself, there was a strong local connection with the English suffragettes. Sophia Goulden, the mother of the suffragette Emmeline Pankhurst, was Manx: she lived at 9 Strathallan Crescent, at the north end of Douglas promenade, near the tram station, where a blue plaque was unveiled in her honour in 2018.

stint in prison for his efforts in 1864, as did other activists – members were eventually first elected by the people in 1867.

Nautical Museum

Bridge St, IM9 1AX ⊘ manxnationalheritage.im ⊙ Apr–Oct noon–16.00 Sat–Wed

In a grand house on the northern side of the harbour, 200yds from the Old House of Keys, overlooking the mouth of the harbour, this is a curious little museum as eccentric as the 18th-century inventor who once lived here. Despite its name, this is not the story of great warships or far-flung naval explorations, but rather the tale of small craft, local power and smuggling, all told through the lens of one man and his boat.

The house belonged to George Quayle (1757–1835), an entrepreneur, politician and shipbuilder. A member of a wealthy Manx family, Quayle was one of the founders of the island's first ever bank and spent 51 years as a member of the House of Keys. He never married or had children, and clearly had a very active imagination. There is also some discussion as to whether he was involved in smuggling (though quite why his house would have had some of the features it did if he wasn't involved is a question worth asking).

A highlight of the museum is Quayle's old 'cabin room'. Built to his own design on the back of the house, it resembles the stern cabin of a Nelson-era ship and was treated like a mini gentleman's club – it was where the most influential men of Castletown would have been free to talk and drink, away from any prying eyes. It also has some gloriously madcap features straight out of a Boys' Own manual: the hidden safe disguised as a fireplace (which would have proved useful for anyone engaging in illicit trade), plus the secret cupboard that could only be opened if you knew the trick.

Upstairs are all the accoutrements of 18th-century shipbuilding (ropes and sails hang from the rafters, while a giant cauldron is still coated with a lining of tar), as well as a sizeable telescope – another of Quayle's interests.

CASTLETOWN: **1** The ancient capital is built at the mouth of the Silverburn River. **2** The ropes and accoutrements needed for 18th-century shipbuilding are on display at the Nautical Museum. **3** The steam train pulling into Castletown station. **4** Eve Adams of Art Squared makes exquisite miniature dioramas. **5** The World Tin Bath Championships have been taking place each summer for over 50 years. ▶

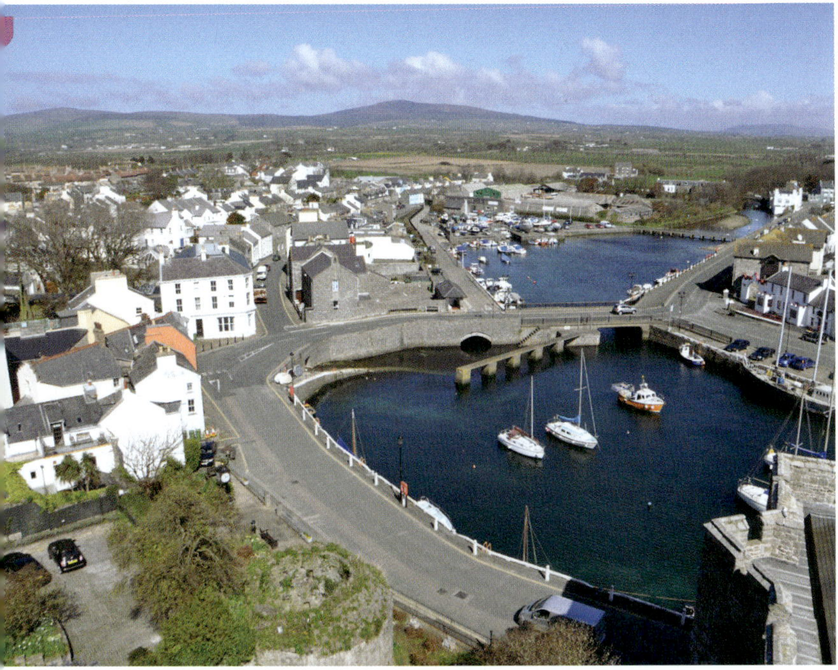

SAMANTHA FLETCHER

VISIT ISLE OF MAN

SAMANTHA FLETCHER

EVE ADAMS

VISIT ISLE OF MAN

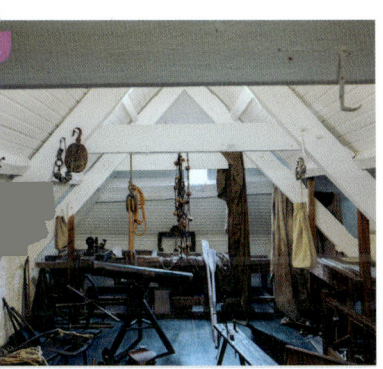

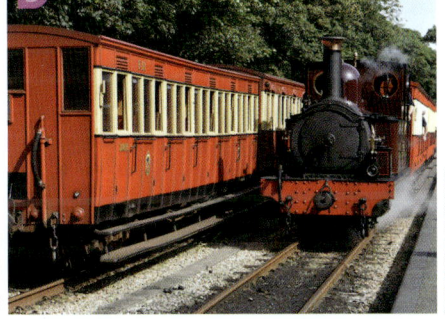

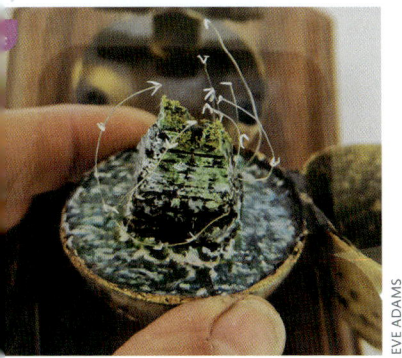

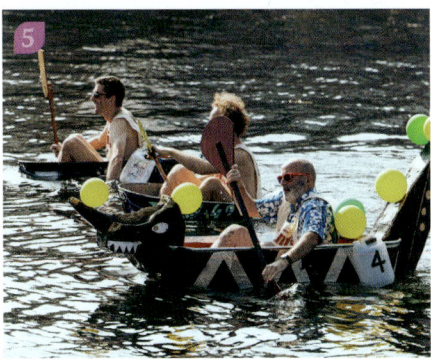

But the most exciting find in the house was made in 1935, when the *Peggy* – the world's oldest surviving schooner – was discovered hidden in the basement. The 26½ft vessel was built in 1789 to Quayle's design, and would have been fast and agile. It had lain forgotten under the house after Quayle's death, when the small private dock leading out to the harbour had been walled up, and the

THE MANX CAPTAIN AT NELSON'S SIDE

Directly outside the Costa at the mouth of Castletown Harbour there is a statue of a rather distinguished gentleman wearing the smart buttoned jacket of a Royal Navy officer and the distinctive wide-brimmed hat of the early 19th century. This man is the Manxman **Captain John Quilliam**, and this statue was installed in 2005 to mark the 200th anniversary of his important role at the Battle of Trafalgar.

Born into a farming family in the south of the island in 1771, Quilliam turned his back on agricultural life and was apprenticed to a stonemason before being press-ganged into the Royal Navy in Castletown in 1791. He quickly rose through the ranks and came to the attention of Lord Nelson after the Battle of Copenhagen in 1801, when all senior officers on his ship were killed and Quilliam, as first lieutenant, calmly took command.

Nelson then appointed Quilliam first lieutenant of HMS *Victory* when she was commissioned in 1803. Part of his responsibilities was to establish an emergency steering system – something that was soon put to the test at the Battle of Trafalgar in 1805. As she neared a French gunship, shortly after Quilliam had helped to guide the vessel into action on 21 October, part of the mast was shot away and the wheel was destroyed. The *Victory* then had to be steered from the gun room, with Quilliam and the ship's master taking turns.

Quilliam remained in the Navy following his great success in helping the British fleet achieve victory at Trafalgar, becoming wealthy in the process. He married Margaret Stevenson, the daughter of a Manx farming family, in 1807, and they eventually made their home at Balcony House on The Parade in Castletown, which stands next to the northbound bus stop on the town's market square (it is easily identifiable from its black wrought-iron balcony and round heritage plaque beside the door).

After retiring from the Navy, Quilliam joined the House of Keys as a politician, and was instrumental in helping Sir William Hillary set up the Manx branch of the Royal National Lifeboat Institution (page 54). He died in 1829 and is buried in the churchyard at Arbory Church of St Columba in the village of Ballabeg, two miles northwest of Castletown. His uniform is on display at the Manx Museum in Douglas (page 63) and more information about his life can be found in his biography, *Favourite of Fortune*, by Andrew Bond, Frank Cowin and Andrew Lambert.

rediscovery caused a sensation. She even still had sealed bottles of Nelson-era brandy stashed on board.

Unfortunately, the vessel had to be removed from the museum in 2015 as its condition was deteriorating rapidly, and it was placed in a controlled environment out of public view. However, there are plans in place to redevelop the museum to allow it to return, and in the meantime the site is an eye-opening insight into quite what the great and the good of Castletown were up to when they thought no one was looking.

Hango Hill & King William's College

Half a mile from the Nautical Museum, at the northeastern end of Castletown promenade on a raised grassy mound on the edge of the beach, stands what remains of a small square building – one side now propped up by a pole after years of beatings from storms and sea. The mound itself, **Hango Hill** (*w3w* pressing.narrowly.represent), is believed to be a Bronze Age burial mound, based on the discovery of a bronze axe head at the site.

The ruined building was once a summerhouse, constructed in the late 1600s by the 8th Earl of Derby and Lord of Man. With views over sparkling Castletown Bay, on a warm day in summer it would have been an idyllic retreat.

But there is probably another reason the Lord of Man enjoyed spending time here. On 2 January 1663, it was the place of execution for Illiam Dhone, who was shot by firing squad for treason for his role in the surrendering of the Isle of Man to the Parliamentarians during the English Civil War in 1651 (page 136). The spot is marked by a small plaque on the ground.

> "The ruined building was once a summerhouse, constructed in the late 1600s by the 8th Earl of Derby and Lord of Man."

Immediately across the promenade from Hango Hill, set back from the road amid broad playing fields, is the Gothic square tower of **King William's College** (*w3w* hairpins.winded.blatant). It sits just back from Castletown Bay, clamped between the ends of the airport's two runways, and its private grounds and building are easily visible from the road. King Bill's (as it is known locally) is the island's only private school – and is the first building many air passengers see on their arrival here. Founded in 1833, it initially only taught boys but went co-educational in

THE EXECUTION OF ILLIAM DHONE

Illiam Dhone is one of the great figures of Manx history, and he is thought of by many as a martyr and patriot (though there is still argument in some quarters that he deserved the label of 'traitor'). Born into the powerful Christian family of Milntown in Ramsey (page 108) in 1608, his real name was William Christian – he acquired the nickname Illiam Dhone (meaning Brown or Dark William in Manx) supposedly on account of his hair colour and complexion.

The Christian family had locked horns with the 7th Earl of Derby early in the 17th century over a change in Manx inheritance rights. But Illiam Dhone curried favour with the earl and his star rose. By 1648 he was the island's receiver-general and was put in command of the island's militia when the earl left to fight for Royalist forces in Lancashire in 1651. However, the earl was captured in battle in England and executed – and Illiam Dhone moved to seek redress for how the Manx had been treated by staging an insurrection with the militia. He surrendered the island to the Parliamentarians and was later appointed the island's governor.

In 1659, Dhone fled to England after being accused of misappropriating funds. He returned in 1660 after the English monarchy had been restored, in the belief that under a general pardon for all crimes committed during the Civil War he would be absolved of his earlier political actions. However, as his uprising had been against the Lord of Man – and not the Crown, as stated in the pardon – this was not the case. The 8th Earl of Derby sought revenge against Dhone and had him arrested for treason. After being held at Castle Rushen, he was executed by firing squad at Hango Hill on 2 January 1663.

The date has been adopted as a day of remembrance by Manx nationalists, who hold an annual ceremony on the hill in Illiam Dhone's honour. Wreaths are laid and speeches are given in Manx and English – a service at Malew Church (page 206), where he is buried, follows later in the day. There have also been several unsuccessful attempts to have the day formalised as a national holiday.

A stained-glass window celebrating Illiam Dhone has also been installed in the Tynwald building in Douglas (page 61), with the staircase it sits on now named after him. His portrait hangs in the Manx Museum in Douglas (page 63), which also has an embroidered cap on display that is believed to have been his. More detail about his life can be found in the book *Illiam Dhone: Patriot or Traitor?* by Jennifer Kewley Draskau.

the 1980s and now accepts both day pupils and boarders, with about 500 pupils across both its secondary- and prep-school sites.

Alumni of note include the island's national poet TE Brown (page 22) and the Reverend John Ellerton, who wrote the hymn *The Day Thou Gavest, Lord, Is Ended*. However, it is probably best known for its

Christmas quiz, officially called the General Knowledge Paper. First set in 1905, the General Knowledge Paper is a fiendishly difficult list of 180 questions that used to be sat by pupils on the day before the Christmas break, then again on their return after they had had time to research the answers. The average score on the unseen test is just two correct answers. Today, the test is sent home to pupils' parents, with a prize for the winning family. It has also gained a cult following among those with no connection to the school, as it has been run in *The Guardian* newspaper every year since 1951. The back catalogue can be found on ⌀ theguardian.com.

SPECIAL STAYS

The Witches' Mill Arbory Rd, IM9 1HA ⌀ airbnb.com. If you want to say you had a truly magical visit to the Isle of Man, then it would be hard to beat staying in the former Museum of Witchcraft (page 194). The 19th-century windmill tower at the Witches' Mill has been transformed into a four-storey cottage, with four bedrooms sleeping up to eight guests. The décor has mercifully been toned down since its heyday as a museum in the 1950s – it now has tasteful cream walls and wooden floors, but maintains a hint of the fairytale with its wooden furniture, a 'magic tree' in one of the children's bedrooms and a display cabinet holding items relating to the building's former life as a museum. However, the real star is the domed glass ceiling at the top of the tower: a cast-iron spiral staircase reminiscent of Lemony Snicket leads up to a floating mezzanine, where stargazers can watch the heavens using the telescope and reclining chairs.

FOOD & DRINK

The Castle Arms The Quayside, IM9 1LD ⊙ 16.00–23.00 Tue–Thu, noon–midnight Fri & Sat, 13.00–22.00 Sun. Squeezed in between Castle Rushen and the edge of the harbour, this iconic little pub is known locally as the Glue Pot – allegedly because, in the days of smuggling, it was tricky to unstick the smugglers from their seats at the bar once they'd finished unloading their goods. It also claims to be the pub that stands closest to a castle wall anywhere in Britain (it is roughly 15yds away), and has the honour of being the only pub to appear on a British banknote (it is in the foreground of an image of Castle Rushen on the Manx £5 note). Filled with dark wooden panelling, low ceilings and cosy corners, and with local Okell's ale on tap, it is a real pub-lovers' pub. A small outdoor seating area also allows pints to be enjoyed while overlooking the tranquil harbour.

The Garrison 5 Castle St, IM9 1LF ✆ 01624 824885 ⌀ thegarrison.im ⊙ 09.00–23.00 daily. Just off the Market Square, this is an old pub with a contemporary feel. The building dates from 1640, but the interior is bright and modern with exposed brickwork, stylish leather seating and fresh, mint-green décor. The food is in solid gastropub territory, such as beef carpaccio or burrata salad, along with elevated classics such as steak and chips. It stocks the full range of spirits from the Fynoderee distillery in Ramsey (page 101) and local Bushy's ale. Try out the games room, with old-school pastimes including table skittles and cribbage, from Thursday to Sunday.

THE FATHER OF MODERN WITCHCRAFT

If you had been wandering through Castletown in the 1950s or 1960s, the chances are you may have bumped into an eccentric-looking gentleman with a pointy white beard, tattooed arms and a crown of hair sticking straight up. This was Gerald Gardner – a former rubber planter, writer and, most memorably, the 'father of modern witchcraft'.

Gardner was born to a wealthy family in Lancashire in 1884 and spent much of his childhood abroad. However, after being influenced by the tribal magic he had encountered around the world, he moved to the Isle of Man to become the 'resident witch' at the Museum of Witchcraft, which had been set up in Castletown in 1951. By 1954 he was running the place and formalising his magical beliefs – also influenced by the English esotericism of the early 20th century – into the modern pagan religion of Wicca.

'Wicca is one of the fastest growing religions in the world, particularly in Europe and North America,' says Jacob O'Sullivan, a museum curator in Scotland and folklorist who has extensively researched Gardner. 'Remarkably, it has its origins in the mid-20th century, largely informed by Freemasonry, indigenous beliefs from the global south, and the occult histories of Britain, Ireland and the Isle of Man.

'Gardner also took extensive influence from Manx folk and fairy beliefs, and established on the island one of the world's earliest Wiccan covens, the locations associated with which can be glimpsed today; from his former home on Malew Street, where rituals took place, to the Union Hotel [on Arbory Street] where the coven would socialise after worship. To the millions of Wiccans practising today, Castletown may even be considered a sacred place of origin; a town of importance akin to Jerusalem for followers of the Abrahamic religions.'

Gardner's museum was at the Witches' Mill on Arbory Road, on the western edge of Castletown, which is now a self-catering holiday let (page 193). The building complex is now private flats, but the red tower of the old 19th-century windmill is easily visible from the road. Old photographs of the attraction, many of which can be looked up on the website of the Museum of Witchcraft and Magic in Cornwall (⌕ museumofwitchcraftandmagic. co.uk), show Gardner standing outside with his broomstick, sitting beside his papier mâché demon, and surrounded by his collection of swords and armoury. He died in 1964 while travelling on a ship off Tunisia (where he is buried), and the museum's contents were sold off to the Ripley's Believe It or Not! organisation several years later.

SHOPPING

Art Squared Market Square, IM9 1LG ⌂ artsquared.im, eveadams.art ⊙ 11.00–16.00 Thu–Sat. The working studio of the artist Eve Adams, who makes exquisite, mechanical little dioramas and automata. She creates tiny, fantastical worlds using found objects such as vintage clock faces, doorknobs and antique keys. Pop by the studio to see her available pieces or to purchase illustrated cards and gifts.

Memory Lane Sweet Shop 1 Arbory St, IM9 1LJ ⊙ noon–17.00 Mon–Sat. A tiny, old-fashioned sweet shop packed with nostalgia. The place to go to stock up on a quarter of liquorice whips, barley sugars or strawberry bonbons. The shelves of jars stretch from floor to ceiling across every wall, and even under the window – you'll be spoilt for choice.

2 LANGNESS & DERBY HAVEN

A mile east from the centre of Castletown sits the narrow, T-shaped peninsula of **Langness** – a windswept, low-lying stretch of land filled with diverse wildlife among the scrubby plants (plenty can also be found offshore in the shallow surrounding waters). Though unpopulated, it holds a wealth of human history, with a scattering of abandoned buildings each revealing a different tale from the outcrop's past. Stretching over a mile from where it joins the mainland to its southernmost point, the two branches of the peninsula help to form Castletown Bay to the south and Derby Haven Bay to the north, which has left it rich with maritime stories.

The flat landscape lends itself to gentle but rewarding walks – though largely unsurfaced – with a loop around the entire coastline of the 'T' totalling about four miles. It is also home to **Castletown Golf Links** (page 40), ranked by Rolex one of the top courses in the world. The peninsula is an easy walk from Castletown, or can be reached by car – there are small car parks on the southern end of the peninsula (⫿ hitch.waffle.bowling) and on Fort Island off the northern end (⫿ medicate.bundles.gripped).

The land itself is what's known in geological circles as a 'tombolo': a rocky island attached to the mainland via a spit of sand. A mixture of limestone, Manx slate and conglomerate (a sedimentary rock made up of small pebbles mixed with finer grains), it also has one of the island's largest salt marshes on the southern Castletown side. The whole peninsula is an area of special scientific interest, recognised particularly for its birds and insects, and is the only place in the British Isles where the lesser mottled grasshopper has been recorded. Waders such as

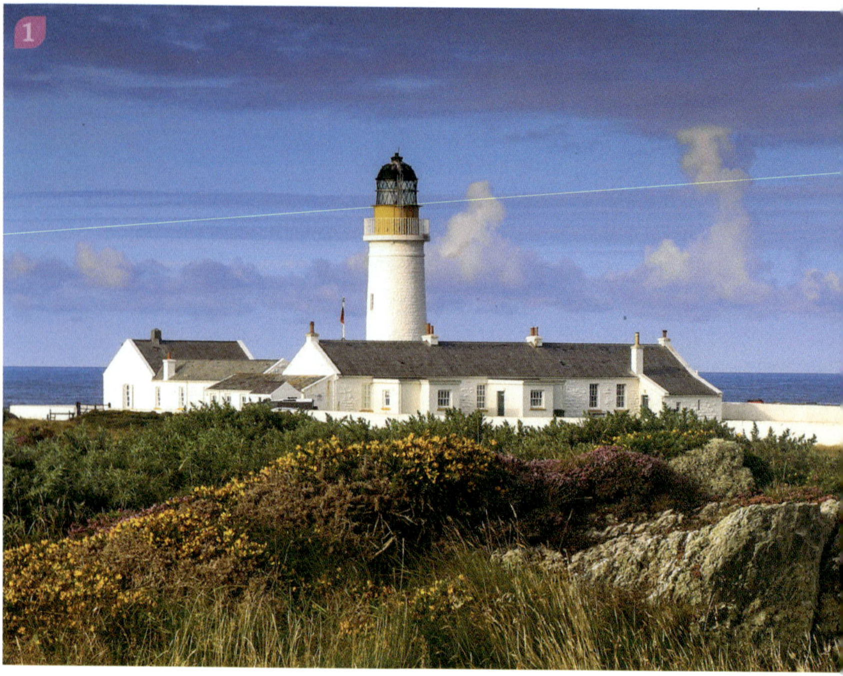

SILVERGULL/S

OTTER/WC

VISIT ISLE OF MAN

TIMOTHY CRAIG

DIANE SHADDICK/S

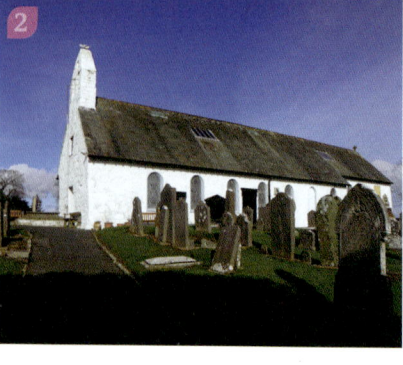

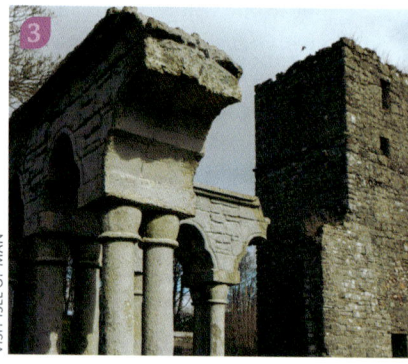

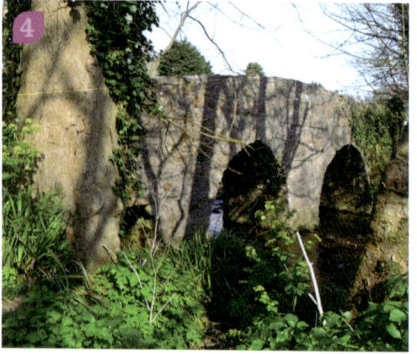

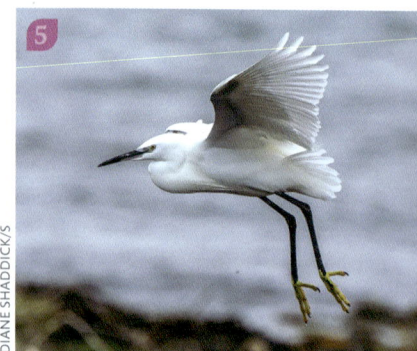

CASTLETOWN & AROUND

lapwings, choughs and ringed plovers can be spotted on the shoreline, while ravens and choughs nest on the rocky coast. Migrant species such as little auks and little egrets have also been seen, and frogs and common lizards have been recorded, along with 15 different species of butterfly.

Offshore, the waters surrounding Langness (the name means 'long point') and the hamlet of Derby Haven to the north are a designated Marine Nature Reserve – the shallow water at the northern edge of the peninsula has one of just four areas of eelgrass around the island, a seagrass which is important for trapping carbon. The eelgrass is also the home of the rare grooved top shell, a tiny sea snail that was found at the site in 2019 after last being seen in 1838 – it is thought to be the most northerly recorded sighting of the snail, which is more common in the Mediterranean. Easier to spot are the grey seals that pop up on the seaward side of Langness peninsula – they are very curious and often tag along with scuba divers, following them as they explore underwater. Risso's dolphins, along with their calves, can also be seen offshore in the summer months.

There are numerous points of interest dotted across Langness peninsula for those willing to explore on foot. The southern tip, known as **Dreswick Point**, is in fact the southernmost point of the Isle of Man (maps generally tilt the island, making it look as though the Sound on the southwestern edge of the mainland is further south). The lighthouse here was built in 1880 after pleas from mariners that the outcrop was a danger to shipping – the now-disused red foghorn can also be seen pointing out to sea. Conflict has also left its mark on the area, with six circular gun mounts made of brick (located near the foghorn) the visible remains of a World War II training range. The islets trailing off the southwestern tip by the lighthouse, known as **Langness Point**, are also marked by the remains of an Iron Age fort – a series of low earth banks are the visible evidence of its existence.

The peninsula is awash with tales of shipwrecks. One such tale dates from 1832 – though it is hard to tell how much is true and how much

---

◀ **1** A lighthouse marks the southernmost point of the island at Langness. **2** Malew Church – the home of some of the area's best legends. **3** The remains of Rushen Abbey, near Ballasalla. **4** Walking through Silverdale Glen, you will reach Monks Bridge, the only surviving medieval bridge on the island. **5** Langness peninsula is an area of Special Scientific Interest thanks to its insects and birdlife, including little egrets.

has been embellished over the centuries. In that year, a ship carrying Irish migrants was said to have been lost, with 32 bodies washed ashore. As was then customary, it was decided to bury the dead where they had reached land, and a mass grave was allegedly dug for them on the southern end of Langness. An unmarked, turf-covered mound near where the lighthouse now stands is said to be their final resting place, and is known as the **Potato Grave**.

Some 400yds to the north of the lighthouse stands an earlier attempt at making Langness safer for sailors. **The Herring Tower**, a round stone pillar inspired by a tower at Peel Castle (page 154), was built in 1811 to act as an unlit landmark so those at sea could at least identify the peninsula during the day. It didn't completely reduce the danger, however – more than 40 wrecks were recorded after it was built. Just to the east of the tower, well hidden among the jagged rocks of the coastline, is the **Provider Stone**: a grey, lichen-covered standing stone about 4ft high that is carved with a memorial to the *Provider*, a vessel that went down in 1853. The sparse monument is inscribed simply with the words 'Provider 1853 All Lost'.

"Slightly confusingly, Fort Island also goes by the name St Michael's Isle."

It wasn't just industry out at sea that left its mark on Langness. Towards the centre of the peninsula stand the remains of a small, square stone building that was once the dynamite store for a small **19th-century copper mine**; the ruins of the mine's smithy still stand next to the car park.

At the northern end of Langness there is a separate, tiny islet called **Fort Island**. Just 300yds long by 150yds wide, it is joined to the peninsula by a narrow causeway and, as its name suggests, is home to a fort dating from the mid-16th century, when Henry VIII ordered coastal defences to be built to see off attacks from France and Spain. The round stone gun emplacement is thought to have housed several cannons, and was upgraded by the Royalist Lord of Man during the English Civil War a century later. It is still in excellent condition, and the exterior can be seen up close using the footpaths that lead off from the dedicated car park.

Slightly confusingly, Fort Island also goes by the name St Michael's Isle, thanks to the dinky 13th-century church that stands on its eastern edge. Easily identifiable from a distance thanks to its short bell tower, the basic structure of **St Michael's Chapel** is still largely intact, apart from being roofless, and sits within an old burial ground (marked by a low earth bank) that is thought to have still been in use by the 18th century. The building is closed to the public, but it is easily visible from the footpath.

Across the bay, the long, crescent-shaped beach at **Derby Haven** is shingly but secluded, and the shallow bay is protected by a breakwater, which makes it a popular destination for scuba divers and windsurfers. It is also a good day out for any plane spotters, as the airport's boundary fence runs along the northern edge of the beach.

WHY HORSE RACING HOLDS A DERBY

The Epsom Derby, which takes place in early June each year at Epsom Downs racecourse in Surrey, is one of Britain's most prestigious horse-racing events. Attended by the great and the good of British high society, the event was a favourite of the late Queen Elizabeth II, who watched many horses run in her colours over the decades she appeared in the Royal Box.

Yet for all its modern glamour, the event actually has its roots some 350 miles away – on the rugged peninsula of Langness. For it was here in the mid-17th century (the precise date is unknown) that the precursor of the race was first run, on the command of the 7th Earl of Derby, then the Lord of Man and for whom the event is named (the bay of Derby Haven is so named because it was where the Lords of Man would arrive when visiting the island). An order from 1670 shows that the riders competed for a plate gifted by the earl.

Historical documents setting out the rules of the Manx Derby for the years 1691, 1692 and 1693 went up for auction in London in 2017, and were described as being of 'exceptional significance for the history of horse racing'.

The documents stated that the race could only be entered with horses born in the Isle of Man or Calf of Man, and set out the route: 'Every rider shall leave the three poles set up on the back of the land near the rocks upon his left hand and the poles around the harbour and the running poles next to William Looreye's house also to be left upon the left hand.' There also seemed to be some concern about unsportsmanlike behaviour, with one rule requiring all riders to conduct themselves in a 'civil manner', at risk of forfeiting their place.

It wasn't until 1780 that the Derby was first run at Epsom, following a party hosted by the 12th Earl of Derby to celebrate the first running of the Oaks Stakes, which is also held at Surrey racecourse. Amid the buoyant mood of the party, a plan was hatched to set up another race at the course – and, as the earl was the host, it was decided it should be in his honour.

The horse racing at Langness has long since ended, but the event is recognised as being the more senior 'Derby', despite being less famous.

FOOD & DRINK

Café Bar Two Six Airport Way, Derby Haven IM9 1TU ✆ 07624 222620 [f] ⊙ 09.30–16.30 daily. Follow the road that runs along the the edge of Derby Haven Bay northwards, and about 300yds after it turns away from the beach you will find the low white building that is Café Bar Two Six. It takes its name from the airport's runway 26, which is just 150yds away (airport runways are given numbers based on their compass bearings). The cosy little café does light, tasty brunches such as omelettes, French toast and a full English, as well as cakes, coffees and champagne for celebrations. The space is small, so booking is recommended.

3 SCARLETT

Visitor Centre car park at /// upper.travesty.hinge

Half a mile south of Castletown is the coastal path round Scarlett peninsula, a must-see for anyone with an interest in geology or who just fancies a bit of amateur fossil-spotting. The area is made of volcanic rock formations and carboniferous limestone, and evidence of its formation and subsequent use by humans is everywhere to see. The half-mile section of the footpath that stretches from the Visitor Centre (⊙ late May–early Sep 14.00–17.00 Thu–Sun plus bank holidays), near the car park, round the southern edge of the peninsula is a designated **nature trail**, with eight stops that make the most of the views, rocks and wildlife – it is a particular haven for birds and butterflies. The Visitor Centre is run by the Manx Wildlife Trust and includes information displays, a short film and a small shop.

When arriving from Castletown, the first point of interest is the **old flooded quarry** beside the car park – the strata are clearly visible in the rocks above the water line. Rock from this quarry, which operated until 1930, was used in the 1870s to build the track and bridges of the island's steam railway; it is now home to swans, moorhens and clutches of water lilies. On the beach side of the footpath, which is the only route around peninsula, are the remains of **three lime kilns**, which were used from the early 19th century to produce quicklime for fertilising the island's acidic fields.

A little way further on lie great sloping slabs of limestone that contain the trapped remains of all manner of ancient sea creatures. The rocks

---

1 Scarlett is a must-see for its volcanic rock formations and opportunities for fossil-spotting. **2** The Viking ship burial in Balladoole; the ship itself was nearly 10ft wide and 36ft long. ▶

RICHARD CHILDS PHOTOGRAPHY/A

SAMANTHA FLETCHER

began their existence some 354 million years ago when the area was near the equator, and creatures living in the warm, shallow seas piled up on the seabed when they died – crushed under its own weight, the debris eventually formed limestone about 1,300ft thick. Scramble down on to the rocks at low tide for a closer look: the most common type of fossil are small disc-like crinoids – distant relations to starfish. Looking south, the domed stack that sits just offshore is a basalt formation (similar to the Giant's Causeway in Northern Ireland) plugging what was probably a volcanic vent.

The **rock pools** here contain a wide variety of living marine creatures, such as red-tentacled anemones. The wildflowers that flourish on the verge alongside the rocky outcrops are at their best in spring and summer: bobbing sea pinks and white sea campion make a beautiful display. Lichens are abundant on the volcanic rocks, while skylarks and meadow pipits can be seen in summer and choughs year-round.

On a less scientific level, a ghostly green lady is said to haunt the large heart-shaped pool that is revealed at low tide about 200yds south of the Visitor Centre – though she is said to be more protective than threatening.

The excellent views out to sea from the coast at Scarlett mean it has been used as a lookout for hundreds of years. The most modern evidence of this is the bright orange **coastguard tower** that stands proudly above the limestone slabs: it was manned continually in stormy weather before it was decommissioned in 1971. The remains of much earlier outposts

STONE GOOD ENOUGH FOR ST PAUL'S CATHEDRAL

Just over a mile round the coast, following the footpath from Scarlett Visitor Centre (page 200), is an unassuming small working quarry separated from the sea by nothing more than the narrow footpath. Great slabs of black limestone sit beside the walkway, sprinkled with sea spray on breezy days and yards away from knots of seaweed swirling in the surf.

It is a far cry from the high-end settings where so much of this rare rock, known as Pooil Vaaish Black Limestone, ends up. First quarried in the 1300s, it contains fragments of fossil and white veins of calcite and achieves a deep, icy black when polished, making it highly prized by architects and designers. Most famously, it has been used as the black floor tiles in St Paul's Cathedral in London, as well as for its exterior steps; it also adorns the ornate façade of Burberry's flagship store on Regent Street.

CASTLETOWN & AROUND

can be found a mile further round the coast from the Visitor Centre at Close ny Chollagh, where the round bank and ditch of an **Iron Age fort** are perched clearly on the waterline beside the footpath. Excavations uncovered possessions including a bone comb, black jet jewellery, a bronze brooch and weaving tools, some of which are on display in the Manx Museum (page 63).

4 BALLADOOLE HISTORIC MONUMENT SITE
/// dishy.rationally.fans

With expansive views out to sea and situated not far from the shoreline, the crest of Chapel Hill in Balladoole would make an ideal final resting place for any mariner. But the Viking who was laid to rest there in around AD1000 – in his mid-thirties, still wearing his luxury gilded belt buckle and carrying traces of a fine linen shirt – was not just any mariner. He was someone for whom it was worth hauling a 36ft wooden ship 350yds up hill, and burying with an assortment of treasures that included a shield, a decorated horse bridle and stirrups, and an iron cauldron. He was a man of great importance: a grand landowner, chieftain or merchant.

Just over a mile to the west of Castletown, the Viking's burial place has become one of the Isle of Man's most striking archaeological sites, and is freely accessible to the public. The location where the Viking ship was discovered is now marked by an outline of large white stones. The site is a joy to explore, with a footpath looping around the main points of interest and clear views over the sea and surrounding farmland. A good distance from the main road, the wide clearing among the gorse is quietly peaceful, and it is not unusual for visitors to find they have the place to themselves.

The site itself – covering the whole top of the low hill, and largely encircled by the outline of an earthwork – is in fact many thousands of years old, with the high-status Viking only the latest in a long series of burials. Humans first left their mark here about 10,000 years ago: evidence of middens has been found, containing large quantities of shells and animal bones – the leftovers of countless Mesolithic lunches. The remains of a stone cist on the north side of the hill mark a Bronze Age grave from about 1000BC, while the clearly visible base of a small, rectangular keill (the early form of Christian chapel, from which the hill takes its name) from about AD900 is linked to a burial ground spreading over the western side of the hilltop, which was found to contain a

THE SOUTH

Walk from Castletown to Balladoole

✿ OS Landranger map 95; start: Castle Rushen main entrance ♀ SC264675; 4 miles; easy (the route is flat but the first half is largely unsurfaced and uneven under foot)

This walk begins in the centre of Castletown and follows the coastal route along the Scarlett nature trail, looping back to Castletown via the Balladoole Viking ship burial and the ruins at Hango Hill.

1 With your back to the entrance of Castle Rushen, turn right and follow the road gently uphill towards the market square (keeping the castle on your right). Follow the road along the edge of the square, keeping the square and the memorial column to your right. The road passes between two bus stops and heads through a narrow gap at the far southeastern corner – head through this gap, following the signpost for Scarlett nature trail. The road

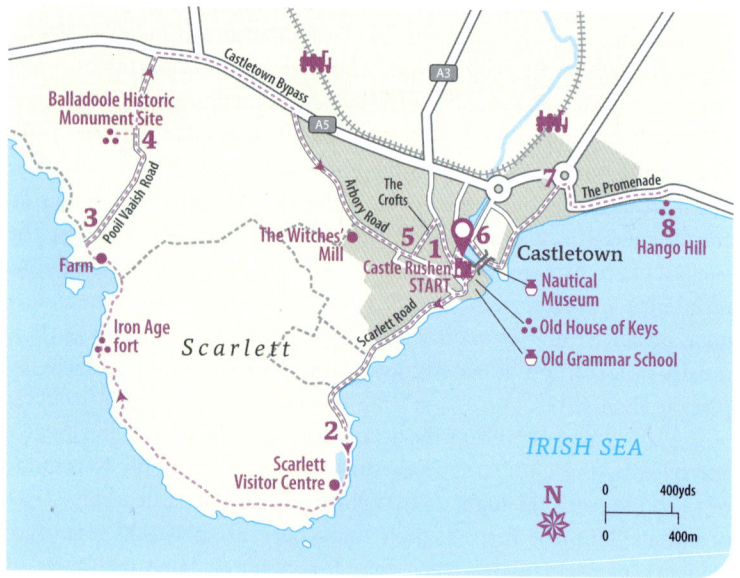

number of early Christian lintel graves. The earthwork that surrounds the site is believed to mark an Iron Age hill fort.

It was this fort that excavators were attempting to investigate when they stumbled across the Viking in 1945. The project was being led by

will take you beyond a row of pretty cottages, and after half a mile you will reach Scarlett car park.

2 Pass through the car park, following the path southwards at the opposite end, keeping the old quarry on your right. Some 200yds beyond the car park, you will pass the Visitor Centre on your right. From here, continue following the footpath around the edge of the coast for about a mile – you will eventually pass the Close ny Chollagh Iron Age fort on your left and Pooil Vaaish quarry on your right, shortly before reaching a farm.

3 Pass through the working farmyard; immediately after the farm, turn right up the narrow road that leads directly inland – there will be a stone wall on either side and a field gate on your left. Follow the road for half a mile until you emerge from a small copse of trees and see a small lay-by on your left and a wide wooden gate in the wall, marked by a signpost for the Viking burial (page 203). Head through this gate and follow the path to explore the burial site if you wish, then return to the road.

4 Continue along the road in the same direction as before, until you reach the main road after 400yds. Turn right and follow the main road for 600yds; when you reach the triangular traffic island, bear right down Arbory Road. Follow the road for half a mile, keeping an eye out for the Witches' Mill (page 193) on your right towards the far end.

5 Turn left on to The Crofts – a pretty street of smart stone cottages. At the end of the road, turn right on to Malew Street, then after 250yds turn left on to Bank Street and follow it down to the harbour. You can either turn right here and return to the entrance of Castle Rushen to end the walk, or continue out to Hango Hill.

6 If heading to Hango Hill, cross the harbour bridge. On the far side, turn right to follow the road along the harbour, past the Nautical Museum and then as it curves round to the left among the cottages. Continue on the road along the seafront until you reach a fork in it.

7 Bear right, keeping the castellated white house immediately on your right, and continue for 200yds until you reach the promenade. Follow the promenade for 450yds until you reach Hango Hill (page 191).

8 Once you've finished looking around and taking in the view, retrace your steps to return back to Castle Rushen.

Gerhard Bersu, a German refugee, who worked alongside prisoners of war from the island's internment camps (he recorded in his field notes the day a policeman arrived on site to tell them that the war in Europe was over – one can imagine the cheers that rang out across the hillside).

THE SOUTH

The ship itself had almost completely rotted away, but the 300 iron nails used to hold it together had survived, clearly marking out its shape in the ground.

The size and shape of the vessel – nearly 10ft wide by 36ft long – suggest that it was used for carrying cargo rather than raiding and would have had a crew of at least five. The lack of weaponry at the site beyond some iron knives suggests that the man's wealth and status was gained through trade instead of fighting. Some of the earlier Christian graves were damaged during the installation of the ship, though there are varying interpretations of this: some see it as a sign of Viking dominance over the native Celts, while others believe the damage was accidental while trying to create the grave at a place that was recognised as being spiritually significant. Many of the Viking grave goods are now on display in the Manx Museum in Douglas (page 63).

The site can be reached by travelling out of Castletown along the A5 road to Port St Mary (buses 1a, 2a, 11a and 12a from Douglas go along the A5), and after one mile turning south down the narrow track that leads past an old farm. A footpath leading directly up to Chapel Hill is found on the right 400yds down this road, marked by a signpost and wide wooden gate next to a lay-by.

5 MALEW PARISH CHURCH
Church Bends, Malew Rd, IM9 3DJ ⊙ approx 09.30–16.00 daily

Malew Parish Church – a squat, white, stone building on a corner of the A3 just a mile north of Castletown – is the largest of the island's ancient parish churches. Sometimes known as 'the Westminster Abbey of the Isle of Man', it has one of the island's biggest graveyards and contains memorials that attract attention from all over the world. It is also the home of some of the area's best legends, involving fairies, a vampire and an illegal exhumation.

There is thought to have been a church on the site from the middle of the 12th century, and the oldest parts of the existing building date from around 1400. However, two Viking swords discovered in the churchyard in the 19th century suggest it was previously used as a pagan burial site, and carved stones found in the surrounding area are now set up inside the church. One of the stones, dating from the 10th century and known as the **Sigurd Slab**, carries carvings of scenes from the Volsung Cycle – a series of Norse legends first recorded in medieval Iceland but known across the North Atlantic Viking world. This example appears to show the hero Sigurd roasting meat (a dragon's heart, according to the story) over a fire.

The name 'Malew' is thought to come from either one of two saints, or a combination of both. The church is believed to have originally been dedicated to St Lua or Molua, a Celtic saint associated with Killaloe in Ireland. However, the Roman church was said to object to saints who did not appear in its calendar and the dedication was altered in the early 15th century to St Lupus, a 5th-century French bishop.

The building itself is a simple rectangle, though a north wing was added in the 18th century, not long after the basic bell turret was added on the western end. It is bright and airy inside, with plain white walls reaching up to a ceiling spanned by the arches of dark wooden rafters. It is still filled with the old Georgian box pews, and there is a raised gallery at the western end that was added for the prominent local Moore family in the early 19th century (the wealthy Moores were active in law and politics, and also have a private walled burial yard in the church grounds, marked by an obelisk). Almost all the windows are of stained glass, with the altar window believed to be the first modern stained glass on the island – its installation in 1843 caused a bit of a ruckus, with some in the congregation feeling it was 'a step towards Rome', according to John Gelling in his 1998 book *A History of the Manx Church*. Visitors can help themselves to tea and biscuits inside the church, and walkers are welcome to eat their packed lunches in the building.

"It is bright and airy inside, with plain white walls reaching up to a ceiling spanned by the arches of dark wooden rafters."

Possibly the most famous of those to have been buried at Malew is Illiam Dhone, who was laid to rest in the chancel the day after his execution for treason at Hango Hill (page 191) in 1663. A bust of Dhone, designed by the Royal Academician and Manxman Bryan Kneale (page 21), was installed on the wall in the chancel in 2006 and is marked by a plaque. Also inside the church is a now-illegible stone in the wall to the left of the altar, which is a memorial to one Elinor Staffarton who died in 1578; she was married to the receiver of Castle Rushen, and the stone is thought to carry the oldest date of any known tomb on the island.

Outside, the graveyard is a fascinating place to wander. The stile over the wall that leads into the graveyard off the main road is itself made from an old memorial slab (a reminder that graves were once not treated with such reverence after the burial was out of living memory). The churchyard also contains **17 war burials** from both world wars, identifiable from the short Portland stone headstones that are standard for all Commonwealth War Graves. Two of note are the final resting place of merchant sailors: the first, whose body was never identified, was known to have been from the SS *Dalewood*, which was struck by a torpedo in the Irish Sea in February 1918 as she was carrying coal from Cardiff to the fleet in Scapa Flow; beside this is the grave of Alfred Dunthorne, who was a fireman on the SS *Sea Gull* when it was sunk off Anglesey less than a month later.

In the southwestern area of the churchyard, beside a stone wall that marks an earlier graveyard boundary, lies what is known as the 'Vampire's grave'. It is easy to spot: it is the only one surrounded by iron stakes and chains. The tomb belongs to Matthew Hassal and his wife Margaret, both of whom died in the 1850s. Little else is known about their life but there have long been rumours about why the chains were felt necessary. One story goes that while Matthew was being laid out after his death, his body suddenly sat upright and let out a moan – this led to claims that he was a vampire, and a stake was driven through his heart before burial and his grave surrounded by iron (which supernatural beings cannot cross). Another tale is that Matthew in fact took his own life and thus was not really supposed to be buried on consecrated ground; the grave was said to have been dug from outside the boundary wall as a sort of compromise – though this does not explain the presence of the chains.

This is not the only bit of superstition to have become attached to Malew. The story of the fairy cup is a familiar one to locals: the tale goes that a man who was out at night heard beautiful music, which he followed until he came upon a fairy feast. They passed him a silver cup to drink from, but one of the fairies warned him that if he did so he would be trapped with them for ever – instead, the man secretly tipped its contents onto the ground and the party vanished, leaving him holding the cup. Not wanting it to do any harm, he took it to Malew Church where it was said to have been used for the communion wine. Another tale is that of an illegal exhumation in 1863, after a woman had mistakenly been buried with knots tied in her shroud. The Manx believed knots left in the clothes of the dead meant their spirit would not be able to rest, and the woman's relatives soon claimed she was haunting them. After being refused permission to exhume the body, her brothers-in-law took matters into their own hands and dug her up early on Easter morning to untie the knots – they were caught and tried, but let off with just a bill for court costs and a severe telling-off.

From the graveyard there is a good view of the field that rises to the west – **Skibrick Hill**. Used for livestock, it is marked by a standing stone on top. The hill itself is a glacial deposit of sand and gravel, but surveys have shown that it once had an enclosure on the top surrounded by four rings of ditches. A bone found in one of the ditches was dated to the late Bronze Age or early Iron Age. The land is private, but the stone is easily visible from the churchyard.

Just up the road from the church, 400yds to the north, is the **Cross Four Ways** crossroads, which joins the road leading to the village of Ballasalla. There was said to have once been a cross at this point, where parents would bring sick children in the hope of curing them. The practice was mentioned in the writings of the island's bishop in the early 17th century.

6 RUSHEN ABBEY

Mill Road, Ballasalla IM9 3DB ⌀ manxnationalheritage.im ⊙ Apr–Oct noon–16.00 Thu–Mon

Two miles north of Castletown, next to what is now the small village of Ballasalla, lie the remains of another symbol of power: Rushen Abbey (both the abbey and Castle Rushen in Castletown take their name from the sheading – or historical administrative area – they are in). The abbey was founded on land gifted in the 12th century by Olaf Godredsson, the island's Viking king, who believed it would boost his reputation. At the time, the estate was secluded and a good distance from any other settlement, allowing the Cistercian monks to focus without distractions.

Like Castle Rushen, the relatively small abbey was made of limestone and was added to over the years – a square church tower built in the mid-15th century is now the most obvious surviving construction at the site. Initially it had 12 monks and an abbot but it was down to just six monks and an abbot at the time of the Dissolution of the Monasteries in 1540.

After the dissolution, most of the building work was dismantled and the materials taken away to be put to use elsewhere. As well as the tower,

THE SOUTH

Walk from Rushen Abbey to Grenaby & back via Ballahott Farm

OS Landranger map 95; start: car park on Mill Rd, opposite The Abbey restaurant
SC278703; 3½ miles; easy (the route is fairly flat and with only gentle climbs, but large parts are unsurfaced and uneven under foot)

This walk follows a route of 3½ miles up the Silverburn River through Silverdale Glen from Ballasalla, then back along country roads and via a footpath that crosses farmland. Uneven under foot in many places, it includes some slight hills that are unlikely to be strenuous for a seasoned walker. The Silverdale Glen Cafe (SilverdaleGlen ⊙ 10.30–16.30 Sat & Sun) offers the chance of a pit stop after the first half-mile at weekends, serving hot drinks, ice cream, cake and light lunches.

1 From the car park, follow Mill Road 50yds east, towards the river. Just before you reach the ford, turn left to pass the bridge and head up the single-lane track marked by two stone pillars. After 200yds you will reach the Monks Bridge – the only surviving medieval bridge on the island. The double arch spans the Silverburn and once gave the monks of Rushen Abbey easy access to monastic lands in the north of the parish. Do not cross the bridge, but stay on the same side of the river and clamber over the old stone stile on the bridge wall (or pass through the modern gate to the left) to carry on along the footpath.

2 After roughly 100yds, you will reach the entrance to the glen proper, marked by two stone gateposts. Pass through them and follow the glen – which is sun-dappled and filled with the scent of wild garlic in spring – for about a third of a mile until you reach Silverdale Park. There are two paths through the glen, both ending at Silverdale Park: if you take the left-hand path when you reach the fork, keep an eye out for the Monks' Well beside the footpath about halfway through the glen. With a semi-circular stone surround and a plaque 'in memory of our ancestors', the well has long been a place to make a wish.

3 After exiting the glen on to the road, cross the car park and climb the steps on the opposite side. (If you took the left-hand path through the glen, you will emerge slightly higher up the road: turn right and walk downhill 50yds to the car park, and turn left to cross the car park and climb the steps). Continue along, around the boating lake, keeping it to your left. Follow the path into the woodland and continue 300yds until you reach the main road. Cross the road and pass through the gate on the opposite side. Follow the footpath along the river for just under a mile until you emerge on to a narrow country road.

4 Turn left and follow the road for just over a mile, ignoring any turn-offs. This will take you to a T-junction with the main A3 road, directly opposite two large houses. Turn right on the main

CASTLETOWN & AROUND

road and walk 250yds until you reach the wide stone gateway to Ballahott Farm. Turn left, passing through the gateway, and follow the route through the farm – when you reach the pair of wide wooden gates, bear left. Climb the stone stile over the wall and continue another 100yds along the edge of the field until you reach the narrow wooden gate – pass through it, climb over the stile and follow the track 50yds downhill to the main road.

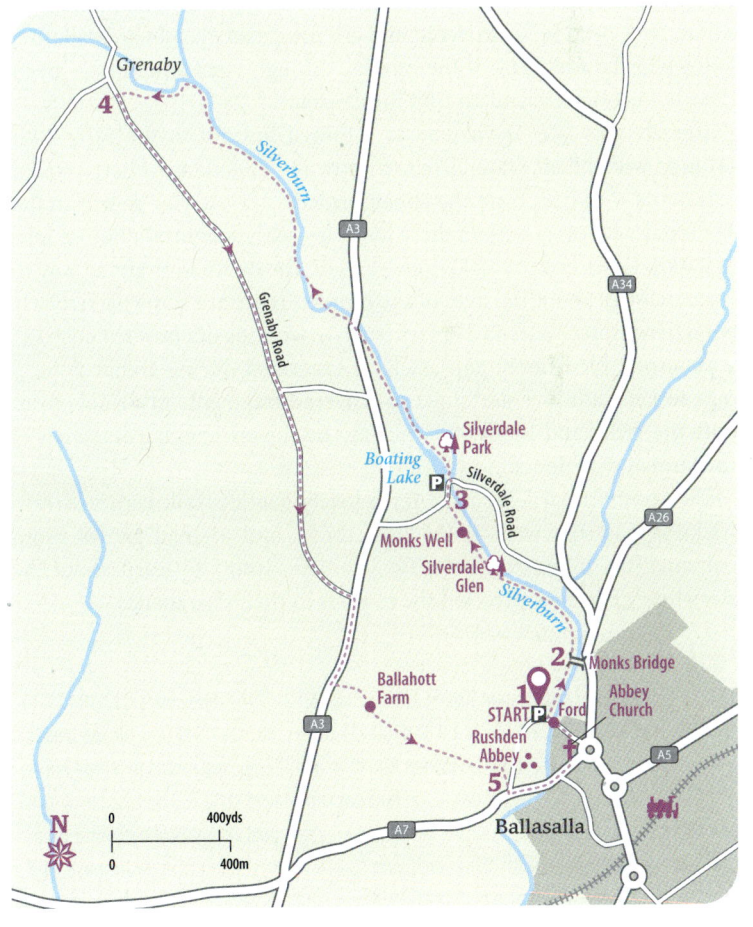

THE SOUTH

> **Walk from Rushen Abbey to Grenaby & back via Ballahott Farm (continued)**
>
> **5** ▶ Turn left on the main road and follow it as it crosses the river and curves round to the left. After 300yds you will reach the Abbey Church on your left; pass through the church grounds onto the narrow road. Turn left and walk 100yds to the ford. Cross over the footbridge to return to your starting point.

visitors today can still see the foundations of the old abbey buildings, which have been left uncovered and are navigated via a boardwalk that follows in the footsteps of the monks, through what would have been their living quarters and around the cloister.

The site was later developed as a tourist hotspot in the early 20th century, with a dance floor, live orchestra and famous strawberry cream teas made with fruit from the abbey gardens. The visitors' centre on the site today addresses both of these histories, with delightful photographs of happy 1950s holidaymakers swirling on the dancefloor giving way to earlier stories about the lives of the monks. There are some particularly good hands-on children's displays (such as working out how to construct a patterned tiled floor) and artefacts excavated during archaeological digs to keep adults entertained (uncovered fragments of urinals from both the 1980s and 1400s offer musings on the unchanging essentials of the human experience).

The compact gardens make for a lovely gentle stroll, with a stream trickling past the well-tended flowerbeds, and a small games room contains fun, interactive ways for younger visitors to learn about the strawberry jam that attracted the tourists in their charabancs.

FOOD & DRINK

The Abbey Restaurant Rushen Abbey ⌀ 01624 822393 ⌀ theabbey.im ⊙ 10.30–15.30 & 18.30–22.00 Wed–Fri, 10.30–17.00 & 18.00–22.00 Sat, 10.30–17.00 Sun. Sitting beside a sun-dappled stream next door to Rushen Abbey, in a building constructed to be the home of an 18th-century judge, this smart restaurant has the relaxed style and polished interior of an old-money country house. It serves classic but elevated British cuisine showcasing some of the best local produce, with dishes including seared scallops, lamb with garlic mash, and Manx honey cheesecake. It also does afternoon teas, and has become a destination for locals celebrating a big birthday, wedding or special event.

7 FAIRY BRIDGE
The Mill House Stables
kilts.flake.tampering

Two miles north of Ballasalla, on the A5, is the Fairy Bridge. Marked by two white stone walls on either side of the fast-moving, busy main road – and a tree covered with notes and wishes – it seems a slightly unlikely place for fairies to want to linger. But according to local legend that's exactly what they do, and it's frightful bad luck not to greet them on the way through.

Coach drivers were said to have encouraged the practice among visitors in the 1940s. Failure to say a cheery 'hello, fairies!' (or 'hello, little people' if you're being truly Manx about it) allegedly results in travel-related misfortune; tales abound of punctures, lost car keys and even, for those on the way to the airport, lost passports. Anyone travelling through on the bus will be reminded to greet the fairies with a short announcement over the speaker system.

There were discussions in the 2000s about whether to install a postbox at the site so visitors could send messages to the fairies, in the hope this would dissuade people from attaching items to the tree. However, the idea wasn't enacted and the tree still attracts mementoes. As there is no pavement and only a slight lay-by in which to park, it is safer simply to say 'hello' while travelling through in a car or on the bus.

THE CHRONICLES OF THE KINGS OF MAN & THE ISLES

The only record of the island's medieval history told from a Manx viewpoint, the *Chronicles of the Kings of Man and the Isles* is a Latin manuscript that sets out events from 1016 to 1316, shortly after the invasion of Robert the Bruce. It highlights the importance of the Isle of Man and Rushen Abbey, and the island's place at the heart of a Viking kingdom.

The main part of the manuscript is believed to have been written by monks at Rushen Abbey in the 13th century, with the entries about later years containing much more detail (presumably as events were still fresh so more was known about them). The ink handwriting on the vellum pages is thought to be from ten different people.

The manuscript passed through private hands following the Dissolution of the Monasteries in 1540, and is now in the care of the British Library in London, though there have been calls to repatriate the document to the Isle of Man.

SPECIAL STAYS

The Mill House Stables Old Castletown Rd, Santon IM4 1EX ✆ 01624 827000
 manxstables. Located just behind the Fairy Bridge is this converted two-bedroom stone cottage, set among the grounds of a 500-year-old mill. Guests have access to a private woodland called the Fairy Glen, which includes a nature walk and a river pool for wild swimming. The cottage has been recently renovated and comes with all the mod cons – including a fully equipped kitchen and en-suite shower room – and has French doors opening onto a patio area to enjoy the peace and quiet of late summer evenings in the countryside. The hosts are extremely welcoming and friendly, and guests are greeted with a loaf of still-warm homemade bread. Despite being out in the sticks, it is just five minutes from the airport and ten minutes from Douglas by car.

8 MURRAY'S MOTORCYCLE MUSEUM

Santon Villa, New Castletown Rd, Santon IM4 1EN ⌘ murraysmotorcyclemuseum.com
⊙ 09.00–17.00 daily

Located half a mile north of the Fairy Bridge on the A5, this is a true place of pilgrimage for TT race fans and anyone who loves motorbikes. Murray's is the oldest established motorcycle museum on the island, having been set up in 1964, and now has a collection of 150 machines on display.

The long, low-ceiling buildings are packed to the rafters with bikes and memorabilia, and every surface is plastered with photos, postcards and vintage adverts, giving it the cosy air of poking round a beloved grandfather's garage. The staff are hugely knowledgeable and are always on hand to answer questions and chat about the bikes.

PORT ERIN & PORT ST MARY

The seaside villages of Port Erin and Port St Mary sit just a mile apart on opposite coasts of the island – Port Erin to the west and Port St Mary to the east. Port Erin is the livelier of the two, with an excellent bucket-and-spade beach, a seafront sauna and bustling places to eat. Yet Port St Mary also has its charms, with its sleepy old harbour and narrow lanes running between the cottages. Both are on the Raad ny Foillan coastal footpath – it is possible to walk from one to the other following the path around the entire southwestern tip of the island, a journey of about seven miles that takes in breathtaking scenery and clifftop views along the way.

PORT ERIN & PORT ST MARY

9 PORT ERIN

The beach at the village of Port Erin is about as postcard-perfect as it is possible to get: a curve of soft pale sand tucked into the cosy bay, it has its own white-and-ruby lighthouse right on the shoreline, beach huts the colour of sugared almonds and comes alive with children wielding buckets and spades as soon as the sun comes out. The headland rises steeply on both sides of the bay, creating a snug inlet perfect for paddling – or more adventurous watersports such as paddleboarding or aquabiking – and offering plenty of walks with stunning views out to sea.

The bay's beauty is perhaps what attracted the mermaids who were once said to come ashore here at night. One was reportedly trapped by locals using a fishing net and, despite being treated kindly by her curious captors, refused to eat until she was freed. Another became stranded by the retreating tide and blessed the women who saved her with easy childbirths. Today the bay is one of the island's designated bathing spots, so visitors can experience for themselves what drew the mystical creatures.

Port Erin, which has a population of 3,700, was a Victorian seaside resort and has blossomed once again in recent years, attracting a raft of unique little businesses that turn a regular day at the beach into something truly special. A dip in the chilly Irish Sea can quickly be elevated to something luxurious by booking a sauna session with **Kishtey Cheh** (⊘ kishteycheh.im ⊙ check website). The barrel-shaped wooden sauna cabins are right on the beach, with round windows framing a perfect view of the bay as you swelter away any stresses and strains.

The promenade itself is delightful, with a row of fishing cottages lining the walkway, overlooking the colourful boats tied up in the bay. The oldest house in the village is the white Christian's Cottage: the double-fronted little home sits just behind Scoops ice cream parlour in the middle of the promenade and was built in 1781. Also on the waterfront, 120yds north of Christian's Cottage, is **St Catherine's Well**, which is marked by a stone arch in the sea wall. Water from the holy well is said to cure the sick, and is said to be particularly powerful in early August.

For those planning a day on the sand, the **Port Erin Beach Huts** (⊘ porterinbeachhuts.com) can be booked individually for the day in summer and each one has its own unique decorative theme, including 'tiki bar', 'fisherman's retreat' and 'pink flamingo'. Extra 'beach packs' can

also be ordered, which include spare sun chairs for warmer days and blankets and hot water bottles for chillier weather. The huts are tucked at the back of the beach beside the squat little lighthouse.

With such a sheltered bay, watersports are a big part of the fun here. Aquabike tours of the bay can be booked in advance with **Aquabike Isle of Man** (⌀ 07624 266221 ▮), and paddleboarding experiences are available through **Port Erin Paddleboards** (⌀ porterinpaddleboards. com) – the twilight sessions with lights attached to the boards are particularly magical. Boat trips to the Calf of Man (page 229) also depart from the breakwater.

Fans of the Isle of Man Steam Railway should check out **Port Erin Railway Museum** (Station Rd, IM9 6AE ⌀ iombusandrail.im ⊙ 09.30–17.00 on days the railway is operating), housed in a building that sits just a few feet behind the buffers of Port Erin railway station, 150yds inland up the hill away from the beach. It has displays of memorabilia and rolling stock – including the coach used by Queen Elizabeth II and the Queen Mother during a trip to the island in 1963. The gift shop has all manner of souvenirs, and with its dark wooden panelling is positively Enid Blyton-esque.

FOOD & DRINK

The Bay Shore Rd, IM9 6HL ⌀ bayporterin.com ⊙ noon–late daily; kitchen: noon–14.00 & 17.00–21.00 Fri, noon–21.00 Sat, noon–17.30 Sun. The flagship pub of Bushy's brewery (page 32), it is enormously welcoming and cosy, with wood panelling, fairy lights and an open fire when the weather turns. Dishes are lovingly crafted pub food, such as locally sourced queenies, duck breast with dauphinoise potatoes, beef burgers or a good old-fashioned chicken pie.

Cosy Nook The northern end of the promenade, Shore Rd, IM9 6HH ⊙ days and times vary from season to season; check ⌀ noa.im and the Foraging Vintners website (page 218). A charming café and beach bar housed in a 19th-century fisherman's cottage, right next door to the beach sauna. It is run as a joint venture between the artisan bakery Noa Bakehouse (page 68) and the Foraging Vintners winery, and is the go-to spot for a weekend brunch or post-swim flat white. It has a tiny indoor seating space with exposed rafters and stone floors – otherwise, seating is all al fresco, with benches and deckchairs spilling out onto the sand.

◀ **1** The picture-perfect beach at Port Erin. **2** Book one of the sugared-almond-coloured beach huts for a day on the sand. **3** Spectacular Bradda Head is topped by Milner's Tower.

MARINE CONSERVATION & THE LEGACY OF PORT ERIN

By Dr Fiona Gell, marine conservation and climate policy specialist based in the Isle of Man, and author of Spring Tides, about her work protecting Manx waters

For over a hundred years, Port Erin was a global centre for marine biological research, and thousands of students and scientists dug in its sands, scoured its rock pools and netted fish in the bay. Very sadly, the Port Erin Marine Laboratory closed in 2006 but its legacy lives on, not least through the **Port Erin Bay Marine Nature Reserve**, which was originally set up as an experimental area to compare seabeds that were open and closed to scallop dredging. Now over half of the Island's inshore waters are protected from scallop dredging and are thriving, and this all started with the very small protected area in Port Erin that convinced the scallop fishermen of the benefits of protecting areas of seabed from dredging.

Port Erin beach and Spaldrick Beach, a pebbly cove just round the bay, are both brilliant for rock pooling. The rocky shore on the north side of Port Erin beach is easily accessible and great for rock pooling with children. Spaldrick Beach requires more scrambling over slippery rocks but the marine life exposed at low spring tides is worth it; overhangs encrusted with orange and green sponges, kelp holdfasts inhabited by whole communities of crabs, molluscs and worms, and so much more.

Out in the bay, you have a good chance of seeing harbour porpoise (which are resident in Manx waters year-round) and from June onwards the possibility of seeing basking sharks. In good years basking sharks are spotted right inshore off the sandy beach and within yards of the shore in Spaldrick Bay.

Foraging Vintners The Old Coal Shed, The Breakwater, IM9 6JA ⌀ foragingvintners.com ⊙ noon–22.00 Wed & Thu, noon–late Fri & Sat, noon & 21.00 Sun. A seaside winery producing non-grape varieties of sparkling wine, such as their rhubarb fizz and elderflower fizz. Linger over something refreshing at their raised outdoor seating area beside the harbour, with stunning views over the water.

Kerroo Brewing Company Former Commissioners Depot, Droghadfayle Rd, IM9 6EE ⌀ kerroobrewing.com ⊙ 17.00–22.00 Fri & Sat. An award-winning micro-brewery with a taproom open to the public at weekends. There are long wooden benches, cool merch and plenty of exposed brickwork; pop-up events are also hosted, so check the Facebook page for the latest updates.

La Gusto Shore Rd, IM9 6HL ⌀ lagustopizza.co.uk ⊙ 17.00–22.00 Sun–Thu, 17.00–23.00 Fri & Sat. Hand-stretched artisanal pizzas right on the seafront. Sit inside and enjoy the view through the wall-to-wall windows, or take away and eat right on the beach.

 SHOPPING

Bridge Bookshop Shore Rd, IM9 6HL ⌀ bridge-bookshop.com ⊙ 09.30–17.30 Mon–Sat, plus Easter–Dec 11.00–16.00 Sun. The southern branch of the small Manx book chain, this dinky bookshop sits right on the seafront – perfect if you realise you forgot to pack your beach read. It also stocks an excellent selection of local-interest publications.

Soaral 36 Church Rd, IM9 6AQ ⌀ soaral.im ⊙ 10.00–16.00 Mon, noon–17.30 Wed, 10.00–17.30 Fri & Sat. A local fragrance company specialising in perfumes and scented candles, it also runs workshops if you would like to try your hand at creating your own. If you'd rather leave the blending to the experts, you can pick up one of its Manx-inspired scents – such as the moody Manannan's Cloak parfum.

10 BRADDA HEAD

On the north side of Port Erin Bay, the headland of Bradda Head is a great place to explore on foot. The entrance to Bradda Glen – and the start of the footpath that leads up to the summit – can be reached easily from Port Erin beach: follow the main promenade road half a mile north up the coast until you find the arched stone entrance on the left, clearly marked with black-and-white signage.

The steep, uneven footpath splits into a lower and upper route, but both ultimately reach **Milner's Tower** at the tip of the headland. The tower was built in 1871 in honour of William Milner, a businessman from Liverpool who adopted Port Erin as his home and became a benefactor of the village. He had made his fortune with the manufacture of safes, and when viewed from above his tower has the shape of a lock and key – it is always open to the public, with a spiral staircase leading to the top. There is also a World War II pillbox at the top of the headland, which makes the most of the vantage point looking out over the Irish Sea towards Ireland.

> "The headland of Bradda Head is a great place to explore on foot."

11 PORT ST MARY

Exploring this sleepy little village, just 1½ miles southeast of Port Erin on the opposite coast, is to see the two pillars of the island's history, fishing and tourism, sitting snugly together side by side. The small community of about 2,000 people spills from high up on the headland above small, cove-like Chapel Beach – where pastel-coloured old guesthouses line the main road – down increasingly narrow, winding streets towards the picturesque harbour with its dinky stone cottages.

THE SOUTH

THE MAGNETIC HILL

/// pecan.goes.buyers

Just to the east of Earystane Plantation, on Ronague Road about 2½ miles north of Colby, there is a small, lichen-covered marker stone in the western hedge with 'Magnetic Hill, Ronague' inscribed on the face. The stone is slightly obscured by bracken and other hedgerow plants, and is beside a small copse of trees. It is here that a curious phenomenon occurs.

A car left in neutral with the handbrake off at this spot will gently start to roll... apparently up hill. The slope is actually an optical illusion – a result of the surrounding hills obscuring the real horizon, making a slight downhill slope look like the opposite, and meaning cars look like they are being pulled 'magnetically' up the road by an unseen force.

The phenomenon is more than a little disconcerting, but there are many examples of the effect around the world, with several videos of the hill at Ronague on YouTube.

The village is believed to take its name from the old Chapel of St Mary, which is thought to have sat on the shoreline at Chapel Beach. The church is long gone, with the sound of bells replaced by the squeaks of oystercatchers scuttling in the surf, but there is still a wishing well named in honour of St Mary on the promenade. The beach itself is a designated bathing area, though a combination of wind direction and sea currents means there can often be a fair bit of seaweed washed up.

There is a handful of shops on the small high street, as well as **Studio 42** (Waverley House, Bay View Rd, IM9 5AE ⊘ studio42gallery.co.uk ⊙ 10.00–17.00 Wed–Fri, 10.00–16.00 Sat), a petite but perfectly formed art gallery that shows work by numerous established local artists.

The squat, stone church that stands on the high street today, **St Mary's** (⊙ 09.00–16.00 daily), was built in 1884 and is open daily for visitors – it is bright, peaceful and welcoming inside, with gentle music left playing to accompany any private moments of reflection. The interior is simple, with white walls stretching up to the high raftered ceiling and colourful stained-glass windows highlighting the village's maritime history.

The **pretty little harbour** is well worth a gentle wander, and can be reached by following the main road down the hill or cutting through one of the numerous steep alleyways that slice between the old fishermen's cottages. The RNLI lifeboat stands guard at its permanent mooring at the mouth of the harbour, while slipways and deep water make the inlet popular with leisure craft – there are usually a few sailors pottering on the waterside doing a spot of maintenance. Boat trips to the Calf of Man (page 229) also depart from the harbour. A giant hare was once said to harass the fishermen of Port St Mary, while a ghostly horse-drawn carriage reportedly travels silently down Lime Street, which curves south away from the harbour, after midnight.

> *"The church is long gone, with the sound of bells replaced by the squeaks of oystercatchers scuttling in the surf."*

A raised walkway follows the outside of the sea wall from the harbour round to the beach, which is particularly fun at high tide with the water sloshing beneath your feet. There is a good walk to be done along the coastal path to Castletown: the route can be followed north from Chapel Beach up to **Gansey**, a popular spot with windsurfers, and round the coast at Scarlett (page 200). Going from Port St Mary to Castletown on foot takes about two hours and the 5½-mile route is almost entirely flat, with a few stiles to navigate and some uneven, agricultural surfaces.

FOOD & DRINK

Cornerhouse Coffee On the corner of Gellings Av and Bay View Rd, IM9 5AQ ⊙ 10.00–14.00 Fri–Sun. A cosy little coffee shop perfect for a pit stop, a light lunch of quiche or a gourmet sausage roll, and a slice of homemade cake. Wide windows offer gorgeous views over the bay.

Kellas Manxonia House, Bay View Rd, IM9 5AE ⌕ 01624 838060 ⌕ kellas.im ⊙ variable, check online. A real destination for foodies, this renovated 19th-century schoolhouse contains a café, restaurant, cocktail bar and farm shop, all showcasing local produce. Restaurant menus are seasonal and based on classic British cookery (think braised lamb or w bream), with homemade sweet treats available in the café – it also does afternoon teas (which must be booked 48 hours in advance). The restoration work itself is top-notch, with the building's original features, such as beautiful wooden rafters, complemented by contemporary artwork on the walls.

The Shore Hotel Shore Rd, Bay ny Carrickey IM9 5LZ ⌕ 01624 832269 ⌕ theshoregansey ⊙ food noon–20.30 daily. Standing proudly on the edge of the sweeping Gansey Bay, a mile to the northeast of Port St Mary, this hugely popular bar and restaurant is the perfect place for a cosy roast dinner while watching the stormy sea outside. Decked out with driftwood-style panelling, fairy lights and squishy leather sofas, it has a gastropub-style

THE MANX AT DUNKIRK

'I'm a Steam Packet nerd,' Matt Cain says proudly, by way of explaining how he came to own a little piece of Manx history. 'I saw her for sale online – I got on the blower to my dad and he said, "we have to save that"'.

What they saved, back in 2008, was a lifeboat that had been on the Isle of Man Steam Packet ship the *Lady of Mann* – one of eight vessels belonging to the Manx ferry company that was requisitioned for the war effort and took part in the evacuation of Dunkirk.

When we speak in late May 2025, Matt is in Ramsgate in Kent, preparing to cross the Channel to mark the 85th anniversary of the evacuation. As membership secretary of the Association of Dunkirk Little Ships, he is joining a flotilla of vessels that took part in Operation Dynamo, retracing the voyage that saved the allied forces – and he is doing it in his lovingly restored Manx lifeboat.

'I'm doing this to tell the Manx story,' Matt says. 'Because the Manx story of Dunkirk is unbelievable. It was one of the single greatest sacrifices of any nation.'

Of the 340,000 troops rescued from the beach in northern France as the Nazis approached in 1940, 25,000 of them were saved by Manx vessels – or 1 in every 13 men. The ferries were unarmed and, as Matt points out, 'they were big, big targets'. Three of them were lost amid the mayhem.

Port St Mary is now home to a memorial to the Manx ships that were lost during those heroic few days early in World War II, and the men who served on them. On a flat patch of grass overlooking the sea at **Kallow Point** – about 300yds south of Port St Mary harbour – sits a large ship's anchor, pointing southeast towards France. The anchor is taken from the *Mona's Queen* – a Steam Packet ferry struck by a German mine on its second approach to Dunkirk, with the loss of 24 men. The anchor was raised by divers in 2010 and installed at its present site in 2012. The other two Steam Packet ships lost – the *King Orry* and the *Fenella* – are also remembered at the site.

The *Lady of Mann* – the flagship of the Steam Packet fleet – survived the ordeal, eventually being decommissioned and broken up in 1971. The No 8 lifeboat was saved and turned into a fishing boat, eventually turning up in Essex in an online advert Matt spotted in 2008. 'It was a virtual wreck,' says Matt, whose grandfather played his own role at Dunkirk as a dispatch rider. 'We didn't know if it was going to end up as a garden ornament or what state it was in. We got lucky.'

The vessel turned out to be salvageable and was restored in time to take part in the Queen's Diamond Jubilee flotilla on the Thames in 2012. Matt, who grew up in Lincoln with a Manx father and whose uncles worked on the Steam Packet, now uses the boat for pleasure cruising with his family, on the Thames near his home in Surrey.

---

menu covering everything from pies to curry. The service is fantastically friendly, and it has dedicated regulars. Booking highly recommended. It also has seven cosy rooms available as accommodation upstairs.

THE FAR SOUTH

The southwestern end of the Isle of Man has been inhabited for millennia, and today is a destination for history buffs, walkers and wildlife spotters alike. Stretching from the high ground of **Cregneash Folk Village** and **Meayll Hill** down to the very southwestern tip of the island, known as **the Sound**, and the narrow channel that separates the main island from the **Calf of Man**, the area is rich in layers of history beneath the rolling farmland, and has a craggy coastline that is alive with the squawks of seabirds and snorting of curious seals.

The **Raad ny Foillan** footpath loops around the whole craggy southwestern coastline, making for a bracing but enjoyable day out on foot. Cregneash and the Sound can be reached using the 8 or 8S bus service, which runs several times a day from Peel via Castletown and Port Erin.

12 CREGNEASH VILLAGE & AROUND

Howe Rd, IM9 5PX ⌂ manxnationalheritage.im ⊙ Buildings that are part of the museum are open Apr–Oct 10.00–16.30 daily

Whatever life you currently lead, it is hard not to imagine giving it all up to become a crofter when standing outside one of the gleaming whitewashed cottages of Cregneash, 1½ miles southwest of Port St Mary. One of the island's rare upland villages, its cosy thatched dwellings look down towards the Calf of Man, the sea sparkling in the sunshine and the sky stretching out to the horizon. Luckily, it is possible to get a feel for this life without enduring any of the hardships, as the village is now an open-air museum and it is the best place to find out how rural islanders were living towards the end of the 19th century.

This scattering of homes – some modernised with two floors, many single storey – has been pulling in the tourists since the 1800s. English Victorians, who were used to the clanging dynamism of the agricultural and industrial revolutions, came here to see a way of life that was rapidly being forgotten elsewhere: horses still pulled ploughs, women worked on their spinning wheels and dinner was cooked in a pot hung on a chain over an open fire. Electricity didn't arrive until 1938; running water arrived in the 1940s. It is this enduring appeal that led to the village becoming the first open-air museum in the British Isles, after the family of one of the residents gifted his cottage to the Manx Museum following his death in 1938. Manx National Heritage went on to acquire many more of the properties, though some are still privately owned and lived in.

The most basic of the cottages are low, white rectangles containing just two main rooms with an upper attic space or mezzanine (children

THE THREADS OF COMMUNITY

Spinning was part of everyday life for the women of Cregneash (page 223). Many owned spinning wheels and would use them to process the wool from their own sheep, with children helping to sort and prepare the fleeces. The yarn would then be woven into cloth by local weavers – one of the houses in the village, known as Crebbin's Cottage, has a special weaving shed built onto the side.

It was during a kindergarten trip to Cregneash that I first saw a woman spinning. Sitting outside Harry Kelly's cottage in the sunshine, she was processing a fleece with a wooden single-treadle wheel, gently pedalling and drawing out the fibres in a slow rhythm – I was mesmerised. The memory stayed with me, until eventually – after years of living in London and wrestling with homesickness – I bought my own wheel. It is now one of my most treasured possessions; a connection to the Manx women who went before me, and a reminder of who I am when I feel lost.

Some 150 years earlier, another Manxie had observed this slow, measured process at Cregneash on a much broader scale. Edward Faragher – a poet, Manx speaker, small-scale farmer and native of the village – was born in 1831 and grew up with full knowledge of the work that went into producing clothes by hand. He was a prolific writer and was championed by leading figures in the Manx cultural revival of the late 19th century (some of the 4,000 poems he wrote in his lifetime can be found at manxliterature.com). He also wrote a captivating sketch of day-to-day life at Cregneash.

'The old folks… were very different from the present generation; they only spoke the Manx language, and were clothed with their manufactured clothes,' he wrote. 'They had a pair of cards in every house to card the wool, and a heckle to heckle the flax, and cards to card the tow [the coarser part of flax]. They very often spun the tow, and made sackcloth of it, and some of the hard-working men had shirts of it. The women spun the flax and the wool, and there were plenty country weavers. I recollect five weavers in Cregneish alone… They made woollen cloth and flannel for singlets for the men that were going to sea, and petticoats for the women. Then they were sent to the mill to thicken it for drawers and coats to work in: the coats were white and bound with black braid, and looked very stylish.'

In an age of cheap, mass-produced textiles, it is a sobering reminder of just how much effort once went into keeping the clothes on our backs.

would sleep on the upper floor, with fishing nets used to stop them rolling off). The thatch was traditionally straw, which could be put on quickly but only lasted two or three years, unlike the reeds used in England which could last up to 30 years.

You don't need a ticket just to wander through the village, but buying one is definitely worth it as it allows you to step inside several of the old homes and see for yourself just how snug – or cramped – conditions could be. Homely touches such as a dresser stacked with beautiful crockery hint at the pride residents took in their homes, while some of the furniture is curiously grand: it was not uncommon for pieces to be bought cheaply secondhand as wealthier households sold up and moved on. Chickens still scratch about between the cottages and among the old pieces of farm machinery, and if you keep your eyes peeled you might spot a Manx cat disappearing over a wall or basking in a sunbeam. One of the houses in the village has been turned into a cosy little **café** (◐ museum's open season 10.00–15.00 daily) with a stone hearth and bare rafters, doing soups, sandwiches, scones and cakes – including the traditional Manx tea loaf, bonnag (page 32).

> *"On a bright day it is truly idyllic, though there are hints at just how hard life could be."*

Cregneash was a stronghold of Manx culture, and staff today still offer a cheery 'fastyr mie!' (good afternoon) on their way to check on the resident Loaghtan sheep. On a bright day it is truly idyllic, though there are hints at just how hard life could be for those who eked out a life here. The thatched roofs were sometimes held down with fishing nets to protect against the ferocious wind, and the small two-room stone dwellings could house a family with five or six children. Ostensibly a village of smallholdings, the men supplemented their income with fishing too, and small weaving sheds allowed local fleece to be turned into cloth.

Meayll Hill

The heather-covered Meayll Hill is a moderately steep 400yd climb up a footpath leading north from the village of Cregneash. The scrubby summit is dominated by a scattering of concrete bunkers and platforms that was home to a **World War II radar station**. In 1940, much of this area became part of Rushen Internment Camp for enemy aliens – the only all-female internment camp in Europe, which also encompassed

Port Erin and Port St Mary (the camp perimeter shifted as the war went on, to leave Cregneash outside the wire, and it ceased operating altogether in 1945).

Continue straight over the summit and onto the north-facing side of the hill via a stile to find much older evidence of human activity: a superb Neolithic chambered tomb called **Meayll Circle**, with views out towards Bradda Head (page 219). The tomb is unique in the British Isles as it is organised into 12 stone chambers, which are arranged in six pairs around an inner circle 25yds across – the circular shape has been found nowhere else. During excavations, the discovery of cremated remains, pottery, flint arrowheads and tools dated the tomb to about 4000BC, and some of the artefacts – including pottery and flint tools – are on permanent display at the Manx Museum in Douglas (page 63).

13 THE CHASMS & SPANISH HEAD

Car park for the Chasms at /// sidestep.shatter.nutrient

Heading half a mile south of Cregneash, down the single-track road leading out of the village from the café there, leads to The Chasms and Spanish Head. **The Chasms** are a jagged set of coves and crevices gouged into the sandstone cliff face by the sea, creating deep vertical fissures where the rock is gradually slipping away. Initially invisible when approaching along the footpath from the small car park, they knife through the headland in the area around the old stone building that was once a café (which is easy to spot, as the only building on the headland), plunging to depths that seem unfathomable from the surface. The headland can be explored on foot, though extreme caution is needed around the fissures as the edges can be obscured by heather and other vegetation. It is a superb place for spotting seabirds such as guillemots and razorbills, particularly in the spring. A rock stack known as the **Sugarloaf** just off the headland comes alive with birds during nesting season.

It is possible to follow the Raad ny Foillan footpath half a mile southwest along the coast from The Chasms to **Spanish Head**, a

---

1 The village of Cregneash is now an open-air museum. **2 & 3** A boat tour is an excellent way to explore the cliffs around the Calf of Man, spot seabirds and visit rock formations such as the Drinking Dragon. **4** The café at the Sound enjoys one of the best views on the island, looking out across the Calf. ▶

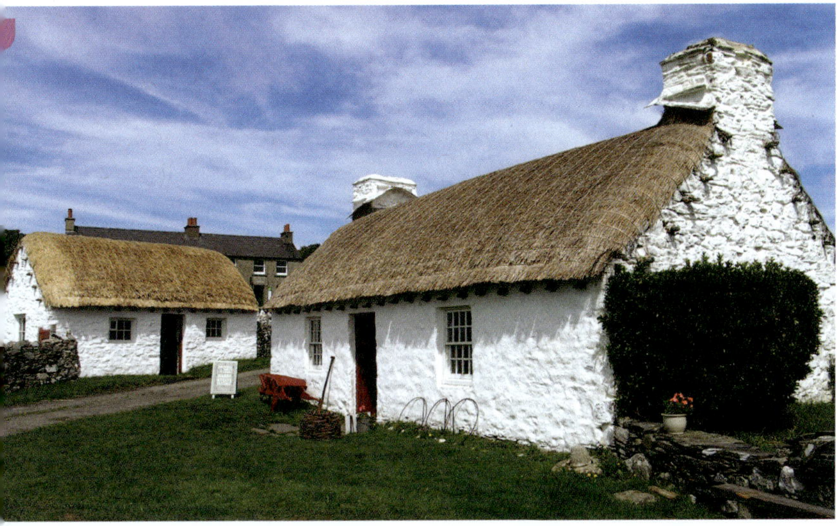

ANNA REGENITER/DT

VISIT ISLE OF MAN

VISIT ISLE OF MAN

VISIT ISLE OF MAN

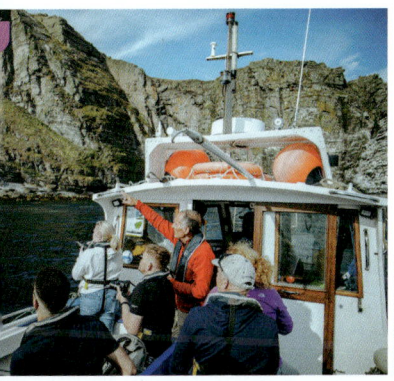

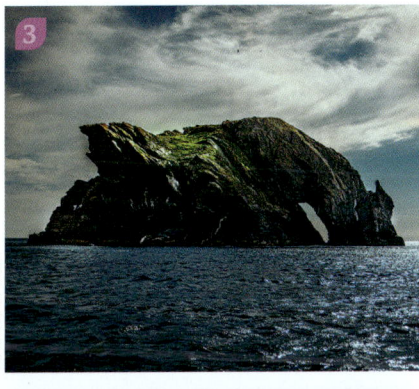

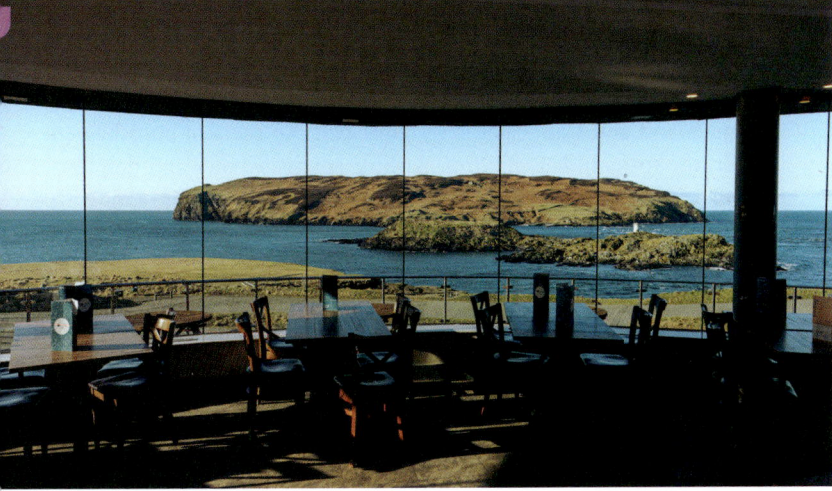

THE SOUTH

promontory of sheer cliffs over 300ft high made of Manx slate, which was once quarried by the villagers of Cregneash to be used as door and window lintels. The name of the area allegedly comes from the Spanish Armada in 1588 – one of the ships was said to have become lost and was wrecked on the headland (there is, however, no evidence for this ever happening). The views out to sea are sensational – the vegetation underfoot is low and scrubby and the clifftop is scoured by the wind, so it feels enormously exposed. The smell of sea spray frequently wafts up from the base of the cliffs, along with the sound of the crashing waves.

The Raad ny Foillan path then continues all the way around this coast as far as the Sound, just under a mile further on, and on to Port Erin.

14 THE SOUND
Car park at /// nevertheless.clams.mammals

The most southwestern tip of the main island, the Sound is where the land tapers to a point just a couple of hundred yards across. It has become a destination thanks to the sweeping views over the Calf of Man and its busy café, which has a good sized car park where you can park up to explore the area. It is a great place for a bit of wildlife spotting, with the flat grass in front of the café much more accessible than the surrounding headland.

The area is treeless, scrubby and exposed – though the land sits much lower than the cliffs at Spanish Head up the coast, putting you much closer to the rocky waterline. The waters that race through the channel between the mainland and the Calf of Man are a favourite with seals, who often pop their heads up to watch the people on land with distinct curiosity (if it's not too windy, there's every chance you will be able to hear them snorting as they gaze at you). They also enjoy a spot of sunbathing on Kitterland – the rocky outcrop in the channel between the mainland and Calf – and it's a great place to see seal pups hauled out on the rocks in late autumn. Basking sharks, whales and dolphins can also be seen, particularly in summer, and it is a favourite spot with kayakers who use the fast-moving current to shoot through the gap between the islands.

If you're keen to stretch your legs, the Raad ny Foillan footpath can be followed from here up both the east and west coasts, tracing along the clifftops on either side of the southern end of the island. However, it is also a gorgeous place to just spend a slow afternoon sitting on the grass

THE FAR SOUTH

with a pair of binoculars watching the wildlife, and the occasional Stena Line ferry passing by the south of the island on its way from Belfast to Liverpool. If it's stormy, retreat to the café, where you can watch the dramatic weather through the panoramic windows.

FOOD & DRINK

The Sound Café Sound Rd, IM9 5PZ ⌂ thesound.im ⊙ Apr–Oct 10.00–17.00 Mon–Fri, 10.00–18.00 Sat & Sun; Nov–Mar 10.00–16.00 Mon–Fri, 10.00–17.00 Sat & Sun. A good-sized, friendly café with arguably the most sensational view on the island: situated just yards from the breakers hitting the headland, the sweeping panoramic windows perfectly frame the Calf of Man. The breakfast menu has all the favourites such as a full English, pancakes, and avocado on toast, while the lunch menu includes delicious salads, sandwiches, and fish and chips – plus restaurant-quality specials such as spinach and ricotta tortelloni, and cheese and caramelised onion pie, all in generous portions. Or just pop in for a slice of cake and cappuccino while you ogle the view.

15 THE CALF OF MAN

Boat trips on the *Shona* leave from Port Erin breakwater and must be booked in advance ⌂ shonaboattrips.wixsite.com/calftrips ⊙ May–Sep. Trips with Port St Mary Calf of Man Boat leave from Port St Mary harbour and must be booked in advance ▪ calfofmanboat ⊙ year-round

If visiting the Isle of Man is a chance to slow down and escape hectic cities, rail networks and motorways, then a trip to the Calf of Man takes this to the extreme. The island off the southwestern tip of Man is roughly a mile square and is home to just four conservation wardens between March and November each year, who live completely off-grid at the bird observatory. With no public transport links, it can only be reached through private boat trips which can be booked from Port Erin or Port St Mary. There is limited phone signal and no shops or cafés – if you're planning a day trip, pack sandwiches.

All this makes for the feeling of a grand adventure. Arriving at Port Erin breakwater first thing in the morning, being strapped into lifejackets and clambering down the steps to board the little blue *Shona* brings on the childish glee of having stepped into a *Famous Five* novel. The *Shona* operates regular sailings to the Calf in the late spring and summer months, with some tours offering landings and others focusing on watching wildlife from the 12-seater boat. Chugging out of the harbour under the guidance of Chris and Dessie – with Chris at the helm and Dessie on tour guide duty – and pootling down the southern coast, it becomes obvious that you are in the hands of experts.

Dessie moves nimbly around the gently rocking boat while cheerfully sharing his extensive knowledge of the area. He spent two years living on the Calf while training for his bird ringing licence, and clearly has a deep love of his subject. His commentary switches seamlessly from highlighting the squawking birds on the cliffs to stories of Viking raiders, smugglers' coves and shipwrecks.

The Calf, which is almost completely treeless and was once used as farmland, has been a nature reserve since the 1950s and is looked after by Manx National Heritage, which works with the Manx Wildlife Trust to run the bird observatory and conservation projects. More than 30 species of bird breed there each year, including kittiwakes, razorbills, shags and Manx shearwaters, the last of which nest in old rabbit burrows. Following a rat-eradication programme (the rodents arrived on the island following a shipwreck and gradually decimated the ground-nesting bird population) there are hopes that puffins might be encouraged to use the Calf as a breeding ground for the first time since 1987.

After a 30-minute journey the *Shona* pulls up in South Harbour near the back of The Puddle, a bay on the south side of the island, where passengers disembark. There are footpaths across the rugged, heather-covered island leading to the three former lighthouses on its western coast and the bird observatory in the middle. Information boards explain more about the wildlife and landscape, and the observatory in the island's former farmhouse has self-catering bunk rooms where it is possible to stay overnight (◯ May–Sep ⊘ islandescapes.im; stays must be booked in advance, slots sell out quickly when booking opens early in the year). Arrival at the natural harbour gives the boat a superb view of the famous **Drinking Dragon**, known locally as 'the Burroo' – an enormous rock formation off the Calf's coast that looks like a fairytale dragon lowering its head to take a drink from the sea.

Looking south, it is possible to see **Chicken Rock Lighthouse** – about a mile off the coast of the Calf, it is the most southerly lighthouse in the Isle of Man and the most southerly to be looked after by the Northern Lighthouse Board of Scotland. It was built in 1875 on a small rocky outcrop that was a hazard to shipping and was manned by keepers until a fire broke out on 22 December 1960 – one of the keepers received burn

THE FAR SOUTH

injuries, and all three had to be rescued by lifeboat. The previous winter, the team had been stuck in the lighthouse for the whole of Christmas and New Year because of storms. It was agreed to automate the light in 1961.

On the return journey, Dessie points out the location of a shipwreck in 1923 which left the women of Port Erin and Port St Mary delighted. The stricken vessel had been carrying a cargo of Singers. 'It was like *Whisky Galore*,' Dessie says, 'but with sewing machines.'

BOOKS FOR MINDFUL TRAVEL

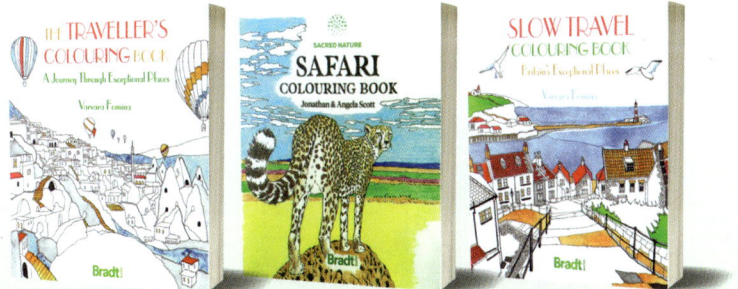

bradtguides.com/shop
@bradtguides

TRAVEL TAKEN SERIOUSLY

THE AWARD-WINNING SLOW TRAVEL SERIES FROM BRADT GUIDES

Over 20 regional guides across Britain.
See the full list at bradtguides.com/slowtravel.

  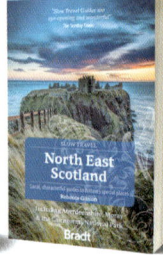

"Slow Travel Guides are eye-opening and wonderful"
Sunday Times

  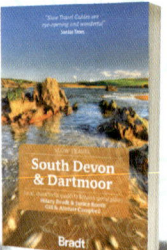

bradtguides.com/shop
@bradtguides

NOTES

INDEX

Entries in **bold** refer to major entries; those in *italic* refer to maps.

A
accessibility 41–3
accommodation 45, 66, 103, 139, 193, 214
Agneash 89
Albert Tower, Ramsey 103
Andreas 137–8
artists and art galleries 21
   Ashby Smyth, Julia 22
   Baillie Scott, Mackay Hugh 74, 183
   Hodgson Loom Gallery 21
   Isle of Man Art Society Easter Exhibition 27
   Kneale, Bryan 21, 207
   Knox, Archibald 21, 112
   National Art Gallery 21
   Sayle, Norman 22
   Studio 42 gallery 21
Ayres Nature Reserve 125, **139–42**

B
Baldrine 50, **77**
Baldwin 72
Ballacosnahan Farm Shop 147, **163–6**
   see also Manx Loaghtan sheep
Ballasalla 209, 210–11
Ballaugh Curragh 126, 134
Ballaugh beach 127
Battle of Trafalgar 190
Bee Gees 64
bookshops
   Bridge Bookshop 104, 219
   Manx Museum 63
   House of Manannan 150
Bradda Head 219
Braaid Viking Farmstead, The 69
Braaid Viking Longhouse, The 50
Bride 137–9
Brown, TE 22, 99, 160, 192
bus *see* getting around the island

C
Caine, Hall 23, 111, 174
Calf of Man 229–31
cammag 147, **171**
car hire 34
Carraghan hill 72
Cashtal yn Ard 116, **120**
Castle Rushen 63, 180, **183–6**
Castletown 52, 179, **180–95**
Cavendish, Sir Mark 37
Celtic Christianity 11, 110, 127, 155, 203
charities
   Manx Peatland Project 35
   Manx Wildlife Trust 16, 160
Chasms, The 16, 226–8
Christian, William *see* Dhone, Illiam
Chronicles of Man 183, **213**
churches
   Agneash chapel 89
   Ballaugh Old Church 132
   Bride 138–9
   Cathedral Isle of Man (Peel) 149
   Christ Church (Laxey) 83
   Kirk Maughold 111
   Malew Parish Church 206–9
   Old Kirk Braddan 69
   Patrick church 162

churches *continued*...
  Royal Chapel of St John's 170
  St Andrew's (Andreas) 137
  St Luke's (Baldwin) 72
  St Mary's (Port St Mary) 220
  St Michael & All Angels (Kirk Michael) 131
  St Michael's Chapel (Fort Island) 198
  St Patrick's (Jurby) 138
  St Patrick's chapel (Glen Mooar) 127
  St Peter's (Onchan) 75
  St Thomas' Church, murals (Douglas) 56
  St Trinian's church 19, 147, **172–4**
Clypse reservoir 75
coasteering 38
Cooish Manx Language Festival 30
Cornaa Valley 117
Corrin's Tower, Peel 153, 154
Cregneash village 16, 27, **223–5**
crofting 63, 223–5
Culture Vannin 170
currency 44
cycling 36, 125
  bike hire 38
  mountain biking 37

D
Dalby Spook, The *see* Gef the talking mongoose
Darts Festival 27
Derby Haven *see* Langness
Dhone, Illiam 108, 137, **191–2**, 207
Dhoon, The 120
diving 38, 40
Douglas 49, **51–68**
Douglas Bay Horse Tramway 55
Douglas Railway Station *see* Isle of Man Steam Railway

Douglas Sea Terminal 34, 50, 51
Drinking Dragon rock formation 230
Dunkirk 222

E
Earls of Derby 12, 108, 136–7, 191, 192, 199
economy 13, 25, 51, 53
events calendar 26

F
Fairy Bridge 18, 213
Fenella Beach, Peel 153
fishing 40
folklore **18**, 43
  bugganes 18, 147
  fairies 18, 208
  fynoderee 18, 20, 107
  mermaids 118, 215
  moddey dhoo 19, 98, 110, 116, **156**
food and drink 31
  Beer and Cider Festival 27
  bonnag 32
  Bushy's ale 32
  honey 102
  Kerroo Brewing Company 32, **218**
  kippers 31
  Okell's ale 32
  queenie scallops 32
Formby, George 64, 150
Fort Island 198–9
further reading 43
Fynoderee gin 22, 32, **101**

G
Gaiety Theatre 53
Gef the talking mongoose 168
geology 167–9, 195, 200–3, 226, 230

INDEX

getting around 34
    Bus Vannin 34, 41, 50, 96, 126, 136, 148, 180
    car hire 34
    Isle of Man Steam Railway 34, 41, 58
    Manx Electric Railway 34, 41, 49, 96
getting to the island 33
    ferry (Isle of Man Steam Packet) 33, 49
    Ronaldsway Airport 33
ghosts 54, 66, 79, 109, 116, 139, 156, 167, 185
glens 36
    Ballaglass 118
    Elfin (Ramsey) 103
    Maye 166–7
    Mooar 126, **127–9**
    Wyllin 126
    Groudle 77
    Molly Quirk's 75
    Port Soderick 68
Great Laxey Mine Railway 85
Great Laxey Wheel 81, 84
Great Union Camera Obscura 60
golf **40**, 195
Greeba 19, **172–4**
Groudle Glen Railway 77
Grove Museum of Victorian Life, The 106

H

health services 45
history 11, 43
Holy Well of St Maughold 113
Home of Rest for Old Horses, The 56
Hop tu Naa 29
House of Keys *see* Tynwald
House of Manannan 41, **150**
Hunt the Wren **30**, 73

I

Ice Age 11, 63, 117, 140
Industrial Revolution 13, 82
Isle of Man Bank 52, 58
Isle of Man Motor Museum 26, **138**
Isle of Man Steam Packet *see* getting to the island
Isle of Man Steam Railway 34, 41, 58

J

Jurby 137–8
Jurby Transport Museum 138

K

kayaking 38, 40
keeills 11, 91, 111, 127, 203
Kennaugh, Peter (Olympian) 37, 74
Kerroogarroo civil war fort 136
King William's College 191–3
Kirk Michael 125, 126, **129–32**
Kishtey Cheh beach spa, Port Erin 215
Knockaloe Centre for WWI Internment 161–3

L

Langness 195–200
Laxey 81–9
Laxey Wheel song 85
Laxey Woollen Mills 82
Leece Museum 26, **149–50**
Lonan Old Church 50, **79–80**
Lord of Man 12

M

Manannan 12
Manx Gaelic 11, 16, 30, 20, 169
Manx Litfest 29
Manx Loaghtan sheep 14, 31, 225
Manx Museum 21, 26, 43, 58, **63–5**

Manx Transport Heritage Museum 150
Manx place names 11, 18, 44
Manx telephone numbers 45
Maughold Head 95, 112
Maughold village 111
May Day 28
Mighty Wurlitzer, The 56
Milner's Tower, Port Erin 219
Milntown Estate, Ramsey 108
Molly Carrooin's Cottage, Onchan 74
money *see* currency
Mooragh Internment Camp 98
Mooragh Park, Ramsey 98
motorsport 23
    Manx Grand Prix 25, 29
    Manx Rally 26, 27
    Southern 100 race 26, 28
    TT races 23, 28, 43, 65, 92, 95, 126, 150
Murray's Motorcycle Museum 26, 214
music 20
    Isle of Man Festival of Choirs 30
    Manx Music Festival 27
    Yn Chruinnaght festival 20, 28
Mutiny on the *Bounty* 75, 78, 108

N

Nautical Museum 188–91
New Year's Dip 27
Niarbyl Bay 167–9
North Barrule 95, **121–2**
North Quay, Douglas 65–7

O

Old Grammar School, The 186
Old House of Keys 187
Old Tynwald Site, Baldwin 73

Onchan 73–7
Ordnance Survey maps 45

P

P50 car 150, 151
parking discs 44
peat 35, 63
Peel 52, **148–61**
Peel Castle 147, **154–7**
Pilates (origins of) 163
plantations and woodlands
    Archallagan plantation 37
    Conrhenny Community Woodland 37, 75, 79
    Corlea Plantation 175
    Cringle Plantation 175
    South Barrule Forest Park 175
Point of Ayre 96, 126, **143–4**
Port Cornaa Beach 118
Port Erin 179, **215–19**
Port Erin Railway Museum 217
Port Soderick 68
Port St Mary 179, **219–22**

Q

Queen's Pier, Ramsey 99

R

RNLI 54, 160
Race the Sun 28
Radio Caroline 104
Ramsey 95, 97
Royal Manx Agricultural Show 29
running
    Easter Festival of Running 27
    Isle of Man Marathon 28
    Round the Island Race 28
Rushen Abbey **209–12**, 213

INDEX

S

Saddlestone, The 72
St John's 147, **169–72**
St Patrick's Isle 153, **154–7**
Scarlett 200–3
shipwrecks 127, 160, 197–8
Slieau Whallian hill 170
slums 58, 59
smuggling 52, 149, 179, 188
Snaefell mines disaster 90
Snaefell mountain 11, 50, 91
Snaefell Wheel, Laxey 85
Sound, The 228–9
South Barrule 37, **174–6**
Spanish Head 226–8
Spooyt Vane waterfall, Glen Mooar 128
Stanley family 12, 185, *see also* Earls of Derby
stargazing 40
stone crosses 70, 75, 79, 112, 131, 138, 171, 206
Sulby Giant, The 133
Summerland fire 67

T

Thomas the Tank Engine 60
three legs of Man 12
tombs and burial sites 11, 50
  Balladoole Historic Monument Site (Castletown) 203–6
  Ballafayle cairn (Maughold) 115
  Cashtal yn Ard (Maughold) 116, 120
  Cloven Stones (Baldrine) 78
  Giant's Grave (St John's) 171
  Killeaba Mound (Ramsey) 102
  King Orry's Grave (Laxey) 50, 86
  Meayll Hill 180, **225–6**
  Quaker burial ground (Maughold) 115

tourist information points 46, 50, 96, 148, 181
Tower of Refuge *see* RNLI
travel cards 34
Tynwald 12, 13, 52, 61, 182
Tynwald Day 28
Tynwald Hill 170
Tynwald National Park and Arboretum 171

V

Victory Cafe 26, **92–3**
Viking Longboat Race 28
Vikings 12, 63, 157, 181, 183, 203–6
votes for women 187

W

watersports 38, 217
walking 35
  Bayr ny Skeddan (Herring Road) footpath 36, 179, 183
  End to End Walk 29
  Millenium Way 36
  Parish Walk 28
  Raad ny Foillan (Way of the Gull) footpath 35, 49, 96, 125, 148, 179, 228
  Snaefell 93
wallabies 126, 135
What3words 45
wildlife 13, 17, 63, 151
  Manx cat 14, 26
  Manx shearwater 16
  seabirds 14, 115, 151, 197, 200, 226, 228, 229–31
  seal spotting 148, 197, 228
  whales and dolphins 14, 49, 115
Wisdom, Sir Norman 64, 139
witchcraft 29, 182, 193, 194
World Tin Bath Championships 182
World War I 65, 99, 161–3, 208

World War II 65, 98, 121, 125, 137, 142, 197, 204–5, 208, 222

world's smallest car *see* P50
writers and writing 22, 29

INDEX OF ADVERTISERS

Bridge Bookshop 123

THE BRADT STORY

In the beginning
It all began in 1974 on an Amazon river barge. During an 18-month trip through South America, two adventurous young backpackers – Hilary Bradt and her then husband, George – decided to write about the hiking trails they had discovered through the Andes. *Backpacking Along Ancient Ways in Peru and Bolivia* included the very first descriptions of the Inca Trail. It was the start of a colourful journey to becoming one of the best-loved travel publishers in the world; you can read the full story on our website (**bradtguides.com/ourstory**).

Getting there first
Hilary quickly gained a reputation for being a true travel pioneer, and in the 1980s she started to focus on guides to places overlooked by other publishers. The Bradt Guides list became a roll call of guidebook 'firsts'. We published the first guide to Madagascar, followed by Mauritius, Czechoslovakia and Vietnam. The 1990s saw the beginning of our extensive coverage of Africa: Tanzania, Uganda, South Africa, and Eritrea. Later, post-conflict guides became a feature: Rwanda, Mozambique, Angola, and Sierra Leone, as well as the first standalone guides to the Baltic States following the fall of the Iron Curtain, and the first post-war guides to Bosnia, Kosovo and Albania.

Comprehensive – and with a conscience
Today, we are the world's largest independently owned travel publisher, with more than 200 titles. However, our ethos remains unchanged. Hilary is still keenly involved, and **we still get there first**: two-thirds of Bradt guides have no direct competition.

But we don't just get there first. Our guides are also known for being **more comprehensive** than any other series. We avoid templates and tick-lists. Each guide is a one-of-a-kind expression of an expert author's interests, knowledge and enthusiasm for telling it how it really is.

And a commitment to wildlife, conservation and respect for local communities has always been at the heart of our books. Bradt Guides was **championing sustainable travel** before any other guidebook publisher. We even have a series dedicated to Slow Travel in the UK, award-winning books that explore the country with a passion and depth you'll find nowhere else.

Thank you!
We can only do what we do because of the support of readers like you – people who value less-obvious experiences, less-visited places and a more thoughtful approach to travel. Those who, like us, take travel seriously.